KV-050-889

Metaphysics and the Moving Image

For my parents, near and far

Metaphysics
and the Moving Image

"Paradise Exposed"

Trevor Mowchun

EDINBURGH
University Press

Edinburgh University Press is one of the leading university presses in the UK. We publish academic books and journals in our selected subject areas across the humanities and social sciences, combining cutting-edge scholarship with high editorial and production values to produce academic works of lasting importance. For more information visit our website: edinburghuniversitypress.com

© Trevor Mowchun, 2023

Edinburgh University Press Ltd
The Tun—Holyrood Road, 12(2f) Jackson's Entry, Edinburgh EH8 8PJ

Typeset in Garamond MT Pro by
Cheshire Typesetting Ltd, Cuddington, Cheshire,
and printed and bound in Great Britain

A CIP record for this book is available from the British Library

ISBN 978 1 4744 9390 1 (hardback)
ISBN 978 1 4744 9392 5 (webready PDF)
ISBN 978 1 4744 9393 2 (epub)

The right of Trevor Mowchun to be identified as author of this work has been asserted in accordance with the Copyright, Designs and Patents Act 1988 and the Copyright and Related Rights Regulations 2003 (SI No. 2498).

Contents

Figures

Acknowledgments

First to my good fortune in *not* having had my way many years ago when a somewhat impulsive plan to commit myself exclusively to the study of philosophy at the expense of film failed to materialize, for it so happened that I found various places and paths, in the university context but also in my own life, where I could investigate film and philosophy together—and literature, for my love of the arts began, if I recall, with novels—as equals making distinct yet compatible claims on my consciousness. While daily life can be all but impossible without a will towards decisiveness and a stomach for small sacrifices, the freedom to think and follow thought where it roams (what Nietzsche somewhere calls "the feast of thinking") can draw inspiration from a certain degree of justified ambivalence in a world of increasing specialization, what I like to think of as a "right" of passage across perceived borders and against the grain of propriety. The pressure to specialize with its promise of mastery and belonging may lead you astray if not careful, betraying you for what is deemed most pertinent and proper, pragmatic and "reasonable," particularly at a time when the sheer wealth and accessibility of knowledge can have the effect of throwing the seeker into submission. My admittedly limited experience has shown that those who truly identify with the spirit of philosophy and the humanities at large—that is, those for whom the throes of committed thought, feeling, and expression are synonymous with "life itself"—rarely satisfy the profile of a specialist or would ever be caught pursuing their own confinement in such a manner, whatever benefits it might afford, and that is a good thing.

The support one receives along the way(s) of circuitous exploration of interrelated objects of knowledge and across overlapping disciplines is obviously crucial. In facing the occasional yet inevitable sense of isolation and lostness that comes with following one's deepest intuitions, allies are indispensable. Such "ways," wayward or not, folly or not, are bound to be met with some degree of skepticism, and I have been fortunate to have been given the benefit of the doubt from my colleagues, mentors, and friends, receiving only the most constructive and inspiring forms of skepticism. I will take a raised eyebrow over a status quo smile, a pat on the back over a steady finger telling you the right or safe way to go—any day. What is the right way, anyway, but the one that is *seen through to the end*? Seeing something all the way through involves seeing into yourself perhaps more deeply than you would like, but when you find out what you're made of, as they say, it is from those materials that the work is built and by those materials that it may fall. You hope you won't outgrow it too soon.

There have been enriching, reviving founts of knowledge and expertise who shined their brightest of lights into the woods of my metaphysics and the moving image. By a form of duty to what I would call a higher calling beyond my purview, Martin Lefebvre keenly commented on all the chapters as they were being written, including material which does not appear in the final work presented here. It was Martin who took it upon himself, with a patience and tactfulness all too rare, to put a hand on my shoulder, a mirror to my face, and interject with the tone of the concerned father: "Let's back up a bit, shall we? Have a look around and collect your bearings. Is that what you wish to say? *This* is what you're *actually* saying." In this way he taught me a great deal, and nothing more important than that constructive criticism helps cultivate the ultimate value of self-criticism, and that no form of criticism is to be feared, certainly not any more than praise. Andre Furlani, Justin E. H. Smith, George Toles, and Nathan Brown also provided thoughtful comments on early drafts of the book as a whole, comments whose differences from each other exposed it to a remarkably wide range of perspectives and methodologies (classical film theory, the history of philosophy, film aesthetics, philosophy of art, poetics, pragmatism, semiotics, postmodern literature, theater studies, and more). It was George who knew best how to ask (in so many words, as alive to me now as when I first heard them as an undergraduate student at the University of Manitoba): "What becomes of the big philosophical questions when a film about which they are being raised—no, a shot from a film, this moment from a film—is permitted to ask these questions first, in its own unique way?" I applaud their stalwart *openness*—clearly perceiving what I was setting out to do and intricately tailoring their thoughts to the internal logic and style of the work, deftly pointing out weaknesses and, just as importantly, drawing my attention to strengths in need of some reining in.

There were times, I admit, when I may have moved forward too swiftly and barged somewhat recklessly through these walls we all face, but I was precisely interested in points of collision, in the crumbling and rebuilding of great edifices of thought, and that spark convinced me that I had to begin, well, at the beginning, or a new point of origin. It was then that the words of another great teacher came to my aid, a figure long gone yet whose works never lose their power to *provoke*: Ralph Waldo Emerson. The audacity of the rhetorical question from the opening paragraph of *Nature* allowed me to close one too many books flying around me like crazed birds: "Why should not we also enjoy an original relation to the universe?" I suppose I sought an original relation to the *universe of film* through a simple question—one which, today, might be called an interdisciplinary question—that took me years to ascertain and justify: "What is metaphysics in/as film? What is film as a form, or deforming, of metaphysics?"

Over the years I have benefited from various types of conversation with colleagues and friends through which aspects of the book both large and small came into finer focus. Here are only some of the cheerful and discriminating voices that accompanied me along the way of writing (and in some cases the *entire* way): Daniel Gerson, Mustafa Uzuner, Denis Wong, John Hunting, Mi-Jeong Lee, Julio Valdés Jover, Shaun Gamboa, and Robert Ray. The roots of this book, as long and twisted as they are, can be traced back to work from two graduate seminars on the themes of Realism and Romanticism, the former given by Luca Caminati in 2010 at Concordia University, where I began to think through cinema's ontological affinity with "nature," and the latter given by George Toles in 2004 at the University of Manitoba, where I experimented with the possibility of putting into practice Stanley Cavell's bold yet unsubstantiated claim from *The World Viewed* that Terrence Malick's film *Days of Heaven* enacts Martin Heidegger's philosophy of Being. I would say something of the spirit of both of these projects remains intact in the finished book. But of course the pinpointing of an origin remains, as always, a mere fantasy, a story at the expense of history. If I am honest with myself, this book is the maturation of ideas and intuitions long held; and in what is a perfectly bittersweet event, now I am free to let go of it all, to watch this work thrive (or not) in the hands of others. I hope to always be there to stand by it should I ever be asked to account for it, and in the plainest speech of which I am capable.

The Introduction, parts of Chapters Three and Four, and Chapter Five were presented in their early incarnations at various conferences and meetings, including Society for Cinema and Media Studies (Chicago, 2017; Montreal, 2015), Spiral: Film and Philosophy Conference (Toronto, 2017), ARTHEMIS (Advanced Research Team on the History and Epistemology of Moving Image Studies) based at Concordia University (Montreal, 2013–14), and Film Studies Association of Canada (Victoria, 2013). The questions and comments I received on these occasions remain, even years later, useful friction in finding one's footing by making possible small yet significant adjustments to one's habitual ways of thinking. Chapter Four is a revised and expanded version of an essay published in *Film International* (Spring, 2015). I thank the journal and its editor, Daniel Lindvall, for granting me permission to publish the definitive and fully contextualized version here, and above all for supporting my early forays into the metaphysics of film.

Gillian Leslie at Edinburgh University Press has been incredibly supportive of this book from our first conversation about it at SCMS in Seattle, 2019. In the timeliest manner she orchestrated an illuminating peer-review process through which I could see the book more objectively as though for the first time. My heartfelt thanks to the anonymous reviewers who gave their time and energy to this process. I am grateful for the editorial assistance of Sam Johnson and Eddie Clark, whose diligent handling of the manuscript and gentle coaxing of its delivery came with unexpected encouragement and warmth during the demanding home stretch. I also experienced fruitful collaborations with Wendy Lee, who copyedited the final typescript, Caitlin Murphy, who designed the book cover (using Tina Leto's stunning photograph), and Zoe Ross, who made the index (revised by Cecile Cristobal). I am grateful to the Department of English at the University of Florida where I teach, for granting me a research leave during the Fall semester of 2021, which allowed me to devote myself to the realization of the final manuscript as envisioned. I would also like to acknowledge the University of Florida College of Liberal Arts and Sciences and Center for the Humanities and the Public Sphere (Rothman Endowment) for their generous support.

The unwavering support of parents such as I have been lucky to have is as immeasurable as it is indescribable. Nonetheless, I will try: the warm lamp glowing in the winter, the fan gently whirling in the summer, the consistent beaming on the other end of the telephone line, and the strange feeling of never having left "home" wherever my travels have taken me. Such unconditional and routine support, I realize, takes great persistence and is hard work unsung. They have never ceased to nourish me in ways uniquely their own, propping me up from opposite sides of my psyche and joining forces at the most opportune times when one believes, mistakenly, that one's independence is without a single debt in the world. Ha! Until very recently both have been there to provide the benefit of their life experience and, in a true stroke of humility and wisdom, have continued their parentage by suggesting that they needed me as much as I needed them.

My wife, Cecile Cristobal, has been with me every step of the way, both in the journey of writing this book and the one which led me to the University of Florida, where I have been teaching since 2018. A long-gestating book tests oneself, hence one's life, hence everyone with whom one lives. Our projects risk justifying an unbridled commitment to—ultimately, regrettably—ourselves, what we call "our work." I will say that the chronic solitude that goes into the making of books or films has the power to exude a sumptuous warmth from a kitchen of ideas—the aroma of quiet and steady thinking from a corner of the house which may, for some, harbor an air of familiarity. I, for one, find such an atmosphere intoxicating when I sense my partner hard at work on affairs of her own, in a privacy and silence that is not for me to know. Just when writerly solitude feels as if it's about to calcify into a snail shell, I relished the sudden shifts from metaphysics to everyday matters, sometimes using the concreteness of the latter to escape my fate to think from what may be too great a height. Fortunately, Cecile is no stranger to the clouds—is that where we met?—upon which our little life (with our little Mia) glides peacefully and passionately through time.

Lastly, I would like to make a panoramic salute to all those with whom I have shared a passion for film, philosophy, and the arts. I am certain that our optimistic, pessimistic, yet always committed and energizing conversations atop these giant peaks of word and image could have occurred only out of school and after hours. (A footnote thanks, or bow, is now in order for the late Stanley Cavell, from whom I borrow this phrase "out of school" and learned to wrestle with the paradox of working and living both in *and* out of school—one of many paradoxes which, far from rendering us powerless, eloquently reacquaint us with the bottomless depths of our humanity whenever we are in doubt of doubt itself—thus making the desire for certainty and its corollary of conformity unbecoming despite all appearances.)

Gainesville, Florida,
Spring of 2022

The Death of God, the Birth of Film, and the New Metaphysics

> The important thing is to tie one's shoelaces, sew back the parted button, and look the world in the eye.
> — Guy Davenport, *A Field of Snow on a Slope of the Rosenberg*

The branch of philosophy known as metaphysics (sometimes referred to as "first philosophy," in that case the *root* of philosophy) is the oldest and most enduring mode of inquiry into the nature of things. Questions regarding substrates of being, the nature of time and space, elemental harmony and entropy, the soul, good and evil, immortality and the existence of God, and all attempts to know something "in itself" (including the very act of knowing) characterize metaphysics as the idealistic and often systematic pursuit of essences or absolutes, the grasping of which would give us "truth," at long last, and therefore something resembling a perpetual cause lurking behind the myriad effects surrounding us and constituting our world—thus redeeming the limits of human finitude as the adventure of insight gives way to the restfulness of wisdom in the lap of the eternal. With a pure love of knowledge tested by daring acts of skepticism, metaphysics harbors a blind faith in the power to wrest the absolute from the flow and flux of primordial life. Such faith, however, seems destined for betrayal, considering that the past 2,500 years or so of Western philosophy (much of it guided by metaphysical tendencies) have seen not a single system of thought, even the most comprehensive, succeed in generating any absolute once and for all. It is as if the concreteness of the absolute, once touched, either loses the grandeur it possessed when out of reach, entering the flow of historical contingency, or retains such grandeur but only as a mere possibility or thought experiment. With our twenty-first-century hindsight over the sprawling history of the metaphysical enterprise, we are left with the realization that even the most rigorous arguments, luminous insights, and airtight cartographies of human understanding of the world as a whole have proven over time to cripple under the weight of philosophical critique or simply lose their power to satisfy the bottomless temptation of truth—for this temptation turns out in the history of ideas to be ultimately insatiable, like a biological need returning daily, breeding distortions of common sense when deprived and revealing more about the agony and ambition of the human condition than that of the world we strive to know.

The long age of metaphysics comes to a close, entering its "twilight" phase, with Friedrich Nietzsche's provocative and perhaps unfathomable pronouncement "God is dead." Delivered with a strange twist of melancholy and joy, irony and fervor, in the aphoristic parable entitled "The Madman" from *The Gay Science*, God is dead is the philosophical prize for an incendiary critique of the metaphysical truth claims or dogmatisms abounding within the dominant discourses of Christian morality.[1] Nietzsche's paradigm shift from the 1880s heralds an end to the old world of religious beliefs by exposing philosophical metaphysics as the *devaluation* rather than the revelation of the world it promised to be—in other words, as the systematic courtship of various after- or under- or possible worlds in place of *this* world—and aspires to usher in a new world of life-affirming values posited by overmen in a festive spirit of freedom and empowerment. And yet, no paradigm shift can hold sway without a measure of resistance or, for Nietzsche, its own fresh set of illusions and ironies, for that which resists change (the friction of thought) may steer it straight and upright, giving form to its future. What philosophy might prefer to dismiss as a mere coincidence, the death of God is inextricably tied to and overturned by the emergence of cinema, which says by way of reply to God's death: "I am the *rebirth* of the world in its own image: paradise exposed."

On the one hand, this idea of the world in its own image is a purely metaphysical idea, a primal glimpse back into the old world of metaphysics, the world-as-such which metaphysics seeks to conceptually reify and deify by turns. But on the other hand, the idea of the world in its own image equally implies *not in our image*, as the world's mechanically generated appearance onscreen is not pre-constituted by consciousness, precedes human consciousness, and operates, I want to say, on its own terms—providing the ground upon which cinema in its many forms is structured and articulated. What is of fundamental philosophical importance is that this cinematic image of "world" constitutes a *transformation* of the age-old and virtually exhausted tradition of metaphysics. Fueled by the revelatory conditions of cinema's audiovisual recording technologies, these cinematic terms, which I will be exploring in detail throughout this work, introduce or inaugurate a seemingly unprecedented mode of valuing the world, a revelatory ontology prior to discourse—or constituting a kind of automatic discourse—which measures the value of things by *the value which things give themselves*, thus reflecting manmade values back upon their makers.

While cinema's first glimpse in time and space at the end of the nineteenth century is, of course, silent and colorless, I see the camera in particular less as a device that captures the world than as a means by which our consciousness is taken hostage by the world—a luminous flooding of the absolute from without and of the repressed "God instinct" from within. And while the world as the image of God fades away, cinema as the world in its own image intercedes, reenchanting the world by appealing not to a creator but rather to the creativity inherent within life itself. Cinema in its infancy embodies its own radical gesture of what Nietzsche calls the reevaluation of all values, a gesture not exactly of human origin, not manmade but machine-made, not intentional but automatic, shifting the terms of belief from an afterworld to this world, or from transcendence to immanence, and positing what I will call the self-affirmation of life as the first principle of a new *cine-metaphysics*. I find deep significance and even a sense of destiny in this moment of contact between two parallel and competing legacies, and seek to analyze its implications for both film *and* philosophy, particularly for the subfields of film-philosophy and what philosophy now refers to as "metametaphysics."[2]

This curious piece of history ties or rather entangles the discrete fates of cinema and philosophy. If the cinema is born, or if the cinema as we know it today comes of age, when the philosopher who launched the most mercilessly rug-pulling and virtually indiscriminate attack on metaphysical truth lost his mind and passed away, then the dawning of the cinematic manifestation of the metaphysical at the end of the nineteenth century roughly coincides with philosophy's first comprehensive, if not catastrophic, *critique* of metaphysics, a critique which exposes truth as an army of metaphors and necessitates the triumphant yet apprehensive declaration of the death of God. Surely, you say, it is a mere coincidence that Nietzsche's death—the death of the man who pronounced the death of God and left our sea of idols in ruins—is followed by the birth of cinema, the rebirth of the world in its own image rather than in our image—this idol of idols, this stone upon which all idols are set: The World. Far from it, though, for herein lies the possibility that the end of metaphysics as philosophized by Nietzsche is, in fact, not the end of metaphysics at all. What philosophy calls the end of metaphysics, sometimes with pride and sometimes with regret, is itself a metaphysical claim, one that Nietzsche never quite brings himself to face, at least not in any straightforward sense (the death of God is declared in the third person by a madman, after all). For Nietzsche, and I suppose for me as well, the overcoming of metaphysics (for that is what is at stake, still at stake in the *return* of metaphysics) depends on an entirely *different* way of thinking, starting with the thought that there will be many ways to think "truthlessly"; and should these ways contradict one another, which is to be expected, philosophy should be the last to raise its arm in self-defense. As for this radical difference in thinking, it will depend, at least in part, on breaking deep-seated habits of mind, body, and expression, those habits which are common to both philosophical critique and systematization (the *same* habits will not do) and that are as old as philosophy itself. Philosophy must look *outside itself* if it wants/needs metaphysics to end, rather than simply call an end to it—and the philosopher, to a certain extent, ceases to be a philosopher. He must *change*, the hardest thing to do, leaving it to philosophy to report that change, which is relatively quite easy. (This is the moment when philosophy becomes autobiography without necessarily becoming personal or even historical.—Change the world? Change thyself.)

When philosophy looks outside itself to face the cinema, and if cinema can be imagined as facing truth—looking the world in the eye—better than we can, then the death of God verdict can be expounded in the following way, as a picture instead of a proposition: "What you perceive onscreen is *all there is* to perceive—there is nothing *beyond*, there is nothing *below*, nothing *holding up* this shining, shimmering vision of the world. The reductive tug of war between good and evil, a binary upon which so many films are built, is actually a rambunctious play of light and shadow, a thick strata of variations and textures of life spreading across the imaginary limits of pure light and dark—these being extremities of exposure which, in cinematographic terms, are all but illegible and therefore surpassed automatically." Should one still be tempted to ask after the substance of this great shimmer (what Maxim Gorky, who was right to be tempted back in 1896, called "the Kingdom of Shadows"), the cinema, deaf in its maturity to the reductive diagnoses of critics, deflects all such questioning back to the *surface* of life where it belongs (where there are no definitive answers)—for now, over a hundred years later, the play of light and shadow has a *history*.[3]

Still, cinema's light on the world *as* world is a relatively new light compared to philosophy's light of knowledge. Abruptly kindled at the turn of the century, it is as if the sun is rising for the first time, spreading a wave of light from a source no longer mysterious and out of reach, advancing towards the future like our sun while keeping an eye on a past to which all films are fundamentally beholden. A cinematic sun waxes and wanes, drawing a perfect circle in the skies of time, thus enacting Nietzsche's most daring philosophical ambition derived from the death of God: the eternal recurrence. Cinema, let's imagine, partakes of this service and splendor of light without origin or destination, a light that now shines from within, emanating from the freedom of all things to dwell, persist, and participate in themselves, a miniature sun for every object that the cinema enables to stare back at us; and not only the freedom of objects to return our gaze, or startle our gaze into action, but also the freedom of space to expand and contract, the freedom of time to recur or spiral, to dance and be spared the logic of progress. Think of the rebirth of metaphysics occurring within the domain of *technology* instead of philosophy: the camera as a machine that captures views of the world and relays them in the form of accidents which, having *already* happened, appear necessary and full of potential meaning. This "post-human" (not necessarily non-human) dimension of "world capture" is the foundation for creating a world buttressed by the *absence* of God, a world where the only proof for existence is existence itself, the absurdity of which only we can redeem. It is a world free for the first time to *perform*, to act out its being (the "misbehavior" of being); a world permitted to unleash the full brunt of its contingent character (force animating all fixity) and thereby thwart our efforts to know it, as if there had never been a time in which we wielded less mastery over it.

Beyond the fact that paradigm shifts are rarely comprehensive across all fields, one might wonder today over the value of a *return* of metaphysics, especially from outside the domain of philosophy proper. Perhaps there is no agreeable value, or no sense in seeking out a progressive or explanatory value, from a return which comes to pass as a timeless *reminder* of what has never ceased to be the case. In terms one could call mythological, a death that is uncannily followed by birth hardly constitutes a smooth cycle so much as an arresting, if not jarring, situation whereby the history of ideas as told by philosophy—particularly the postmodern narrative on the transformation of truth from metaphysical speculation to analytical critique, or from something discoverable in the world to something entirely created as a world in its own right—goes partially unanswered or undigested by the arrival of film because, put simply, the ontology of film posits an "outside" or "out there" that is *a priori* to whatever we might create with it. In other words, the *a priori* comes to us *a posteriori* and thus reconstitutes the quest of metaphysics in a different form. Perhaps film's residual *a priori* puts pressure on the practical capacity of our will to live, not to mention flourish, within the aftermath of the death of God, for Nietzsche knew that such a will on the level of the individual does not necessarily operate in stride with the major evolutions or revolutions of thought occurring on various levels of culture and which are genealogically rather than psychologically determined. In casting the voice of madness over reason in the role of declaring God's death by human hands, a philosophically decisive yet essentially literary device deployed throughout *The Gay Science* which psychologizes the deed, Nietzsche suggests that we have killed God without realizing what it means to have committed such an act or, what amounts to the same thing, without being able to bear the burden of this unbearable knowledge—out of sheer gravity or shame—and repressing it in various ways, resulting in strange and often degenerate sublimations like "the cult of atheism," which the parable of "The Madman" boldly satirizes by addressing a group of what I will call *believing disbelievers*. Some consequences of this ironic situation, in which a great and irreversible deed both is and is not done, are imaginable as follows: what we want to call progress is not necessarily *made* by the human beings who profess it; for every part of ourselves overcome there are parts left behind; for every piece of knowledge acquired the path to wisdom may be *less* apparent (knowledge would be to blame for the silly word "path"). If an awareness of regress becomes a part of the complete picture of progress in a fit of Nietzschean irony, and if the untimeliness of the world in its own image makes possible for such an awareness, then there opens before us a window of opportunity to rethink the value of progress itself—say, by assessing its hidden costs or exposing its hidden agendas, perhaps redeeming the *relapse* as vital to the continued work of progress over time, leading us beyond the purview of our time in which it may be seen to pay off.

I am proposing here that cinema delivers a grounded image-reply to Nietzsche's lofty word of madness: when God was declared dead, something else took its place—not quite a new God and more than a mere idol. The world in its own image is like an unmasked absolute staring us in the face, manifesting from out of the dark and *finding us* just when philosophy called off its futile search. From what I recently described as "a machine's first glimpse in time and space,"[4] the cinema's historically steady movement towards greater intensities of audiovisual totalization, its routine upholding of various depictions and distortions of reality (the act of world-bearing is implied by the art of world-making), signals to philosophy that the cinematic absolute continues to permeate and expand human consciousness, and with no less force in the digital age. So in the eyes of philosophy, cinema's raw material or ontology (that is, the world in its own image, which we experience in the form of *dispossession*[5]) appears strikingly as the "physicalization" of metaphysics; and it is through this "world material" that film theorists and filmmakers can succeed in doing what metaphysics never could: to speculate about the world by withholding the terms of speculation, that is, until the world has first disclosed itself as a vital organ of any living worldview. When interpreted through the moving image, metaphysics appears as a philosophical tradition that strives in vain to see through or otherwise bypass its own inevitable worldviewing procedures, a tradition which strives to represent the world through thought in a way that the ontology of film seems to do *automatically*. For film, to represent the world is to record it in its own image, recordings which then become the basis for cinematic discourse or inspiration for cinematic revelation, what I will call a metaphysical film style—but the precision of these recordings hinge, interestingly enough, on a form of thought *deformed*, as it were, untethered to the old philosophical solid of the "I", free to waft about and wander amongst an expanding multitude of autonomous objects which register and speak the world in its own image.

———

I have settled on the term "moving image" because it is itself a mobile concept open to further technological and aesthetic development. As a literal description of cinema's raw material in the digital age, and with its scientifically strategic yet psychologically shy avoidance of history, artistry, and the individual movies which characterize and exemplify the medium, we welcome the most recent attempt from film studies to disown film and replace it with a virtual blank.[6] We see the vast, expansive, and changing field of inquiry behaving like a discipline and moderating itself: a discipline eager to catch up to, so as to better anticipate, the historical movement of the medium from material to immaterial objecthood, from expressions of light to constellations of digits, from the otherworldly offerings of elusive specialists to the everyday fragments of a routine image-making consciousness. Scholars and spectators alike probably suspect that this change means that *more changes* are on the way and that it is best not to become overly accustomed to any term of reference in this context, even one which honors precisely the immediacy and versatility of the great mobile medium. By emphasizing the *constant* rather than the substance of movies—in other words, the persistence and proliferation of movies of various kinds despite the mutable immateriality of the digital medium (or lack thereof)—it is unclear if, by talking about the moving image, we are even talking about movies at all anymore, especially given that this resurgence of the concept priviliges animation over the photographic, not to mention casting the widest possible net to include works we might not recognize as "movie-worthy." Perhaps by avoiding what is essential to an artistic medium (art) we embrace the essentialism of a discipline (data). When a discipline is in crisis over the fate of its object and the fear of its irrevocable loss, the instinct—more biological than logical or methodological, more survivalist than strategic—is usually to overcompensate for it or repress the problem altogether, to attempt to cure it rather than cope with it, succumbing to the fantasy of a cure in its own reification (film studies studies itself). And it occurs to me that this desire to cure uncertainty, instability, and contingency, rather than cope with what history—not to mention biology—proves to be inescapable realities, is also the greatness and weakness of metaphysics in all its forms: just when the concept of the moving image manages to liberate the medium from ties to a particular material base, it confines itself to a watchtower where its own ability to think is lured by totalization and thus risks dematerialization.

The moving image as an infallible concept is perhaps better suited to keep pace with a moving world, over and above that of a changing discipline. The problem is that the discipline of film studies cannot, in fact, adequately *discipline* its object (a source of its popularity and methodological plurality, no doubt), for this particular object (if that is the right word) is such that it both moves images and images movement—a double movement worthy of the world from which it grows and returns to as an immaculate representation, a world it has never been able to successfully capture once and for all for the simple reason that when changes occur at the level of "the world" they are inevitably if inconspicuously reflected in the moving image, and this is so regardless of how they are used to represent it and even if those representations are flagrant distortions. In this respect the history of film is conceivable as a moving image of history itself, an avant-garde dream narrative rife with resonant tensions, non-sequiturs, and contingencies beyond our complete comprehension. The moving image is, in principle, radically open, taking in as much of the world's light as its frame will allow, a frame whose paradoxical openness moves beyond itself into the offscreen where the world as a whole nests. In this sense the moving image is hospitable to the vagrancy of light, light being one of philosophy's oldest and most recurrent metaphors for what can be apprehended and ultimately known, be it through the senses or through reason or, at last, their synergy, at the risk of melting. And so, in studying such images and the movies they move, we have the opportunity to free them from our stultifying grasp in order to learn from them, pay attention, open up to an ontological openness. Projects of mastery are quite out of place, if not hopeless, whether one chooses to be a scholar or practitioner or, as is common today, both. I like to think that this elusiveness is partly due to the fact that moving images and the movies they constitute are still subject to the mastery of *machines*, cameras and projectors and now computers, as these machines have become commonplace today as vehicles of aesthetic experience and a new kind of "image-utterance"—they are more human or we are less human—and no longer serve as factory-bound tools of the trade, hidden away or even locked up by institutions like the Hollywood dream machine (the studio-era movies which tend to conceal the process of their own creation for the sake of viewers who are generally assumed to have no inkling whatsoever of how movies come to be).

Since the very beginning of cinema, fledgling and more experienced theorists—some tending towards mysticism and others to science—have been quick to point out, or report, that cinematic representation boasts a form of resemblance to reality that is structurally uncanny: the familiar is experienced as unfamiliar because, having been radically displaced into the image, it can be seen for what it is—say, as dream-like—and not taken for granted as merely "real." The uncanniness also stems from the way cinema naturalizes the paradoxes of its own representational system, as in the following: "truth of an illusion," "depth of surface," "the representation of presence," to name but a few.[7] The first paradox recalls cinema's origins in magic where the sublime power of the trick in its moment of conjuring renders the illusion, for a moment, true. With regards to the second one, while philosophical reflection on the world can partake in an act of gross objectification and establish conditions for the tyranny of knowledge, philosophical reflection upon film's world order is forced to resign itself to the sensation of surfaces whose luminosity cuts deep yet slips through our fingers. A reflection of twilight skies in water or on glass can lead us down into the depths of the atmosphere itself where, once submerged in "surface," we are at a loss for what to call it, if not completely and utterly lost in the world of the image. The third paradox registers the sense that films *represent* worlds yet *present* them as existent, found, contingent upon themselves: representation taking the form of presence, presence deriving its power from a necessary absence, absence throwing into relief the importance of *our presence* before the screen as a measure for whether the world in its own image makes an *impression*. These are the primary paradoxes of the moving image which are destined to tread the waters of metaphysical thinking.

Despite the many technological transformations and aesthetic revolutions across a relatively brief history, the moving image of cinema has been, in varying degrees, at the mercy of *exteriority*, a concept at the heart of my reading of *The Thin Red Line* (Malick, USA, 1998) in Chapter Four. An eventful combination of separateness and the incoming, cinematic exteriority casts a world whose claim to self-sufficiency and indifference to our practical motives entangles human expressivity and complicates the realization of our *own* world, whether that world be a product of a single imagination or that of a more collective orientation. The moving image has steadily borne up the world in this way, out of reach and in our midst, carrying it on its shoulders, and enduring it like Atlas—the ancient Greek titan who holds up the sky in isolation and without reprieve, providing unconditional shelter for ungrateful mortals. But we are grateful, whether we like it or not; we show our support by receiving support. When I gaze upon the landscape of cinema and juxtapose the earliest films side by side with those most current, I notice a similar interest in—commitment to, gesture towards—a form of world-making contingent upon world-dependence.[8] While it may be the ancient powers of narrative which ultimately make a world, what continues to distinguish "film worlds" is that they can appear to us *unmade* or better yet *readymade*, not unlike the way we take up our world on a given day by taking it for granted, first existentially and then ideologically. Filmmakers specialize in transforming their ideas into reality through the logistics of believability—in a word, *architecturally*—and they tell stories not through oral or written expression but through a process of *actualization*, showing them or filming them as if the world opened by a narrative is a fact and not a fiction, staging them offstage, as it were, adjacent to the theater where the city hums with the indifference of wind. Basking in the light of a film world, I register what there is to see and hear onscreen, noticing that the only way to "read" these images and sounds, rather than be carried away by them without a second thought, is to think aloud—against the grain of my experiential silence—the embodied intuition that movies use reality itself to construct a view of reality, or can create worlds inhabitable for their characters or penetrable by viewers only insofar as they belong to the world itself (that is, *this* world), which is, by its very nature, fundamentally inconclusive and unfinished, what literary critics sometimes call "ambiguous." Great films open onto a world that is always greater than them, larger than art, so to speak.

This approach registers my unwavering sense over the years that while movies are fictions or at least constructions, they have the tendency to draw from the mysterious rhetoric of the everyday (the familiarities and repetitions that can make almost *any* world inhabitable) in proportion to the so-called flights of fancy tied to "escape" (the escape from ourselves), for when these fictions depart from what is possible/practical and turn their back on what is most familiar and true, the escape is short-lived, about the length of shock (whose effects can certainly linger before demanding yet another). The escape from the everyday faces a *new* everyday—and in facing it, films discover the secret ingredient that blurs the boundary (what boundary?) between everyday life and dream. So our experience of these particular fictions is also one of fact, the rather crude fact of more or less trusting what we are experiencing, because *what* we are experiencing onscreen strikes us, so very often, as similar to or reminiscent of *how* we experience or pass through the everyday: a sublime fit of aesthetics, technology, and the human sensorium that allows something completely fabricated to constitute real/relatable experience and be a factor in our formation as individuals. When I watched movies as I came of age, in tandem with my everyday life and most formative years, I was affected by them rather than influenced or merely entertained by them, and I dreamt about them rather than spoke about them—and it has been one of my callings since then to read the skin of my consciousness as exposed by *two* worlds whose affinity and friction "leave room for thought."[9]

Despite evidence and consensus to the contrary, I still find myself leaning towards the view that movies are *of* the world rather than autonomous worlds unto themselves.[10] To speak of them as worlds unto themselves, as we may be tempted to do with fantasy films or films with an overbearing sense of style, is to disregard or at least significantly diminish the fact that these alternative worlds are still made, let's say, of the rawest "world-material"—the ballet of light and dark, the betrothal of time and space, wild sights and sounds, and the lidless frame which opens up beyond itself, never blinking.

Now this material may congeal into autonomous worlds and we may refer to such worlds as "movies," but my suggestion is that this status is not possible without the prior condition of the moving image's being-in-the-world or world-dependence. This prior condition is a historical fact about movies which shapes equally how they are made and how we tend to view them: movies are like elaborate tapestries woven out of organic fibers harvested from the brute physicality of life, and even if filmmakers today can artificially create life through digital means—in unison with the ambitions of modern science, genetics, and artificial intelligence—the tapestry must hold together and the mosaic for viewers must open up and crystallize, a phenomenon that works best when the diffuse experience of cinema sits atop a foundation of elementality or dimensionality. While this condition may be a mere truism that holds in various degrees for all representations—insofar as all representations are intentional and reference the world in some way (as a concrete existent or pure possibility)—most films use actual photographic exposures or digital captures of the world as a given, and it is noteworthy that those which forgo the world almost always end up creating what we call a "possible world," a mere riff on our own. This is to say that the world is relied upon, leaned upon, even when it is being manipulated or dismissed or altogether forsaken. As long as a recording or an *idea* of a recording holds sway onscreen, and as long as images are brought together to signify a world greater than the sum of its parts (such that it can *stand apart*), then this condition of world-dependency is duly honored. As for the replacement of the photographic by digital technologies, in most cases this has not managed to unhinge the perceptual criteria of the photographic as an aesthetic precedent for cinematic discourse. The camera, whether analogue or digital, retains its photographic spirit onscreen as a kind of world-opening narrator; and even if no camera at all was used in the making of a film, most viewers—and perhaps a part of every viewer—tend to perceive or perceptually read in the passage of audiovisual events what William Rothman has called the "I" of the camera.[11]

It is for this reason that the "I" of philosophy, while gradually working towards an overcoming of the childish games of metaphysics (through the analytical procedures of logic or the phenomenological outpour of description or the existential escapades of inward liberation), is suddenly stalled and filled with wonder by the forms of cinematic revelation, interrupted by a vision of one of its original callings: truth. In film, truth begins as a representational correspondence rhetorically strengthened, or neutralized, by the lurking possibility of non-representational world-dependence. In other words, cinema's world-dependence enacts our intimacy with the world, a primordial intimacy deeper than the proximity of photography to the real and our false sense of proximity to digital instantaneity. This is why the cinema became the tool of an art rather than a science, despite obvious parallels between camera and microscope, between exposures of surfaces and X-rays of what lies beneath: film's mechanical or systematic openness discovers an *affect* of truth to be fundamentally ambiguous, if not overwhelmingly so, which is a letdown for the enterprise of practical knowledge but a starting point for the enterprise of poetic knowledge. Perhaps the films that attain or at least strive for a certain poetic height are those compelled to remain open, to correspond to a truth of which they are the creation: the value of the world is never settled, is infinite, which means we need not hold onto old values for the world to have meaning—in fact, the need for new values is proof enough that the world means on its own.

———

It is worth stressing that throughout this work I am indeed experimenting, above all with the thought that the medium of the moving image thinks humanly *mechanically*, as it were, through a process that is often referred to as one which escapes the intervention of the human mind. In this way film realizes the dream of metaphysics to know the world beyond the senses and the categories of human understanding, a dream epitomized by Kant's noumenon or thing-in-itself. Film sneaks up on the world and catches it off guard—the world as that which is irreducible to our knowledge and experience of it, a "pre-worded" world—as if the camera-eye caught a hypothetical glimpse through closed eyes such that the world in its own image becomes *possible*. This thought marks a decisive moment of encounter between film and philosophy, a moment which is not a philosophical approach to the understanding of film *per se*, nor a summoning of film to render concrete or otherwise shine a light on philosophical concepts which tend to evade a more quotidian expression. Rather this is a moment when the philosophical tradition of metaphysics comes into contact with a material enactment of some of its most enduring tenets and ideals—and, what is more, at the same time comes under the death-dealing scrutiny of the linguistic turn in philosophy where metaphysics is tested against the criteria of grammar. When a compelling school of philosophy discovers that its ultimate province is language and not the world, it becomes possible to see film and its theorization of the moving image—specifically the realist mantras of classical film theory and aspects of the contemporary branch of film theory known as film-philosophy—as renewing the metaphysical enterprise unselfconsciously and without disciplinary incentives. This "new" metaphysics is to be found in film theory instead of philosophy: it is at work in André Bazin's bold proposition that the photographic image "shares, by virtue of the very process of its becoming, the being of the model of which it is the reproduction; it *is* the model"; in

Siegfried Kracauer's revelatory vision whereby "in recording and exploring physical reality, film exposes to view a world never seen before, a world as elusive as Poe's purloined letter, which cannot be found because it is within everybody's reach"; in Jean Epstein's sweeping provocation that "the cinema is true, a story is false"; in Christian Metz's paradoxical insight that "the cinema combines the raw presence of the world and the subtleties and refinements of human speech"; and in Stanley Cavell's Heideggerian response to *Days of Heaven* (Malick, USA, 1978), to which I will be responding in detail later on: "objects participate in the photographic presence of themselves; they participate in the re-creation of themselves on film; they are essential in the making of their appearances."[12] I am surprised to see that an art historian like Erwin Panofsky reaches for one of the more blatant and perhaps credulous descriptions of cinema in contrast to painting, calling it "physical reality as such."[13] In more contemporary theories of the image, metaphysics returns in the revival of interest in the photographic index as an act—Martin Lefebvre calls it an "art"—of *pointing*, one with the capacity to bear witness to the world and perhaps reenchant the photograph's increasingly squandered powers of documentation in the digital age.[14] The paradigmatic phenomenon or reversal has been partly historicized in what Malcolm Turvey has called the revelationist tradition of classical film theory where the cinematic apparatus is endowed with the power to reveal that which exceeds the finite range of human perception, functioning also as a response to or reprieve from the Western philosophical tradition of skepticism.[15] Indexicality as a reenchantment of the referent; the relocation of the philosophical concept of "essence" from beneath reality (where it is static) to the surface of reality (where it becomes dynamic); the technological underpinnings of a revelatory aesthetics of automatism; the self-manifestation of life as the ubiquity of the mystical or of mystical moments in film … these are some of the fundamental events of a new metaphysics that takes the moving image as its starting point. And so we watch metaphysics migrate from the word to the image, from reason to experience, from human consciousness to mechanical unconsciousness, resurfacing under a new guise: cinema's moving image of the world and those film theorists and filmmakers who are the proponents of a new metaphysics "post-metaphysics." They may be quite unaware of their calling, and perhaps *because* they are unaware of it, metaphysical thinking is reinforced as a largely unconscious and cyclical human activity.

Philosophy's grand attempts to realize its metaphysical dream have brought nightmares in equal measure, sliding into religious dogma in Nietzsche's critique and into conceptual confusion or grammatical nonsense in Wittgenstein's (nonsense which befalls philosophy when it decides to make truth claims instead of solve problems, the latter of which are often caused by the former). So for this dream to be realized mechanically and from the outside—from outside of human consciousness and outside the domain of philosophy—comes as a surprise, even a shock, with results that are both fascinating and free of abstraction. In the late nineteenth and early twentieth centuries, when philosophers like Nietzsche and Wittgenstein were practicing their critiques of metaphysics (for criticism is nothing if it is not regularly and ardently practiced), the majority of early film theorists whom we now regard as exemplars of classical film theory conceived of cinema's raw material in what Turvey calls the "revelationist spirit," praising with renewed zeal cinema's capacity to deliver an image of the world precisely in its own image and the achievements of filmmakers who create films with that image in mind and in hand—a metaphysics transformed when photographed and projected and viewed by humans who have finally found a way to unite consciousness and unconsciousness within the concept of the camera-eye. While there are as many, perhaps far more, theorists who remain steadfastly anti-metaphysical in their approach to cinema (for example, formalist theorists who claim that cinema cannot become an art if it unconditionally accepts what the camera gives it, or critics of the apparatus who claim that to trust the camera is to be taken in by a capitalist mode of production, seduced by the ideology of Western perspective), classical film theory and its timely resurgence in the digital age can nevertheless be thematized as a heated debate surrounding the nature, purpose, and potential power of this strange finding—what the camera finds (the world) and what the majority of filmmakers do with this finding (make a world). This easily overlooked strangeness, this sudden presence and "upfrontness" of a world as seen by no one firsthand (a world undergone yet amenable to creative cultivation, hospitable to the prism of worldviews), is a discovery that the new metaphysics must learn to accept, insofar as it substitutes immanence for transcendence and aesthetics for ontology in its thinking and as its first principles. One way of understanding what may amount to a compromise is as follows: when the world on film exemplifies both the metaphysical concept of "world" and the epistemological quest to know the world (not *as* we know it but as we *cannot* know it), exemplifying it as a luminously concrete image rather than as an immaterial idea at the mercy of our language, there is the possibility for great disappointment in this, an almost unacceptable disappointment for the philosophical imagination when the final teleology of reason and redemption of our existential finitude must be set aside—and we too must be beside ourselves when consciousness is found thinking through the eye/"I" of a machine. This place outside the world from which we must reenter it through a machine-made image is a strange place indeed—it is one of the things about photographic representation that Cavell describes as making us "ontologically restless"[16]—and it is where we find ourselves when the quest of metaphysics has been undertaken technologically rather than philosophically, or when the aesthetic product of a technology becomes the embodied principle of a philosophy.

A metaphysics in the moving image can, at the same time, be found philosophically satisfying in ways that metaphysical systems leave us wanting, for while cinema only approximates the appearance of the world, in revealing it to us it sates our senses more fully than what might seem possible from a mere two-dimensional image; and while the desire for certainty in traditional metaphysics is so strong that the search becomes as elusive as it is never-ending, setting up the conditions for a life spent wandering the deserts of skepticism, a skepticism which, as Cavell has pointed out, is naturalized in the film image itself and thus no longer plagues the film viewer who can now see (beyond a doubt) that the apparent world is the only world. For the sake of argument or experiment, this new metaphysics can then be thought of as radically inverting, as opposed to reenacting, Plato's parable of the cave, insofar as the world in its own image can give us back the world as such, as if a reverse route to the eternal forms passed through contingency, finitude, and even the unconscious. But as we perform this experiment, we would do well to keep in mind the following:

1. At stake is an image of the world, one whose immediate experience can distract us from actually thinking the world (hence Plato's decision to exclude the poets from his version of the ideal city).
2. This image which makes a claim on the real is unconditionally granted an authenticity in excess of consciousness and a referential capacity more solid and, let's say, instantaneous than language.
3. What is logically determined in this context to deliver or rather "charm" the metaphysical through philosophy's "back door" (the non-human representation of the world by way of the mechanical reproduction of a particular film world) will come in the form of what Cavell calls "the world as things," as opposed to "the world as facts," the latter of which, according to Wittgenstein in the *Tractatus Logico-Philosophicus*, do away with things altogether by positing the logical relations *between* things, encompassing the context of our own specific relation to those relations, as it were.[17]

To elaborate a bit more on the third point, the world as things—as one of the fundamental principles of a new metaphysics—marks the unhinging of things from facts; the things of the world, stripped of the logical relations that endow them with inherent, perhaps *a priori* meanings, are revealed onscreen to be naked or stranded, objects of an alien world or building materials for a new world. This leads to the realignment of facts with things—fact on film being the "fact-free" quality of cinematic thinghood, the empirical rather than logical connections between things, and the continuity between on- and offscreen environments (with a touch of logic to bind the actual with the hypothetical, in this case). A world of things is a fate from which we too cannot escape, for humans are also things within this picture, the objects that stare back, inspiring the inanimate to join our gaze.

An exploration of the relationship between metaphysics and moving images must, in the end, bring into conceptual alignment philosophy's active pursuit of essences and cinema's passive or automatic exposure of the underlying essences of reality through its *surfaces*, a feat which is ultimately dependent upon the aesthetic activation of passivity or exposedness, a discursivity of revelation. This surface reality is fittingly a projected reality that in a sense precedes the projecting mind. With good reason the form of cinematic projection is often described as "coming to us" and "imposing itself": making an appearance onscreen analogous to the impression made on film, transferring the primal exposure of the cinematic substrate—be it through celluloid or digital code—as an undiluted force before being transfigured into pure light, light being the condition of possibility for a world to appear as a world apart, separateness being a criterion for the presence of what-is insofar as what goes by the name "world" is precisely what exists, as Cavell never tired of saying, *without me*. One can also express this relation between the experience of the world on film and the quest of metaphysics more candidly, albeit somewhat formulaically: what philosophy strives to know, cinema takes on faith; philosophy is human striving, cinema is mechanical revealing, and so on. No doubt philosophy and cinema exceed or even oppose these characterizations or caricatures—in fact, both have arguably outgrown or left behind, depending on your outlook, their respective metaphysical and revelatory phases—yet what concerns me as a theoretical preliminary or foundation for the analyses to follow is this point of intersection between philosophical and cinematic metaphysics, one which approaches the world in different ways and so with different outcomes. With philosophy and the moving image, we have before us two radically distinct modes of epistemological inquiry, describable through the following series of binary oppositions which we may still find to be of some use: knowledge and faith, the desire to know and the desire to be known, explanations and descriptions of events, words and images ... And if we continue to follow these modes further along their respective paths and unto the opposing poles of the human mind, philosophy can be imagined as a discourse driven forward by metaphysics and cinema as a process made receptive by what we call ethics—a new metaphysics, therefore, involves a transformation of the old metaphysics *into* ethics—and I again borrow a piece of Cavell's refined terminology, one which runs throughout almost his entire œuvre, in saying that the business of philosophy is to *know* the world and the business of film is to *acknowledge* it, or at least to acknowledge a particular way of knowing the world through contact or submission (keeping in mind that openness to the world and others does not guarantee meaningful dialogue—that is where the *art* of film comes in). This double movement between the resonating worlds of philosophical and cinematic representation is its own dialogical discourse, commonly referred to today as an interdisciplinary discourse; and excluding the conventions which have come to narrow and harden such a discourse over time, it is ultimately indebted to those occasions of intersection where two competing voices passionately echo each other even when they deny each other, accepting a mutual destiny which neither is capable of realizing on its own merit.

I do not maintain that film is a philosophically privileged artform. Like the other arts, film is an "other" to philosophy, but unlike them, film is conceivable as an "other" to art as such. Film is not a pure or absolute art with only one medium at its disposal. Rather it consists of multiple mediums insofar as it is shaped by the influence or inheritance of the other arts; the other arts helped to justify it artistically and economically, protecting it from the poverties of a mechanized mimesis. However, this automatism will always root one of film's two feet, as it were, into the earth of the world in its own image, a readymade yet aestheticized image with no equal in language or thought and which the tradition of metaphysics has been coveting like the holy grail. And so, the medium of the moving image can be seen to stand outside both philosophy *and* art as a possible bridge between them, spanning the end of metaphysics and the ontology of the work of art as the virtual site of truth in the modern world.

The terms and conditions of such a reconciliation between philosophy and film's respective world-image will serve, in part, therapeutic ends, for beneath each of philosophy's attempts at knowledge there lurk secret attempts—longings—to overcome the authority and prestige of knowledge itself. These attempts can no longer be called attempts to know but simply *to be*, knowing full well that we have strayed from such a simplicity. Non-knowledge is better suited to the arts, especially cinema's naïveté of representation and forms of faith. At the same time, these resonant points of intersection between philosophy's logical/empirical investigations of reality and film's mechanical recreation of the world in its own image—a fact of film that is ultimately dependent upon being amplified (that is, valued) by fiction's discourse of revelation—are not always or necessarily discernible when it comes to reading film and philosophy one through the other. The reason for this is that it is not always clear from the outset which field or audience such encounters are meant to address. Indeed, it is not even clear if the philosophy perceived through art or the art perceived through philosophy can yield propositions that will be recognizable to any "specialist." Perhaps the ideal reader will be a wandering member of the so-called general audience with ties to neither, or the generalist hiding within the specialist with a passion for both, be they near or far from one's lot, or completely without name. "Methodological good faith" (to borrow a perfectly placed phrase from Maurice Blanchot) dictates that such readers will be more at home than I am in Chapter Three's "Primer" section—the book's subconscious center. As you approach this center, you may find that Chapters One and Two can also be taken as their own cumulative primer for Chapters Three through Five, which I recommend reading in the free time that may otherwise be spent watching films.

Image Breakthrough: Disclosure and Derailment in Painting, Photography, and Film

I. ART IN THE WAKE OF METAPHYSICS

The philosophy of film is ostensibly tied to the philosophy of art as one of the many branches of aesthetics, and philosophers have been writing on art for centuries, a tradition that goes back (all the way back) to the ancient Greeks. It is well known that the Greeks were generally quite critical of art, or rather suspicious of it, a position epitomized in Plato's *Republic* where the poets in particular are accused of blocking the light of reason by skyrocketing the soul into an enlightenment that philosophy insists must be earned slowly and in stages. Since the Greeks knew enough about art to fear it, I would say this makes the philosophy of art into a tradition as old as philosophy itself. But it was not until much later, amidst philosophy's "visual turn" and experimentation with the senses, that art was approached as something far more radical, inscrutable, wholly *other*. In the modern period, art could appear as something whose essence is as irreducible as it is undecidable, open, and active: the work of art becomes the very site of its own absolute *working*. This term "work of art," despite its relatively recent emergence in the field of aesthetics, is one whose meaning—like so many—evaporates with every casual or dramatic utterance; and yet such terms do grant the artwork a singular autonomy that cannot be fully reclaimed or mastered by the human beings—artists and spectators—standing on either side of the mysterious equation, and this is what I wish to emphasize here. A work of art as a special type of meta-object may point to an object beyond itself, something perhaps otherworldly in comparison with itself; and upon being experienced in this way, it reaches out and grabs hold and commands our attention towards specific ends which are disproportionate to, if not irreconcilable with, it would seem, the material means. In this sense the artwork's ontology is akin to a ritualistic materialization or enactment of the mode of *allegory*, a literal launch-pad of experience beyond the everyday, a phenomenological catapult stationed within endless plateaus of habituation and utilitarian orientations of mind and body. But whatever the work puts to work, as it were, it is ultimately its own entity, its own being, a thing which reveals things, a world which makes room for itself and only itself, lighting the room that is the world in a frame. In throwing a light on being—I hesitate to say the Being of beings, just yet—the work of art shows beings as creations and only then as revelations.

As a reader of the philosophy of Martin Heidegger, especially the late philosophy, I have always found it interesting, if not slightly ironic, that some of his most penetrating and impassioned analyses of metaphysical concepts can be found in the context of an investigation into the ontology of the work of art. In his fascinating yet at times convoluted or cryptic essay "The Origin of the Work of Art," Heidegger sets out to formulate not only the truth value of the artwork but the work of art *as truth*.[1] After the dust of our affinities and disagreements over the question of art has settled, and after all our historical and theoretical models of understanding start to wear thin or entangle in a cacophony of vacant pleas, for Heidegger it is the artwork's absolute ontology or origin, prior to any particular artistic manifestation, that is declared through reason and in faith to protect the concept of truth—or some vital part of it, for Heidegger the very *possibility* of it—from the contingencies abounding within the history of ideas, myriad cultural contexts of human discourse, and prevailing notions regarding best available logic. The work of art (not art *per se*, but art as the powerful and inimitable *work* of art, art as non-utilitarian "work") is held by Heidegger to manifest the actual structure of truth, the non-propositional *form* of truth, because it is a thing whose function is pure manifestation, pure purposelessness. Our various and competing ideas *about* the truth must therefore come after the fact of truth's concrete setup and disclosure. Truth's disclosure within this context is a complex mixture of fact and value whose propositional form and rhetorical tenor belong to its own conditions of possibility, conditions most hospitable to what is possible in art. In somewhat simplistic terms (though this is always an oxymoron when discussing Heidegger, especially Heidegger on art), art lights truth because it lights and nothing more; it is a lighting up; it *shows* what we would normally have no choice but to *say*, if only we could say it in such a way that our words could show it. And even if art's "metaphysical show" does *say something* in the end, it is the task of philosophy to show its showing by saying it (and falling short)—this and nothing more.

As unlikely a candidate as an artistic image may be as a vehicle for truth, Heidegger suggests—and as the essay goes on, takes on faith—that art is the setting up of truth, the happening of truth, truth put to work.[2] He develops the entire essay around this formulation without being the least bit swayed or encumbered by the fact that philosophy has a lengthy history of skepticism towards the truth value of images. For the most part, philosophy finds the force of the grammatical proposition and the rigorously tested rudiments of logic to be more adept in handling the assurances and aspirations of

epistemological progress, the fund of knowledge and its occasional translation into responsible human action, the technical welding of thought upon
thought into belief systems we can trust—because to embark upon thought
step by step is already a sign of trust in what Wittgenstein calls "a form of
life." But it is precisely the nature of this form of life that Heidegger seeks to
analyze on its own terms within the aesthetic, whereas Wittgenstein's analyses
imply only that this form of life is at work all the time, in what we say and
in what we do, and we cannot access its inner or autonomous workings for
the simple reason that it lies out of reach for those inescapably bound by
it, like hinges on a door or scaffolding, to borrow images Wittgenstein uses
in the posthumous collection *On Certainty*.[3] If Heidegger's abstract methodology seems immodest or tactless or even reckless in comparison with
Wittgenstein's, then saving his philosophy from the wrath of extreme anti-
essentialism means remaining sensitive to a method of thinking that appeals
to and proceeds by *listening*, one that is receptive to what he names "the call
of Being," which becomes sharply interrupted and potentially nonsensical
when thought sets upon silence in a manner that Western thinking is trained
to do and takes prides in doing well, given an admirable record of graspable
results—yet results they remain.

Heidegger's sole example of the metaphysics of aesthetics is a painting
of a pair of peasant shoes by Vincent Van Gogh **(Fig. 1.1)**. (Is it a good
example?—One example is as good as another. Let's say it calls to him,
chooses him. If these shoes could talk they would say ...) This being a relatively modest work by the painter, I am quite struck by the individuality of
each member of the pair, the togetherness and separateness of the shoes, how
in certain places they dissolve, in accordance with their own demise, into a
wild abstraction of wear and tear, especially along the folded cuff of the one
on the left which can no longer hold itself upright, drooping like a dog ear
or wilting like a dying rose—the pathology of the poor thing is actually quite
moving—and yet Heidegger, so disinterested in this kind of formal analysis,
will not rest philosophically until what is being moved here occurs at the level
of Being itself and opens up a world unto itself. What is interesting is that
for Heidegger the expressionistically painted and strangely unrecognizable
shoes or work boots *are absolutely there*—absolute "thereness"—not under-
neath the formal breakdown but in plain view, broken in, viewed from the
angle of human feet. And they are there—present and alive, presencing and
enlivening—in a manner paradoxically denied to the model shoes themselves
(if they could be held up for the sake of comparison), as if only a thoughtfully painted *image* from an artist's imaginative commitment to truth could
express what these shoes embody metaphysically: the gravity-bound burden
of feet, the old soul of the wearer, harsh life in the fields or on the streets, the

Figure 1.1   *Heidegger discovers the truth of Being in a painting of peasant shoes:* Shoes *(Vincent Van Gogh, 1886).* Credit: Van Gogh Museum, Amsterdam (Vincent van Gogh Foundation).

residue of armor hearkening back to medieval times—what Heidegger calls the equipmental character and fundamental temporality of the shoes which become palpable, it would appear, only if the shoes themselves are left out of the picture. For a "picture" is what we need in order for the shoes and the world they imply to resonate: the painter has captured them unawares and gestured them into being through all phases of their being. Now the shoes can transform the floor into an extension of themselves: the earth. They bring the outside in. And their being/Being crystallizes long after the people (the real workers) have turned their backs or gone to sleep—for this is that moment when the world is and shines because, with shoes worn out yet unworn, we are not merely the beings who trudge through the mire of daily survival or destructive conquest.

But if Van Gogh has found a way to let the shoes "be," it must be their use—that is to say, their life—which he paints, and in painting, lives; he lives through that which makes life on earth so much more bearable—*shoes*, which take a beating, as do we, says the painter, particularly those who take to the fields. (Perhaps the impetus behind our equipment or technology has always been less a matter of progress than protection.) Van Gogh's painting can therefore be said to reveal the shoes not because they clearly resemble an actual pair of shoes but rather because they are, real or not, what we call "true to life"—true of how shoes in themselves are lived/loved by the wearer. One can imagine (can I?) a full-length film about the spirit of these shoes—life from the perspective of the equipment which makes human toil possible. But to achieve this kind of ontological realism beyond mere accuracy, one would have to capture the lived-in aspect, the *usedness* of the shoes which makes them loved by the wearer and abhorred by others. A photograph or film emphasizing this usedness/oldness would, in theory, bring out details extraneous to beauty or utility, thus setting itself apart from an advertisement featuring brand new shoes as scripted and soulless as the prospective owners they posit as incomplete, that is, until the shoes engulf their feet and promise never to sully or wear away.

Of equal concern here is that to take an image for the real thing—or for an image to *overtake* the real thing—may imply that it is precisely the realness of things which fail, or have failed far too often, to make a deep enough impression on us. Falling within our immediate range of experience, useful when needed yet otherwise cumbersome, the feast of things within our midst tends to go untouched. After all, things have been made for a purpose and so exist for our use—to perceive things philosophically as things-in-themselves is actually to miss their point; letting them be does less of a service to their being than becoming a part of their being by using them in accordance with their equipmental nature. In the end, according to Heidegger, only the work of art can excise a thing from the roar and flux of functionality—pluck it from a transient world and inscribe it within a more permanent world, some refer to it as an image world—where its presence will be readable against the horizon of truth. The "thingliness" of the artwork as a whole is what the artist activates, only to abandon it to an autonomy without utility, a form of work without a means–ends agreement, as it were, an autonomy not unlike the artist's own existential constitution and predicament: perpetual self-definition and, as is often the case in the culture of modern art, self-justification.

In *Art's Claim to Truth*, Gianni Vattimo extends Heidegger's investigation into a comprehensive account of the ontology of the work of art amidst what he and many contemporary philosophers obscurely and perhaps prematurely call "the wake of metaphysics." (Now I say prematurely because my own self-consciousness in this matter restrains me from attempting to settle debates regarding the end of metaphysics and the beginning of "something else," let's call it art. Throughout the course of my own thinking on the so-called philosophical turns (all of which seem to want to *turn away* from metaphysics, in part or in full), one can nonetheless sense that when a long-standing tradition underlying even the most radical historical change is felt to come to an end, it usually means that the period after the end commences a scrupulous, sometimes heartfelt, recollection of what it is that has been lost, only to discover that, in picking up the pieces, the logic of their assemblage becomes apparent as they are pieced together for the last time as if for the first time. If metaphysics dawns most vividly in the wake of metaphysics, then it is perhaps better able to serve our deepest, loneliest sense-making aspirations; and if the end of metaphysics makes the search for certainty logically or even technically impossible, then, the impossibility of it is likely for some to increase the desire and absolve the perversity of epistemological transgression. With the slightest degree of separation from tradition, accompanied by a whisper of nostalgic regret over the death of God that saw the prevailing of truth over spirit, metaphysics can now be documented or photographed, monumentalized and honored, perhaps even mourned. And just because our knowledge has turned out to be psychologically limited and historically contingent, our self-consciousness as knowers may not guarantee the overcoming of the metaphysical aspirations intrinsic to knowledge itself.—I look into the mirror and look at myself looking at myself and say to myself, "There I am." To add the qualification, "There I go, I come and go with every glance," or the famous Shakespearean confession from *Othello*, "I am *not* what I am," is not the logical if contradictory *step* it appears to be. Taking such a step takes courage, experience, and Dionysian willpower (if there is such a thing), and remains a largely private affair among one's various "selves"—between who one is and what one wishes to become—an existential rite of passage where an immense uphill of will and testing suffering oversees so many scattered projects of self-realization worthy of the name "life's work," even if none of them ever comes to an end.)

According to Vattimo, the end of metaphysics amounts to the aftermath of the great epoch of Western thought, an epoch defined by the possibility of objective certainty in our representations of the world. Think of it also as the end of our trust in philosophy's faith in *discovered* as opposed to *created* truths. In this "wake," the goal of art in particular changes internally and irrevocably—in a word, ontologically—not just historically or ideologically but *in its very essence*.[4] As a consequence of irreversible movements of thought, or rather critically self-conscious counter-movements of thought, art's new essence will also encompass, first and foremost, every individual's actual experience of an actual artwork, which means that the essence of the human is imbricated and at stake in the restated question of the ontology of art. With instruction and inspiration from Hans Georg Gadamer's *Truth and Method*, Vattimo's idea of an end to metaphysics implies that the ontological bearing of art now grounds a fundamental *hermeneutics*: more specifically, the *a priori* command to interpret and the haunting caveat that truth must be perpetually formed and deformed by human hands—the self-consciousness of the pressurized moment of encounter where the *value* of truth is inescapably ripe, hanging in the balance of every twist and turn of thought. The artwork's truth-value is now expressed as the activation of a new perspective on truth: truth *as* value. In other words, that which strikes us as "true" is now secondary to the condition of possibility for truth to emerge, forged as if out of the fires. And the work of art throws this condition of possibility into relief, throws a light on this lighting or clearing, as Heidegger would say, making consciousness self-conscious (calibrating consciousness) and an accomplice in the creation of meaning—creation being the necessary if paradoxical condition for meaning's revelation and discovery in the world.

Vattimo's response to life in the wake of metaphysics is therefore generally an aesthetic one and a specifically Heideggerian one (capitalizing on the latter's reconsideration of the potential primacy of the aesthetic): "After metaphysics, a work of art is beautiful if its wholeness is rigorously dominated by its own internal law."[5] When truth-bound thought ceases to be governed by immutable external laws or overarching absolutes forming a fixed world picture, then some form of compensation or victorious respite can be found within the ontology of the work of art as a world unto itself constituted by human creation. At the same time, such compensation may not be our first response or priority, even on a purely subconscious level where the decay of the absolute compels deeper, more desperate forms of attachment entirely unmotivated by reason. For it is a possibility worth considering that the end of metaphysics is precisely demarcated or made philosophically public by the emergence of the work of art's radical self-definition, what Vattimo calls its own internal law, as if a work of art worthy of the name is a creation of something completely natural, something reminiscent of a living ecosystem of thought and feeling, significance and speculation, *a* world constituted within *the* world, that is, when the latter no longer holds sway as a site of truth. When it becomes clear (or semi-clear) to us that our pursuits of truth have routinely met with disappointment, with shadows of futility cast by truth's fundamental non-existence or relativity, then what has happened—at least for those who continue to believe in truth or insist that we simply cannot live without some version or salvaging of it (thinking without it does not entail *living* without it)—can also be interpreted as a monumental shift in the nature of truth from something factual or propositional that corresponds to or in some cases touches its object to something best described as "evental" (no thing, in fact). Here, nothing propositional or otherwise is put forth, as the content of truth is handed over to the form of art in whose presence truth *happens*, is put to work or gets underway, in terms through which Heidegger never tired of expressing the autonomous working of truth amidst hardworking human hands. The appearance of beauty for Vattimo, then, is not an impression of harmony so much as the experience of conditions of possibility for art to impress itself as *work*; and in the process the work demonstrates that the most certain or at least enduring of truths have always been the most artful and immanent, emancipatory rather than dogmatic in their various aims and influences, fit to build with and live by insofar as they foster human striving.

Since my aim in this chapter is to situate the metaphysics of cinema in a larger context of image-based arts, all of which historically precede the cinema, I will now turn my attention to recent attempts by two art historians with philosophical ambitions who, late in their careers, explore the metaphysical possibilities of painting and photography in a post-metaphysical age where the work of art, as we have seen, enjoys the status of worldhood. In this context a decisive possibility of the post-metaphysical is discovering the metaphysical *within* the image, a place traditionally off-limits to it. But what a painting or photograph shows of the world is not necessarily to be taken for granted as a representation of anything guaranteed to be objective or held in common, for "to show" is no longer a systematic and richly codified process of visual communication through what art history has termed "the natural attitude."[6] Rather it is the gestural wagering of a worldview calling for consent or critique and where the possibility of community hangs in the balance.

In *Picasso and Truth: From Cubism to Guernica* by T. J. Clark, the metaphysical configurations of modernist painting (that is, the seismic relocation of truth from the security of the external world to the suspension of worldviews, or from that which exists in cold mind-independence to that which is made/unmade in bold feverishness) are brought down to the micro-level of pictorial detail, the hidden depths and inner workings of that thinly painted surface, right into the heart of Picasso's pictorial thought.[7] Such thought, if we can call it that, is fleshed out in the form of spontaneous color, speculative line, spatial (dis)orientation, and the radical disfiguring of the everyday which nonetheless declares itself inhabitable, giving rise to an uncanny normalcy. As we can ascertain from almost any work of Picasso, the sense of disfiguration and destruction can seem completely natural or solid, if not sublime, as if we could feel perfectly at home in a kind of ordered chaos to which our lives invariably return despite all our attempts to regulate and make sense of things.

Clark's first major step in rising above Picasso's persona to the living, breathing worldview of his work is to register the painter's persistent exploration of the physical and mental interiors we inhabit as a kind of gestural cartography of modern consciousness. For Picasso—Clark places the greater emphasis on late Picasso—our private abodes have become public spaces that mirror the tenuous patchwork of the modern world and the nagging insta-bilities of the day, aesthetic as well as political instabilities which have finally managed to penetrate the excruciating decorum of the bourgeoisie. A perva-sive, portentous, and contingent sense of exteriority is now being established in terms of *interiority*, which amounts to saying (pictorially) that our private abodes are material externalizations of the ruptured psychological interior. So if we can be said to inhabit a world at all, it is none other than the embodied microcosm of *the room*: the valve of a door, the grafting of floor and ceiling, the window as eye and the anatomy of objects, all radiating an atmosphere which sticks to our bodies like a foreign scent—and the more we become a product of this atmosphere, the more profusely and, for Picasso, grotesquely will we secrete ideology **(Fig. 1.2)**. (Perhaps only the man without a room to call his own can actually reach the world outside the mind. The elusiveness of the outside implies that rooms exist because the world is generally felt to be inhospitable, an unyielding enemy to the homeless wanderer whose "room" is at best the butterfly's cocoon.)

The monstrousness of the world in Picasso culminates in Clark's reading of *Guernica* (1937), a monumental painting that reconfigures the interior in terms

Figure 1.2 *"The floor of a world . . .":* Mandoline et guitare (Mandolin and Guitar, *Pablo Picasso, 1924).* Credit: The Solomon R. Guggenheim Foundation / Art Resource, NY.

of "proximity but not intimacy," a place "neither outside nor in, exactly, but the floor of a world as it might be the very instant 'world' was destroyed."[8] Here "the world" gains a foundation of support—a floor—in the wake of its destruction, with a loss of totality and sizing down acting as a domestication of worldhood, affording a provisional and revisable sense of stability into the future and whatever disasters lie in wait. When an ancient idol is destroyed, we are both freed and afraid; and when we roam about the shards, who among us will not be tempted to take one as a token? Are we ready to have the floor drop from under us to find ourselves completely on our own? Absolute truth, horizons of intelligibility, the historical resonance of humanity's most nourishing deifications, these cannot be logically refuted until the conclusion is borne out in the hearts of men—vitally "gay" hearts in Nietzsche's imagination, the golden symptom being that of beating laughter over stone-cold seriousness. The wake of metaphysics delivers truth as ruins, remainders, lifeboats; the earth-as-floor and sky-as-ceiling and world-as-things; the everyday as a relentless tide of familiar tokens that few can withstand without arranging at least a handful of them into their so-called right place.

Looking hard at the paintings, both through and at them, leads to the discovery of Picasso's iconoclastic pictorial thought—that is, the painted line's transmission of the artist's embodied perception, or the gestural interrupting/rupturing of Western perspective's reduction of visual communication to mimetic operations. Such an approach to Picasso's achievement opens up the metaphysical dimensions and possibilities of certain paintings, not surprisingly those of great ambition and experimentation. These so-called metaphysical aspects are not blank slates or stable immutabilities or bland conditions of possibility at the expense of actuality; they are not the truths of the paintings, are not to be extracted and translated and upheld as laws of discourse; rather they are the finished work's conflicted reconciliation with its own making, resulting in a form of representation shot through with abstraction, with internal self-criticism, with the very thing which will emancipate a picture from ocular lines of reference and keep a truth claim from infringing upon the truth itself, as it were.

Clark's unembarrassed search for truth in Picasso's late work also draws on decisive yet conflicting moments in the philosophy of Nietzsche and Wittgenstein, less as a case of influence on Picasso than as a way of making sense of what the paintings make possible. (Picasso may or may not have read Nietzsche and he certainly could not have anticipated Wittgenstein's ideas on perspicuous representation and acts of picturing.) Lured into the depths of difficult passages from Wittgenstein's *Tractatus* and Nietzsche's *On the Genealogy of Morals*, Clark is faced with two very different visions of truth, of equal value yet apparently incommensurable. On the one hand, there is Wittgenstein's insistence that the power of the image belongs to a representational reaching out towards reality, a reaching guided by a friction against forces external to our own mind and action (Clark refers to this as Picasso's extreme exactitude). And then, off to the side, there is Nietzsche's adamancy that the noble project of a will to truth typically (and tragically) delivers life-denying deformities of spirit, hypocritical and head-shaking "results" which indulge various grand illusions/delusions of progress and bring Nietzsche the iconoclast a whole lot of grief—for that which free spirits claim to be the bottomless fuel of their will to power is actually antithetical to life and an enslavement to an inescapable *belief* in truth (that is, the truth that there is no truth—*this* truth being so invincible that it can ironically repress or perhaps even reverse the death of God, one wonders). Standing naked in between these two philosophical visions—let's call the former representational and the latter non-representational—Picasso's late paintings not only accommodate but also warrant both perspectives on truth: the early Wittgenstein's perspicuous *reaching out* via the smooth logic of propositions and the late Nietzsche's recalcitrant *holding back* via sanctions either to stutter or to sing.

The inherent availability or amenability of Picasso to the remote peaks of the analytic and continental philosophical traditions in their most critical moments is exemplified by the paradox, perfectly logical in painted pictures and to a certain extent in all forms of picturing, of an extreme pictorial exactitude *without* a known—and perhaps unknowable—visual referent, be it for the eyes that see or the mind's eye that otherwise senses. Since Picasso simply thinks in paint, he rethinks or, better yet, questions reigning representational conventions through the hand rather than the mind, the mindful or autonomous or truly emancipated hand, the hand as the "mind" of the body, by turns caressing and crushing the world. Such thoughts, I want to say, are made possible only by way of the pictorial: philosophy will not be able to prompt *these* particular thoughts, if only because they transpire by looking at that which disorients—puzzles—rote perception: touch. The difference, then, between a rigorous pictorial thought and a reckless one can be measured by the productive tension between seeing and thinking, as opposed to the naïve harmony between seeing and believing—tensions out of which the painter might show what has yet to be seen, what is *to come* for those brave enough to face *what is*. Compared to countless other painters working within specific traditions or genres, Picasso's audacity is bold in the extreme, stationing himself within the "war zone" between figuration and abstraction in an almost systematic way, creating a dialectics of destruction which, at its most pictorially precise, covers the entire canvas and engulfs the world in a blaze of possibilities foregone.

Regarding the metaphysical possibilities of the medium of photography, and keeping in mind photography as a vital precursor of cinema (not to mention the currency of cinema's photographic basis still in wide circulation, even in discussions of the digital), I turn to Michael Fried's philosophical analyses of the photographic art of Jeff Wall. Wall is best known for staging elaborate, large-scale photographs reminiscent of monumental history paintings, exhibiting them using backlit lightboxes which punch them into a vibrant glow before the belittled viewer. As a modernist alternative to the immortalization of politically charged or proudly partisan historical moments, Wall turns towards everyday life in all its banality, intensity, marginality, and corporeal absorption in the world of things.[9] Boldly bringing to bear key concepts from Heidegger's *Being and Time*, which harbors both metaphysical and anti-metaphysical motives, Fried is compelled to develop his reading of Wall's photography as a measure of the medium itself and its singular powers of revelation and concealment. Is the practice of taking pictures to be taken seriously anymore? How far are we prepared to follow the photographic or indexical referent *into the world*, and to what extent can viewers of photographs remain attuned simply to the absolute openness of the photographic itself, an openness whose sheer endurance constitutes an occasion to which viewers must rise (no mind can open as wide as the eye of a well-made photograph)? Are we justified in saying that photographs are documents, proofs, witnesses, as a description of an object that enters our consciousness prior to any particular aim or use we might have in store for it? Do we actually *believe* ourselves when we say that photographs are "records of the real"? Is it a matter of *using* photographs in accordance with the ambivalent terms of their disclosure, or should we rather *let them be*, perhaps naively in accordance with an aspect of the world coming to presence in the light of its own image as if seen for the first time? And if we are so bold as to adduce the unconcealing powers of *alethia* from the photographic disclosure, is it not ultimately the province of consciousness that plays host to the disclosure of what we call "world," or what, for Heidegger, philosophers used to comprehend by the word "Being"? Is there such thing as a "photography of consciousness"? ... Such questions belong to a mode or mood of *questioning* that the medium of photography has the power (or is it a burden?) of spurring within our minds, modern minds which have clouded over from an increasing lack of concern with what concerns us most—Being, as Heidegger understands it—for we have become beings (have we always been such beings?) for whom the *mastery* of Being is the preferred means of disclosure.

On Fried's reading of Heidegger, the photographic disclosure is first and foremost a product of absorbed practical activity on the part of the photographer, and so any attempt at aesthetic neutrality based on the premise of the medium's mechanical indifference is a form of withdrawal and loss of control, symbolizing anxiety and not clarity as an increased consciousness of being-in-the-world. If you think about it, a painting might be a more accurate document of this disclosure because it photographs, so to speak, the painter's "sustained absorption over time in the act of painting."[10] It is an animated trace of the past, more alive than, say, a fossil or footprint. However, a photograph's inherent lack of tactile or durational expressiveness is what gives it special access to the drama of human absorption as a momentary— and perhaps momentous—banality, whether this banality be mechanically routine (a bad everyday) or domestically intimate (a good everyday). Both possibilities are at work in Wall's *A View from an Apartment* (2004–5), a photograph of two women immersed (enmired) in the everyday as agents of the automatism of domestic routines, which are also a form of life known only to them **(Fig. 1.3)**. In this deceivingly uneventful photograph, the woman on the right is shown reading a magazine on the couch while the other woman, presumably her roommate, folds laundry while apparently doing or at least thinking of something else (daydreaming). This is a topography, if not a choreography, of the excruciatingly solitary and multitasking nature of modern life—whereas if we still lived "in nature," the task would probably always be the one *at hand*, distractible by urgency alone. Both women are fully absorbed

Figure 1.3 *Social solitude in a world of things* A View from an Apartment *(Jeff Wall, 2004–5).*

(to use Fried's beloved term) in their respective activity (pastime and chore), an absorption, or self-absorption, which presents itself in the context of a togetherness that is neither exactly reciprocal nor oppositional. The separate "cocoons of consciousness" strike me as warmed by the presence of the other person who is in some sense felt all along, if not relied upon, such that the sometimes unavoidable slide into privacy and silence is not necessarily one of avoidance or defiance, a case where the Cavellian act of acknowledgment may be on autopilot, for better and for worse. Indeed, the combination of distraction and contemplation, of togetherness and apartness within a sea of daily minutiae, carves out a *social solitude*. What for philosophy is the problem of the other person (referred to as "other minds" by analytical philosophy, and simply as "The Other" by continental philosophy) is here, in photography, the labyrinth and hearth of "the friend." Cavell, a generous reader of Fried's art criticism, might say that such a photograph helps us to see that the coldness of knowledge dwells side by side with the warmth of acknowledgment. And if we follow the photographic referent all the way through to the fly on the wall of this shared life, going so far as to imagine the life *beyond* the referent before us, the image can reveal *multiple truths* from which consciousness conveniently takes its pick: two friends become, for an instant that drags on endlessly, strangers amidst the thickets of a nervous silence, or two strangers become, for an instant all too brief, the key to the other's completeness without so much as an exchange of words or glances.

Our practical absorption *in* the world may be the primary mode of world disclosure, and yet with this criterion in place the world so disclosed can still assume the material and fragmentary form of things—the world itself, the being of things, is entirely missed. Now, how might the tyranny of things and saving of worldhood function in the photography of the everyday, particularly as exemplified in the work of Jeff Wall? Fried struggles to apply the pristine Heideggerian redemption of the everyday where Being is encountered through a reflective (sometimes poetic) engagement with particular beings—the world's readiness-to-hand and equipmental character standing at a distance, calling us, and waiting for our acknowledgment while we persist, stubbornly, in our efforts to know it, eschewing patience. There is a dark side to the everyday, too, when the human absorption in things makes humans *into* things. For Fried this reading most likely jeopardizes Wall's intention (always separate from the created result) to use photography to unify the social and ontological dimensions of life (not unlike Picasso's pictorial thought), as if to say that our living spaces are the very flesh of those who dwell there, our possessions our very bones. Sharing these spaces with others means sharing our solitude and ultimately revealing our secrets: the woman on the left creates order, the woman on the right disorder; one folds laundry and stows ("where does this go?"), the other unfolds a magazine and dreams ("where do I go from here?"). But for every artistic intention there is a technical limitation, a medium specificity or idiosyncrasy that must turn its key, in this case a camera consciousness set with the task of showing that while these women to a certain extent *are what they do*, they will soon awaken from their absorption and meet face to face—but by then the camera will have shut its eye.

I will now work through three influential ontologies of the photographic arts, in what will inevitably be a non-systematic and far from exhaustive account, albeit one which will help prepare the ground for cinema's deepening of the revelatory powers of the aesthetic. Roland Barthes, in his well-known ontology of photography, *Camera Lucida*, is irresistibly drawn inside the silence and distance of the photographic experience, illuminating it with a confident fusion of thought and feeling, theory and personal reflection, allowing the photograph—or certain photographs—to burrow deep inside his consciousness, blocking predictable paths of perception and interrupting certain habits of being-in-relation with the starkness and stubbornness of their permanence.[11] His concept of the *punctum* is a significant factor in opening up the world of the photograph, as a detail or moment that wounds the spectator, referring the photograph as a whole back to the world which has wounded it in order to give it life. The punctum, therefore, is not the sole property of the photograph itself; rather, it is precisely the point in the phenomenology of photography where spectator and photograph forcefully meet, where personal associations may take over upon not only seeing the photographic referent as if it were actually there, but being directly *affected* by it as if it were inside oneself. The experience of the punctum—this hand, shoe, tear of the cloth, tear in the eye—has the power to eclipse the entirety of the photograph as photograph. Film too can be said to afford similar experiences of being pricked or jolted by an event onscreen, but the question is whether the stasis of the photograph is somehow essential to the emergence and pressure of the punctum and whether cinema's movement as conditioned by mechanized time and expressed by various patterns of narrative is fundamentally at odds with it. I also wonder if the temporality of consciousness requires or benefits from the *absence* of temporality in order to be meaningfully interrupted by the photograph's uncanny breach of human finitude.

A dramatic friction between the stasis of the photograph and the movement of human consciousness can, if tended to, sow the seeds of patience, enabling us to see differently and inviting our reflection upon moments of time anonymously suspended in amber, memories belonging to no one as history in the flesh. It is my sense that the photograph provides a viewer with ample time either to open or to close the spaces of consciousness, to undergo its display of otherness or to reduce it to an image to be registered at a glance and quickly set aside. The moving image, on the other hand, is routinely imbued with other images, or at least implies the coming of new images, and is almost always organized according to a particular discourse of literary, theatrical, or poetic substance, discourses which the cinema willingly inherits, inviting its own possession by outside forces like a body miraculously immune to disease. The moving image is the basic building block out of which films are made, whereas the photograph is the realization of the medium of photography itself, even within the context of seriality. A significant psychological difference can then be discerned between still images and moving images with respect to their modes of *displacement*: in photography, the viewer abandons the still image, whereas in cinema, the moving image abandons the viewer. The perpetual presence of *other* moving images, organized through continuity editing and the stylistic grammar of much narrative cinema, conjures the illusion of a single moving image mass that flows like a river of time far greater than the sum of its parts. The parts of this "mass image" that stand out, punctuate, and strike us viscerally or intellectually are often referred to in conversation as "moments," and the resonance of certain moments can linger long after in the imagination, not unlike photographs. Do photographs resonate like films when they strike us hard? If so, they may be the more powerful. But is it not the case that, generally speaking, we are less inclined to stop to look at photographs for any length of time? Perhaps the act of stopping before a single static image of the world requires more patience than can be mustered in an age in which the image (one after the other) reigns supreme. This suggests the possibility that photographs are passed over cinematically: the knowledge question "who is that?" or "what is happening?" overrides the often bewildering realization, "this is happening *now*—this *was*." And if that is the case, the photograph's metaphysical provocations will have lost their edge—its connection to the past, testament to our mortality, echoing mockery of the primordial longing to stop time. (Recent talk of the banality of photography, for example, suggests a loss of interest, or belief, in the past as that which cannot be passed over without losing one's way in the present.)

As we know, photography and its powers of revelation have a history of being scrutinized by aestheticians for not being adequately artistic and by cultural critics for lulling viewers into a passive acceptance of their apparent evidence; and even though cinema received its fair share of such skepticism in turn, it was photography upon its arrival in the mid-nineteenth century that bore the brunt of this widespread assault. André Bazin described the situation well by turning the tables on photography's various critics, stating that photography is the only artform to derive a decisive *advantage* from the "absence of man," allowing aspects of reality—presumably "reality itself"—to be partially unveiled in a way that artists sometimes call chance but which the human ego is typically blind to in its various efforts at control, usually in opposition to the whims of chance.[12] Bazin's perspective ultimately puts forth a metaphysical claim about photographic artlessness as the basis for a new revelatory aesthetics. In the essays "The Ontology of the Photographic Image" and, to a lesser extent, "The Myth of Total Cinema," the existence of photography introduces a new image-making possibility whose automatism gives form to the metaphysical unknown, staging it outside the domain of philosophical thinking and in the realm of the aesthetic enactment, what I described earlier as the *work* of the work of art. The arrival of photography, and before that the camera obscura, placed in our hands, seemingly without warning, the means to create an image with our hands tied, a point which Bazin crystallizes when he writes, quite famously, "photography affects us like a phenomenon in nature."[13] This idea persists today in the landscape of contemporary film theory and criticism: for example, in Robert Ray's most recent book, where he describes the mechanical principle of automatism as receptive to, if not generative of, the accidental possibilities of "life crowding in at the edges of the frame."[14] But, of course, these aesthetic contingencies can affect us this way only if rendered as a palpable *effect*: the power of photography's unbridled automatism must be harnessed, directed, ultimately utilized, lest the absence of human intervention—that is, the artistic possibilities derived from a medium's preliminary usurpation of human agency—be completely meaningless to us, justifiably dismissible by us as a mere theoretical curiosity with no real ramifications, and perhaps also ideologically harmful if the reality reproduced by photography and film turns out, as later *Cahiers du cinéma* critics like Jean-Luc Comolli and Jean Narboni suggested in the 1960s, to be the *same reality* engineered by the prevailing narrative–stylistic conventions so elegantly masked by classical Hollywood's rhetoric of transparency.[15]

The true value of photographic and cinematic ontologies also depends on their corresponding *psychologies*. Bazin's notion of the world in its own image is meant to be a description of a world which has imaged itself, given birth to itself, and in the case of the moving image, a world which also passes away, slipping from the hands of our eyes, as it were. Of course, neither photography nor film can offer exhaustive representations of the world—in fact, it can be argued that they show far less than they reveal, that their finitude is what is most on display. And yet, neither one seems able to escape the promise, for some, of representational perfection and exhaustion—for Bazin a "total cinema" that is always to come insofar as it *precedes* the cinema's advent a-historically, like a prelapsarian mimesis in which image and world are one and the same. Because representational totalization is a conceptual fantasy of the greatest amount and depth of reality, the ontology of cinema's finite instances is always leaning in the direction of the infinite without ever arriving there, reaching towards infinity in a manner analogous to the psychology of belief and perhaps even to prayer (and Bazin was, in fact, a religious man).

It is no exaggeration that the twentieth century and its voracious appetite for photographs and films (especially films) saw a more natural way with images of the world than with the world itself, the condition of experience in modernity being so eager to flee the grit and grime of an increasingly complex everydayness under the redemptive tutelage of culture and the arts. The ontological question, then, of how the world appears in photographs, films, television, and now the internet, becomes equally a matter of the viewer's mode and mood of appearance in what I already referred to as the psychology of ontology. The bond between image and world is strengthened by a belief in the *vow* of representation in the age of the worldview, a betrothal that we find ourselves gazing upon like witnesses amidst an apathy of consciousness—a consciousness configured, for reasons too complex to explore here, to take the image for the real thing. For evidence of the power of the moving image in particular, I suggest we shift our attention from the moving image itself—whose spatio-temporal depiction of the world is arguably the more robust of pictorial representations—to our various modes/moods of attention, especially when coordinated in the context of a movie: the intensity and absorption of the look or gaze, how the act of looking *at* can be experienced as one of looking *through*, refocuses the great paradox that most images onscreen are, for all intents and purposes, what they appear to be: they are transparent because they invite us (most of the time) to look at them *that way*—through them despite all artifice. Even the most self-reflexive image designed to stifle our absorption has the immense challenge of making the denial of its world-dependence (a kind of techno-solipsism) look believable as a worldview, for naturally no worldview can be *all* view, just as no point of view, regardless of how limited, can be completely blind.

I am drawn to the fact that we are drawn to make such ontological claims about film in the first place, for the context of these thoughts (a speculation, conversation, or reverie) is always too close to *and* too far from the object in question—harking back to a rather peculiar experience of film whose sense is split between a blinding proximity and an alienating pathology. This is how I perceive the significance of Stanley Cavell's confession of self-consciousness at the start of his book on the ontology of film, *The World Viewed*, in which a tidal change in his experience of film broke what he calls his "natural relation to movies."[16] Since *The World Viewed* is not a work of autobiography but rather philosophy, or philosophy as autobiography (a distinct and deeper matter altogether), Cavell does not explicitly narrate the twists and turns of his awakening to the philosophical importance of film-as-such. I think this change can be explained as the emergence or dawning of nothing other than the idea of movies themselves, a modernist idea of the purity of artistic mediums that, for Cavell writing in the 1970s, reverses the relationship between screen and projector such that the movie becomes what moves on the screen as the dance of light, and what moves on the screen becomes the film itself, the celluloid running through the projector, a repeat run of its passage through the camera, the machine that produced the images up there on the screen in the first place. Before long, an awareness of the camera itself starts to encroach upon the individual images, which are now called "shots." The very concept of the shot projects the camera itself back onto the projected image, and so on. The medium itself can be systematically foregrounded within, and to a certain extent at the expense of, its actual received manifestations, which become simultaneously expressive of both meaning and being, revelation and reflexivity.[17]

Now it is not as if we had never thought about what we had seen and heard onscreen when our natural relation was intact, but rather that we had yet to think past a *particular* instance to a set of conditions underlying *all* instances. This breach in the natural relation to movies has opened up a new *unnatural relation*, exemplified by philosophy's love of difficult or unanswerable questions combined with the cinephile's voyeuristic shock of separation from the object of love—loving without the possibility of reciprocity, also known as obsession. The effects of an unnatural relation are as numerous and varied, healthy and unhealthy, dramatic and comical as any committed relationship to a beloved artform. The shift from faith to knowledge and from pleasure to the pain of love is the decisive moment of this or any ontological quest. As a search for a permanent or absolute set of conditions, we know it to be misguided, if not doomed. We know cinema keeps changing, that there is no such thing as a single global cinema, that ontology is forever haunted by ideology. But what if we angle the search to the search itself, as it were, and recall that this search is not linear, not safe, but inextricably relational, a way of relating to *an* object that takes it to be *the* object, and in so doing takes it to heart? (In the age after innocence, happiness requires pursuit.) It seems that for Cavell what grounds the ontological quest is precisely his phenomenological reflection on the film medium as inherently reflective of the world. As a series of worldviews, film reflects reality that much more sharply and brightly in the context of a philosophical reflection that has broken away from its object by turning it into an object of study. Perhaps the experience of film has a kind of Lacanian mirror stage in which, one day, amidst the twilight of innocence, we see not so much ourselves reflected in the image as the image itself supporting our deepest fantasies—the image wrested from its everyday usage and thrown into uncanny relief, as if the act of viewing became the mirror through which the medium of film *recognizes itself* for the first time. The only clue Cavell provides for this turning point in the experience of film can be found, quite fittingly, out in the open of the book's very first sentence: "Memories of movies are strand over strand with memories of my life."[18] Memories of movies are such that they can weave themselves into the fabric of our own memories; so if movies can produce real memories, and if those memories have the power to define us, then our experience of their reality must be similar enough to our own for the two to blur in this remarkable way. For all these reasons, Cavell is compelled to describe *The World Viewed* as "a metaphysical memoir," although no rationale can fully account for the cinematic experience Cavell is attempting to elucidate in this strange little book, what he boldly admits to being "a sometimes incomprehensible book."[19]

Questioning the ontology of film leads Cavell further along the digressive if not divergent course of philosophical contemplation and discovery, primarily because of the peculiar way that film, as "a succession of automatic world projections,"[20] denies or withholds the very world that it makes appear onscreen.[21] On film, a view of the world can be shown indiscriminately and in full, "as it is," but according to Cavell it necessarily comes at the price of its absence from viewers. Responses to the prospect of the presence of the world onscreen through cinematic representation tend to take the form of a skeptical denial or deflation of the power of the index, often through the claim that in the digital age the index has been severed, repudiations of one form or another that strike me as no less paradoxical and extreme than the gross naïveté of blind affirmation. And one can express such denials with the same depth of conviction, despair, or elation regarding the existence of, say, the divine. It might be said that the divine dwells in things by lurking *behind* things, just as the world appears in a moving image on the condition that it not appear, that it remain absent. Absence can become the source of tremendous power, for believers and skeptics alike. The death of a loved one and, of course, the death of God are obvious examples, but consider also the solution to a riddle, the back of a house, the silence of nature, ghosts, homesickness or nostalgia, authors, and something as seemingly routine as tardy arrivals (which are often—perhaps too often—described as fashionable): absence is always ontologically in vogue. The price of knowledge, a great irony, is also in effect: the more you try to know something, the more distant you can become from the thing itself; and yet from this position of absence, the presence of the world has never been more pristine or profound. The "absent presence" or "present absence" of the world on film *brings us back* to the world, as if we found our way back home through the poignant realization that home cannot be returned to, only recreated. The way back to a world we no longer know how to believe in—in part because belief, as Gilles Deleuze suggests near the end of his two-volume study of cinema, still takes the form of a bodiless knowledge in the modern era[22]—goes through the back door of the cinema screen in what is ultimately the recreation of the world in its own image. I will have more to say about this in Chapter Three.

For Cavell, the moving image becomes the primal actor, or enactor, of a clandestine and uncanny revelation. The dynamic concept of an enactment, which has already made an appearance in those perspectives on art which seek to undo or transform mere exemplification, is very instrumental for Cavell's ontology of the moving image and for all his philosophical readings of artistic mediums, movements, genres, and individual works. Near the end of *The World Viewed* (the best is often saved for last because there it is earned) the moving image is described, perhaps without precedent, as a "moving image of skepticism."[23] Skepticism being no mere philosophical problem so much as the wellspring of philosophy's susceptibility to doubt, conjuring as if by blackest magic the fundamental problems of metaphysics, reality is thereby transformed into something that is both existent *and* non-existent when we doubt it for no empirical reason but rather because we *can* doubt its existence and *do*, in fact, doubt it when we find ourselves shunning or altogether repudiating the everyday. And this possibility of human thought and feeling, this fatality of the human propensity for looking away, withdrawing, white-lying or play-acting with matters of great importance, is for Cavell and many philosophical interpreters the blessing and curse and alien idiosyncrasy of the human condition. Cartesian skepticism harbors no immanent threat over our lives, over our daily interactions and decisions by undermining them as potentially unreal, unless we mount the perch of philosophy and then embark upon that peculiar metaphysical detour—breaking our natural relation with people, things, and the world as a whole for the sake of the all-too-human desire for absolute certainty. The skeptic (naturally? greedily?) wants absolute certainty of the world and in the process loses touch with the world he or she strives to know by turning it into an object of knowledge and being perpetually dissatisfied with its value as knowledge. The end result is that the desire for certainty is forever shadowed by the fear of uncertainty—knowledge appears to be chasing down the truth, but in doing so it also runs away from this truth *about* the truth: namely, that in the form of absolute certainty it is a philosophical fantasy painful to outgrow. By taking seriously the possibility that the moving image of the world is the world in its own image, or what Cavell calls the world viewed, the return of metaphysics within the image coincides with its overturning by the presence of absence, by *re*presentation. And that is how it has always been with the tradition of metaphysics: to know what cannot be known is to dream, and to awaken believing in the truth of the dream—like Dorothy at the end of *The Wizard of Oz* (Victor Fleming, USA, 1939)—is to be in possession of unsharable knowledge, what you might call mysticism. What makes sense as art will not always make sense as philosophy, especially when fantasy and reality are never completely separable (human nature confuses them ever so naturally, and the nature of art captures that confusion just as beautifully).[24]

As for how film embodies skepticism as a metaphysical problem, Cavell goes so far as to describe the world onscreen as revealing itself not only despite its absence (which is strange enough) but as a *consequence* of its absence (stranger still—skepticism's estrangement of self and world). The world appears onscreen precisely because it is withheld, just as, in the paradoxical logic of skepticism, the world enters consciousness at the very moment it is denied. Film exhibits the world in such a way that to view the world is to hit its vein: "viewing it is all it takes," with such views occurring as if "from behind the self" or, in my own interpretation, from within the self.[25] Cavell's extraordinary and unnerving encounter with the workings of skepticism comes through most sharply in his interpretation of the cinema screen: a moving image of the world is projected on a screen that functions in the end to "screen us from it"—the world we view becomes a view from behind the screen of our consciousness of the world.[26] Cavell's conception of the mechanical automatism of the cinematic medium as world projection at our own expense suggests that the cinema does not make us skeptical so much as offer a picture of what skepticism *looks like*, what he describes as the self-sufficiency of the world and our obsolescence as horizonal beings. Cinema is defined as a moving image of skepticism not because that is what moving images actually are, but rather because in Cavell's idiosyncratic understanding of film the philosophical concept of skepticism is what the moving image enacts, or stages, or dramatizes, rather than merely conceptualizes. It does so for many reasons, some of which I have hinted at, the heart of which exceeds the scope of this project. But regardless of the potential accuracy and underlying autobiography of Cavell's elaborate philosophical interpretation, I take it as a shining example of how an artistic medium, especially one in its infancy, can change the discourse in which philosophical concepts are embedded by seeming to escape discourse altogether (through an act of showing rather than one of saying) and bringing the philosopher outside the parameters in which his thought "normally" functions. When we are shown something that we did not expect would speak so clearly a language external to its own (cinema enacting skepticism), it is here that we come to appreciate the universality or commonality of our concerns with respect to skepticism: that it is a fundamentally human horizon rather than a mere philosophical problem for specialists to gnaw away at. There is the chance to better understand what we know—or what we thought we knew—more intuitively and affectively rather than conceptually or theoretically; and in that moment which we did not expect would be so pregnant with meaning, we may be prompted to take on an idea that suddenly appears more alive than it ever did as words on a page. The artistic enactment of philosophical ideas also shows that such ideas are not confined to philosophy alone, demonstrating to philosophy that its acts of self-definition ought to be in the service of its availability or hospitality, ideally as support or sustenance for self-creation; and by tracing them throughout the arts where human existence is represented in all its glory and terror, philosophy is expanded beyond itself or perhaps returned to one of its original callings: the decisive moment of truth where truth itself, such as it is, is either practiced or preached.

Whether the presence of the world on film outweighs its absence or vice versa, cinema make us, in Cavell's words, "ontologically restless."[27] Ontological restlessness suffers the inscrutable encryptedness of an object in plain view, an object like film whose view is anything but plain, hence whose fundamental unknownness qualifies it, now in the apt words of Cora Diamond, as a "difficulty of reality,"[28] an impasse the burden of which it is the job of philosophy to take on, to explore while simultaneously accepting or resigning itself to, without treating it as a mere problem to be solved—a problem which gives us grief only in a rudimentary "textbook" manner. When Cavell calmly states that we do not know what a photograph is, we can hear him stress (perhaps with a chuckle) that we *still do not know* (and if we still don't, of course we never will), as if knowledge here is unsuccessful or incommensurable with our experience of photographs and films, that the photographic basis is in practice—during experience—fundamentally unknowable.[29] A sign or symptom of having given up on knowledge in this case is when the photographic no longer enchants us with its mystery but rather, as suggested above, disenchants us with its banality, as though we have become fully acclimatized to ontological restlessness. If so, then the experience of representational recording imagery has itself become the norm of human consciousness. One wonders if such imagery, in all its forms and throughout history, has always provided a better, more meaningful fit with our consciousness than the objects represented, the representational aspect of consciousness being calibrated to receive the world through representations of the world, as if the only thing in itself that consciousness could lay claim to is an image: hence the inclination to regard images of "things-in-themselves" as possible breakthroughs within the increasingly confined and catatonic condition of consciousness. Ontological restlessness and what I will call ontological ecstasy are closer than we think.

II. The Myth of the Lumière Leaf

As a response to Cavell (and it saddens me that a conversation with him is no longer possible), I propose the idea that the viewer's presence *to* the representation of the world is a factor in the prevailing of presence over absence *within* such representations, so that a viewer's psychology becomes instrumental in activating an artwork's ontology. I concede that the existential basis of this or that movie, video, photograph is equally if not primarily intentional, aesthetic, cultural, and so on. In fact, these two bases—call them nature and culture—are inextricably and intricately intertwined; and while the latter might be more meaningful, the former, the existential, is defined by potential, and has the power to touch us—to make *us* present. But what makes us present? What are the conditions of possibility for a spectator to become not just active or passive but *present* to the image? Cinema may have mythically begun with the world in its own image as seen in the actuality films of the Lumière brothers, but how exactly did it present this image and what was our response to it? The world in its own image is an ontological breakthrough with metaphysical ramifications which must, after all, be aesthetically articulated and phenomenologically received. And it turns out that, at least in this respect, the cinema begins *twice*, each beginning accompanied by a significant or telling gesture of consciousness yet with only one having emerged dominant over time (very little time, in fact): cinema as narrative. The other beginning which concerns us here remains hidden underground, as it were, ironically whence film came: cinema as . . .

If truth be told, that which begins twice does not begin at all. The cinema does not begin in the heavens but on earth, and what is more an increasingly industrial earth—the dawn of the twentieth century. There is no platonic inauguration of cinema, or of any artform for that matter. Cavell wagers that cinema comes from *below* the world: that is, from magic and the occult.[30] But I see two distinct spells cast by the Lumière films, one trance-inducing and the other geared towards transcendence. The former refers to a primal scene that we are all overly familiar with: a train moving from the background to the foreground, towards us, a movement which moves beyond the finite parameters of the image, receding not into the distant horizon which inscribes the infinite but opting instead to crash into the theater's ancient fourth wall. The latter refers to the lesser known and easily overlooked poetic scene with which the medium can also be said to "begin": the leaves of a tree gently rustling in the wind in a remote corner of the background, all but hidden by a domestic table scene occupying the foreground. The swaying tree draws us into the depths of the image's world-dependence, perhaps out of boredom, perhaps a few cinephiles in search of poetry or contingency **(Figs 1.4, 1.5)**.

Figure 1.4 *Cinema's primal myth of shock:* L'Arrivée d'un train en gare de La Ciotat *(*The Arrival of a Train at La Ciotat*, Lumière brothers, France, 1896).*

Here we have before us two Lumière creation myths in direct competition with each other: shock versus insight, distraction versus contemplation, meaning versus mystery. Both endure to this day, resonating in the optical unconscious, guiding cinema into the future, forking its fate in polar directions even before a certain film magician by the name of Georges Méliès took the medium to the moon, as it were. And yet, whether we like it or not, only *one* myth has held the seat of "master narrative": an image of the world that *rejects* the world, an image in which the arrival of a train from the distance constitutes, in fact, a sudden departure of distance itself, the very distance upon which a sense of presence—of the world and of ourselves—depends. In Walter Benjamin's terms, such a shock speeds up the decay of the aura of art or snuffs it out in one fell swoop.[31] From background to foreground, from distance to nearness, from the screen to the seats, from presence to absence, from the world to ourselves, the moving image moves away from the world by instead *moving us who view it*. The poetry of presence, on the other hand, will move us by invitation, to each his own, and often by accident—on the outskirts of what is intended and against the grain of what, as viewers, we tend to look for when following a film the way we are "taught." From the

Figure 1.5   *Cinema's primal myth of poetry:* Le Repas de bébé *(*Baby's Dinner, *Lumière brothers, France, 1895).*

very beginning the cinema is dissatisfied with itself, with its capacity to record the world, reveal reality, represent presence, as though unaware of its status as an ontological breakthrough which need not break us to make us present in turn. For cinema, the world after all is a given, and with the world as given what does the cinema do with it? ... It gives the world the ultimate makeover of the spectacle. But the quiet poetic myth, that tree blowing in the wind, reminds us that the world in its own image can steal the show at any moment and without warning, and with nothing more than the gesture of its presence.

The train arriving at the station poses the standard narrative question "What is happening?", while the leaves rustling in the distance declare, or whisper, like a photograph come to life, the poetic fact "It happens" or "This *is.*" This remarkably illustrative distinction is offered by Jean-François Lyotard in his essay on the sublime,[32] to which I will be returning in more depth in Chapter Four where I investigate the metaphysics of nature in film. For now, I use it as a platform for the following set of fragmentary demonstrations from films in which the narratological "What is happening?" is briefly yet pointedly interrupted by the poetic/philosophic "It happens"—interrupted in such a way that the latter subsumes the forcefulness of the former, derailing it like a speeding train. These film moments, excised from an array of genres and narrative fiction contexts, each in their own way orchestrates an aesthetic setup or "trap" for presence and a possible sentience of world-dependence to strike, moments which deliberately yet spontaneously digress from the narrative and invite the world of/beyond the film to impose itself, allowing the narrative to come off its rails, to breathe, and ultimately be caught off guard by a contingent and often sublime intrusion with the power to heighten the consciousness of the characters, the spectator, and perhaps even the film itself. Such pieces of the whole, in breaking away to become their own living whole, suggest not only that there is a tradition of presence in cinematic representation, a tradition in which presence itself is paradoxically represented, but also that the dominant regime of representation—"the train" of narrative progression—is not unstoppable. The train can be taken off its tracks to explore the vast countryside of cinema. It is a vital tool in itself for filmmakers committed to aestheticizing the index, preserving a sense of the photographic contemplation of the world within the onslaught of cinematic time, and moving from the engine room to the seats. Let us now gaze out the window of cinema's mobile medium and embrace the subterranean myth of the Lumière leaf.

Stalker (Andrei Tarkovsky, USSR, 1979)

Near the end of what many describe as a metaphysical film—set in a post-apocalyptic wasteland called "The Zone" believed to possess supernatural powers originating from a mysterious room that, upon entering, will grant one's innermost wish born of suffering—a telephone call interrupts a crucial conversation between one of the cynical seekers and the guide or Stalker over the methods used by the latter to reach their final destination **(Figs 1.6, 1.7)**. The telephone interruption on the threshold of the elusive wish-room, though briskly handled by the cynic-seeker who does not think twice to answer it, has an uncanny resonance at this stage of the film in that it suspends, if not altogether breaks, the ominous, mystical mood, which is fixed from the beginning and peaks at this very juncture of moral confrontation. Such a sense of eerie foreboding in the presence of what might be a supernatural force—albeit one intertwined with the human psychology of religious belief—is to a certain extent established by the science fiction genre of which the film is a member, perhaps a reluctant member, despite its insistence upon stylistic contemplativeness, a moral sense of the unknown, and spiritual concerns related to one's specific calling in life. Amidst the rich greenery and rusted ruins of the Zone, where the only human presence is that of the three main characters, the ringing of the telephone gestures, if not

Figures 1.6 and 1.7 *Did that just happen? … The call of the outside world:* Stalker *(Andrei Tarkovsky, USSR, 1979).*

points, to a world beyond the film, a world free of the pressures of the film and even the genre which addresses them in a specific way and to a specific audience. The question which undoubtedly enters the minds of the characters and, without being able to give voice to it in the same way, can be said, I think, to cross the mind of the spectator absorbed in the mounting tension of a much-anticipated revelation, is the following: Who on earth could be calling this abandoned building, these ruins lodged within the cordoned-off Zone? And how on earth—this particular earth of widespread decay and desolation, silence and sinister beauty—is a profane telephone line still in working order? One of the seekers, by profession a writer of fiction, picks it up, says hello, tells the person on the other end that they have not reached anything like a clinic, and quickly hangs up to resume the cumbersome conversation, the spiritual quest, the film itself, as do we. But do we? Do they? Is everything as it was? It is the sort of moment in which we find ourselves as viewers questioning our cinematic sense data and asking ourselves, "Did that just happen?" "Did the outside world come calling?" Before long the three characters onscreen acknowledge the uncanny event through a silent exchange of knowing glances. Then the scientist character quickly reaches out for the phone despite the urgent protests of the Stalker. It is, after all, a way of contacting the outside world, where some normalcy still prevails, where the struggles of the soul are swept aside. And there is always an "outside world," beyond the here and now, concealed by the here and now—a potential alternative to and escape from the pressures of the inner world. The Stalker as guide does not want for anyone in his party, himself included, to be tempted by fear; meanwhile the telephone call seems to shake him out of his own romantic attachment to the ruins of the Zone, which in his case provide a reprieve from the unrewarding difficulties of life back home. Perhaps we all come to the realization that the Zone is not completely cut off from the world/home, that it is simply a way of confronting the world and ourselves undeterred by distraction or the pride that comes in "knowing the way."

Sideways (Alexander Payne, USA, 2004)

Two middle-aged men on a trip through the California wine country have pulled over to the side of the road next to an orchard. Jack, celebrating his final week of bachelor freedom, has just broken the news to his best friend—and best man—Myles that the latter's ex-wife, for whom Myles still has romantic feelings and hopes one day to reconcile with, has just recently remarried. Outraged that Jack has kept this a secret for so long, that the revelation comes mere days before they are to meet again at the wedding, and heartbroken over the final nail sealing the fate of his failed marriage, Myles impulsively grabs a bottle of red wine from the back seat, pulls out the cork with his teeth, and darts down into the orchard in a frenzy. Jack runs after him with whatever words of wisdom and comfort as the hysterical Myles continues to chug the wine while racing through endless rows of grapevines, eventually running out of steam and stopping in the middle of the orchard to catch his breath. Holding the now half-empty bottle of wine, whose contents seem not to have affected him, Myles notices two bundles of red grapes baking in the sun and reaches out to touch them. While gripping the wine bottle tightly by the neck, he very gently cradles one of the grape bundles in the palm of his free hand and wipes a thin layer of dust from the surface of a few grapes with his thumb. Still breathing heavily yet no longer panting, the expression on his face looks to be one of intense calm for his character, but it's hard to tell: he may just be physically spent or intoxicated **(Figs 1.8, 1.9)**. The scene here comes to an abrupt end, leaving us stranded without any psychological or symbolic resolution. And Jack seems to have disappeared. The shift in Myles from rage and despair to something like tranquility or even awe, from being absorbed in himself and overwhelmed by his emotions to being completely captivated by the glistening grapes which make the wine he loves possible—which grow from the earth and sit quietly in the sun, gathering nourishment from the surrounding elements—is one of extremes for which the term "epiphany" may be in order. And since epiphanies in art tend to dangle and go unresolved, in reaching this precipice the film departs from its narrative trajectory so as to confront the raw essence of its main metaphor of wine, coming to a poetic standstill when faced with it. Before these grapes are fermented and transformed into this drink called wine, bottled and corked and labeled with the method and memory of the vineyard, they epitomize the wild feast of unbridled innocence. Who am I? What might I become? What is possible in this world? I am the fruits of this earth ... The knowledge required to grow grapes just right and realize a wine's *full potential* calls less for hard facts and figures than for loving hands. Therein may lie the difference between aging and maturing.

In the Bedroom (Todd Field, USA, 2001)

Two men are digging a grave in the woods at the crack of dawn. One of them has just killed the man who killed his son. The other, a friend, is assisting in the execution of this absolute form of revenge. It is obvious from their tormented demeanor that neither one has ever been the cause of, or an accomplice to, a murder. They are completely out of their element. How do you dig a grave? ... Regardless of the degree of professionalism in such matters, the shocked or possessed state of the vengeful murderer's guilty conscience, having passed the point of no return, is always liable to open

Figures 1.8 and 1.9 *Therapeutic grapes:* Sideways *(Alexander Payne, USA, 2004).*

the way for costly errors in carrying out the perfect crime. While digging in anxious silence, a soft rustling in the woods alarms both men, causing them to jerk up in the direction of the sound, frightened at the thought of having been spotted. Instead of confronting a witness to the clandestine concealment of such a deed, they find a deer standing behind a row of trees, grazing on some grass or shrubs (it's hard to see for the light is so faint). They ought to be relieved by the sight of the deer, but the deer, sensing the presence of the humans, lifts its head to face them and stares at them through a narrow gap in the trees **(Figs 1.10, 1.11)**.[33] The pair, exposed by the wild stare of the deer in the night, cease to dig for an instant that seems to drag on endlessly. The deer

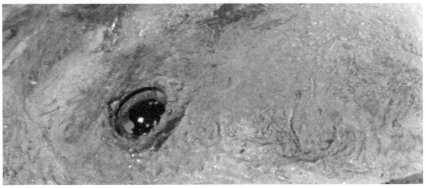

Figures 1.10 and 1.11   *"It just keeps staring!" Marcello and the fish-eye:* La Dolce Vita *(Federico Fellini, Italy/France, 1960). See endnote 33.*

does not relent—animals are known to be either extremely shy or extremely bold during these rare encounters—and the men, knowing they have not been in any way caught in the act, soon cut themselves loose from the deer's singular stare in order to resume the time-sensitive labor of traceless murder. The film also picks up from where it left off and everything goes on as if nothing happened, even though something did, in fact, happen—exactly what, no one knows. The killers manage to cover up their tracks and escape the "eye" of the law, which acts against the sometimes irrepressible urge to steal an eye for an eye. Avenging the murder of one's grown-up child makes one into a very committed yet reluctant killer with a conscience, wrestling with the paradox that one must commit the ultimate injustice in order to restore justice, in the full awareness that the world is simply not just. But after this incident with the deer, the two friends, forever bonded by another man's blood, cannot claim to each other, or to themselves, that their misguided attempt to right a wrong was not, let's say, cosmically noted, that they were not directly observed in the act of hiding the once living piece of evidence which will haunt them for the rest of their days; nor can they heedlessly go to sleep and carry on with their lives and their friendship (what is left of it) without acknowledging that they had also been clearly and incontrovertibly *judged* in some powerful way by nature itself (whose vicious hierarchy knows nothing of the barbarism of murder).

The Thin Red Line (Terrence Malick, USA, 1998)

This example comes from a film I will be discussing at length in my analysis of nature in Chapter Four. The moment I wish to draw attention to here is, significantly, not one of the film's many instances of natural beauty, ugliness, nearness, remoteness, fleetingness, or pervasiveness. The company of American soldiers (Charlie Company) have just landed on the island of Guadalcanal and are making their way along the edge of the jungle towards the Japanese position atop a series of cascading hills. They march quietly and with dread of what is to come—bracing themselves for exposure to the real horrors of war—and all within surroundings one could hardly fail to describe as the embodiment of beauty and peace. From the distance, a figure walking towards them slowly comes into view. Remarkably, no one suspects any danger by shouting out, reaching for their weapons, or looking to each other for reassurance. The short, bearded, half-naked figure turns out to be a native man from the island. The members of Charlie Company—tall, strong, fully clothed, and laden with artillery, but so very young and afraid—witness him as he passes them by, one by one, on the path towards safety and home, for the soldiers the stuff of dreams **(Figs 1.12, 1.13)**. A stealing glance from the local man ricochets back; there is no mutual exchange of looks, voices, gestures, not even a half-hearted indication of a common humanity of which, to be sure, there is barely the faintest trace, at least from the perspective of the soldiers. Where this man has come from and where he is going is a mystery because he, at this moment, is a mystery; his world is not that of the soldiers (nor, by extension, that of the viewers), and yet it is his world, or turf, on which they find themselves at war. His is not the world of the film either, even though the film does indeed begin with scenes of AWOL American soldiers living in the sort of tribal village that one might expect this man to come from. If we as spectators identify with the soldiers here, it is because we have identified ourselves as *trespassers*. Through the coming and going of this "free man" on foot, both the soldiers in the film and the viewers of the film have a palpable, albeit inscrutable, sense of "the other world" which Private Witt, the most spiritual and contemplative of the platoon, associates with a paradise that he previously thought resided only in his imagination. The "What

Figures 1.12 and 1.13   *The clash of ideological worlds:* The Thin Red Line *(Terrence Malick, USA, 1998).*

is happening?" question implied by the war genre, by the inevitable collision between the American and Japanese forces, is interrupted by the "This is happening" reality of an even greater collision between first-world soldiers in pursuit of victory and a local man out for a stroll in paradise—paradise *lost*, it would appear, for all of the characters in the film. Interestingly, the man does, in fact, approach the soldiers—and us too—along a background-to-foreground trajectory that holds us captive, just like the Lumière train arriving at the station; but if we look more closely and examine what is happening here more deeply, we will discover that the perspective of this man needs accounting for. From *his* perspective, the soldiers are the speeding train, fueled by the engine of the camera in the rear; and while his presence sparks a fusion of wonder and doubt in their faces, giving them pause, it is not strong enough to stop them or compel them to vacate this hidden nook of the world unspoiled by commercial warfare, for the latter, after all, is one of the logical conclusions of the Western alliance between capitalism and colonialism.

The Straight Story (David Lynch, USA/UK/France, 1999)

Alvin Straight, a man in his seventies, decides on a whim deeper than any debated plan to drive a lawnmower 240 miles from Iowa to Wisconsin to visit his estranged brother, who has just suffered a stroke. Early on in the journey, after he has hit only a couple of bumps in the road (obstacles which are merely signposts for the real obstacles to come), storm clouds gather to the sound of thunder, boasting imminent rain. Alvin notices an old barn off to the side of the road which appears to be abandoned and steers up the path towards it for shelter. The barn seems tailormade for him and his mower vehicle to rest, consisting of nothing more than a vacant driveway open at both ends—perfect shelter, perfect timing. He pulls inside the shell of this barn at the precise moment the rain starts falling in sheets, with lightning flashing up the gloomy interior of the barn, giving it a kind of electric decor. To make a good thing even better, a soft moment even sweeter, Alvin grabs a cigar from his pocket, lights it, and starts to smoke, watching the storm from this ideal vantage point while cozily protected inside the shelter. The ensuing panoramic panning shot reveals his perspective as a solid fixed point around which his vision glides over the fine contours of the open, rain-soaked landscape. He looks enviably comfortable, calm and content, despite the difficulty of the precarious journey, the great majority of which still lies ahead, a journey he begins so close (perhaps too close) to the end of the journey of his life as a whole **(Figs 1.14, 1.15)**. The lawnmower posing as automobile allows Alvin to experience the landscape more intimately, without the mediation of a window and the stuffy enclosure of a car, and more slowly too, for even the best mowers move like turtles compared to almost any other mode of transport you care to imagine. And yet, Alvin's moment of respite, parked and sheltered in complete and utter solitude, is one of the few moments along the way to his estranged brother where he is shown appreciating the natural surroundings so abundant in the American Midwest—and it serves to meaningfully pivot the "What is happening?" aspect of the quest for reconciliation towards the "It happens" aspect of Alvin's moment-by-moment experience of the non-linear journey of self-discovery. As long as Alvin is on the road, perched atop his John Deer lawnmower, his gaze is a sharp, forward projection towards his sick brother and the possibility of a reunion long overdue. When nature turns ugly, he wastes no time escaping it, and once he is safe and sound under the cover of the barn where nature can no longer touch him, he turns back to devour it as ideal nourishment for the soul. The appreciation *of* nature here implies protection *from* nature. Such a reversal is subtly expressed when Alvin cinches the opening of his plaid coat around his chest and neck before finally sitting back to watch the storm unfold. Seated spectators

Figures 1.14 and 1.15   *Leaving the straight path to take shelter from the rain:* The Straight Story *(David Lynch, USA/UK/France, 1999).*

primed for the long haul of a feature film seem to do something similar, quieting down the body before the film (or play or performance) begins, and it is hardly a coincidence that most heavy shifting and fidgeting fade out in tandem with the lights. It is also worth mentioning an earlier scene prior to the journey, one which the scene I have been describing explicitly echoes, when Alvin first learns of his brother's near fatal stroke while watching a storm rage at night from the comfort of his home. While I concede that the two scenes are linked, and in light of this we may choose to perceive the second through the lens of the first, nonetheless the pre-journey storm is more clearly intended to be a premonition, indulging in a strong version of the pathetic fallacy where the news of Alvin's brother's illness is presented as a cataclysm of negligence and discord in need of immediate rectification. The second storm, by contrast, appears by chance and unfolds autonomously, existing for itself rather than for strictly narrative or thematic ends. It is connected to Alvin's being only in a literal phenomenological sense as a perceptual event bracketed from his mortal mission. The rest stops of life are reserved for those who boldly venture out.

Snow Angels (David Gordon Greene, USA, 2007)

This is a film which involves the death of a child, hence a film in which what we might call "the unrepresentable" comes to presence. The child, named Tara, is at that very tender age when she is still learning how to speak and, in what is an even more challenging rite of passage, why speech is an inescapable hall of mirrors in the world of adults. Her mother, Annie, is at home nursing a routine yet debilitating flu, and she is found rising from an involuntary nap to the piercing alarm of silence in the house, further amplified by the soft hiss of television static streaming from an off-air channel. As if awakening into a nightmare, her daughter is nowhere to be found. Search teams are sent out within this small, well-acquainted community, among them an adolescent boy who catches a glimpse of a pink mitten that seems to point towards a small patch of winter clothing locked beneath a membrane of ice **(Figs 1.16, 1.17)**. Tara's drowning was not pictured onscreen, but its absence does not belong to that species of erasure which functions so well to provoke the imagination. Despite the excruciating lucidity of the aftermath, offered to us as the least amount of visual information necessary to register the tragedy, it seems to me that one *cannot* imagine the unfolding of it, the undergoing of it, for the innocence of a child and her single mother. What force obstructs the language of the imagination to speak for itself that which has been left undisclosed in silence? There are some things that we just cannot imagine—because we dare not imagine them. We do not have it within us to know that which we are emotionally or experientially unfit to support; the imagination's morbid curiosity kills conscience like a cat. Nevertheless, the "blank" of the death of a child at the hands of nature or the madness of contingency (in a world where adventure always entails danger) is irresolvable within the revelatory realm of cinematic representation. It is as though the eye, mind, and heart cannot be reconciled over a traumatic truth, the fact of which is accepted yet the brunt of which is denied insofar as it cannot be endured. Such a paradox is an apt description of the mother's reaction upon learning the truth of her daughter's death: acknowledged, accepted, understood, but *disbelieved*. And what is disbelieved, not so much out of denial as necessity, is the child lifeless beneath the surface of the river or lake where her body is discovered—her tiny body frozen in a time before time, a lifetime unlived. My sense of this image, when it first appeared onscreen for what felt like a flash, is that it was filmed with trepidation and reluctance. What are the cinematic signs that betray such a fear to gaze upon one of the greatest difficulties of reality? In what way can an image

Figures 1.16 and 1.17 *Traumatic traces of a lifeless child:* Snow Angels *(David Gordon Greene, USA, 2007).*

register or resonate an *awareness* of the unrepresentable? By way of an attempt to answer such questions, standing in the light of a certain inexpressible tact-fulness of representation, the undeniable presence of the lifeless, water-filled child is shown in the image as a fleeting sense or impression as opposed to the fixed object *of* a sense or impression. The distinction is a crucial one, not only as it applies to the adolescent in whose consciousness we gain this unbear-able glimpse of reality, but as grounds for a display of aesthetic responsibility towards the limits of representation. The unrepresentable image, I want to say, is filmed, not shown, seen without being sensed. That is to say, it is *in the process of* being shown, of being known (though that will never be), in contrast with a more stable image grounded in convention or exposition. It is not exactly presented *to us* as left suspended in the form of the presence of an absence: a horizontal rip across two vertical cuts makes an incision into the body of the consciousness of the witnessing adolescent. Trauma, we see, is an instantane-ous penetration of mind and body whose resonance—like a flash of light between two mirrors—amplifies and quickens over time. The first thing the boy's mother says to him upon his return home is to take precautions against repression, to speak about what has happened, to put into as many words as necessary what he has seen and felt and must live with. Avoiding the pain of therapy, thus paving the way for a life of suffering in self-misunderstanding, is precisely the risk she admits to having taken throughout her troubled life. "That's what I do," she confesses with resignation, the flight instinct woven into her very identity. What is to be so carefully avoided is the bracketing of difficulties of reality and a shunning of the unrepresentable within oneself, mental shortcuts which only exacerbate "the problem" by laying it on the back of an unsuspecting and deeply cyphered future self.

All the above examples should be taken not only as illustrations of a world poetics of film but also as accounts of an *experience* of an "It happens" moment in which the ontology of art—not just the ontology of cinema—stages the condition of possibility for truth as unconcealment and thus the return of metaphysics within the general domain of the aesthetic. Throughout this chapter I have emphasized the visual arts with respect to metaphysics, a move which situates cinema in a wider discourse of art's unique, oblique, off-kilter claim to truth. In retrospect, I would offer five reasons behind the proposition that the persistence of metaphysics is *aesthetic* and hence not exclusive to film (nor, of course, to philosophy):

1. The world cannot appear in its own image without an image external to ourselves, and the image with the sharpest degree of "externality" is the visual image, framed or projected.
2. The metaphysical ontology of art is as much a property/possibility of aesthetics as the techniques or technologies of representation used to explore it.
3. The idea of the world in its own image made possible by modes of representation, primarily that of photographic/cinematic technologies, can be brought to light in various ways, according to various styles, by artists who can be said to do metaphysics non-philosophically.
4. The mechanical automatism so vital to the return of metaphysics in art is based not solely on the absence of human intervention but also on the prioritization of the presence of the medium in various acts of human creation.
5. While the visual arts are, of course, representational, the artist is always free to steer representation in the direction of presence, which, in the

case of narrative film, might involve a *loss* of direction—a veering into the realm of poetry and the avant-garde.

Now what I suggest we take from these brief readings of "image breakthroughs" is that when an image can be said to point at something, what it shows must be unlike anything human consciousness could point out in its predominantly rational understanding of the world. For when the pointing capabilities of the image take on a renewed interest or forcefulness, are we not then pointing at the possibility of pointing *as such*, a possibility which, for us, points out *the impossible*? And is the (im)possibility of pointing as such not a properly metaphysical (im)possibility of picturing? ... The increasing stakes (not only semiotic and aesthetic but psychological and, in some cases pertaining mostly to photography, *ethical*) surrounding the matter of indexicality in the age of the image (i.e., that certain images can reach their objects, if not touch them, more effectively than human subjectivity can reach around itself, as it were) appear to have taken what is a specific branch of C. S. Pierce's semiotic taxonomy of signs and placed it at the very root of the sign as a whole, a sign whose powers of pointing are engaged just as we lose control over our speech and even our perception.[34] Perhaps that is why the art of pointing as performed in perpetuity by art itself is generally met with *agreeable* silence or confusion.

The idea of an image breakthrough also hinges on our own capacity to be so affected—malleable if not breakable; only then is it likely to be positive and empowering. This brings me to the ethical perspective on the metaphysical ontology of art with which I would like to conclude this chapter. In the phenomenological ethics of Emmanuel Levinas, human consciousness is a closed system of meaning, a highly organized and routinized cage which must be rattled to take the full measure of itself as *belonging to others*.[35] Here it is the other person who has the power, unbeknownst to him or her, to upset the tendency for an individual consciousness to reduce the world and others to extensions of itself. Such an ethics is powered by a radical indebtedness to "the other" to break through the walls of consciousness (this is what Levinas calls "alterity"), and yet at the same time consciousness is conceptualized as impervious to such a rupture. While consciousness contains the germ of alterity within it, as soon as this alterity is brought to the surface of consciousness it seems to deny it or repress it, drowning it for the sake of its own self-preservation. I believe this is why Levinas, like Heidegger before him, looks for examples of this phenomenological reversing and unnerving in certain artworks—for him it is literature which does it best, particularly Shakespeare's tragedies—because ethical consciousness will always struggle in the face-to-face encounter to implement the criteria of openness, passivity, and vulnerability—criteria which are as if automatically embodied, if not idealized, by the revelatory ontology of art. The knowledge that consciousness must be broken does little to break it—it may even keep it intact. The face of the other is bright like the sun and we look away at the very instant of the other's unbidden intrusion. We need help in this, help *out* of this ethical predicament, in order for the self to be dismantled under less threatening conditions which may placate the instinct of self-preservation to retreat from the world (a world of others and otherness). Such conditions are created, I believe, by the enduring powers of art to open onto the world and invite the unfolding of consciousness; and when the world at last succeeds in breaking through the image (and by extension, our own self-image), the result will be a luminous breakthrough held intact by the aesthetic as opposed to a shattering breakdown amidst the shadows of ethics.

On the level of its ontology, a given artwork is constituted not by images of itself (as we often are) but by images of the world: that is to say, images of breakthrough. The meaning of an artwork is coterminous with the happening of the world, what I referred to earlier, after Heidegger, as the artwork's *work*, its destiny of revelation; and to experience this phenomenon—to undergo it—is to expose consciousness to the fact that its rote reduction of the world to various kinds of object functions on the same register as a love for the world as a site of patience and respect, transformation and truth.

CHAPTER TWO

The Evolution of the Concept of "World" from Philosophy to Film

> The world—how grand, how monumental, grave and deadly, that word is: the world, my house and poetry.
>> — William Gass, "In the Heart of the Heart of the Country"

I. THE WORLD IN THE PALM OF PHILOSOPHY

Words like "world" stand heavy and tall like majestic mountains in the distant horizon of the mind. They are not yet facts, or were once facts, or express the sort of fact that is difficult to check without attempting to untangle an ancient edifice of associations. Crossing them out is a minor protest which usually results in a synonym. Law-like and stratified with thought accruing over time, such words are difficult to rewrite or rethink or restrain, for they give us something to write and think and talk about in the first place. Much writing takes place on the "page" of these words or within their house, to echo Gass above. The words we believe we select with great care in expressing ourselves and acknowledging a shared world are as firmly planted as a tree and as real as the chair on which we sit. They are part of the world insofar as they tend to posit the *same* world over time. They are instruments; entire philosophies can be composed in their key; and when we put them to work towards this or that end, such words work miracles of revelation and paint pictures more vividly than any brush. It is like the mystery of facts so basic to daily intelligibility that we can no longer pinpoint as being true or false; of beliefs that cannot be so held because they have a hold on us first; of ideas carried along the winds of our words and imparted like secrets to those in search always for the right words. If the beginning is the word, it is because language is always already speaking, shouting in the case of big words like "world." For this reason, the act of thinking, when it is genuine, can feel like the interruption or silencing of thought itself.

Philosophical concepts originate from words, more specifically from nouns. Metaphorically, they are as stars lining the history of ideas, monoliths of both worship and desecration, gathering places of the mind for those in search of community as much as truth. "World" is one such word which philosophy has at its disposal as a term of reference for the location and limit of all things pertinent to life as we know it, and throughout its history philosophy has been known to philosophize the world as a whole as if it were alive and twitching in the palm of its hand. When historically examined unto its transhistorical origins, such an epic and all-encompassing term could turn out to be as old or ancient as philosophy itself, at least in the West. In fact, philosophy may date back to this great realist dream (some skeptics might prefer to call it a delusional nightmare) to know the world-as-such: that is to say, *everything* there is to be known, where even the unknown is but a temporary obscurity waiting to be lifted. The most obvious precedent of this myth is Plato's unenlightened cave of consciousness which reduces the world to mere images of it, holding the mind in an immature and antiquated state of being lest consciousness can bring itself—with the help of philosophy—to face the blinding truth of the light outside, the "real world" as that which exceeds mere appearance via the five misbegotten senses. And of course, no notion of "world" can exclude all the perspectives and pictures of the brilliant blue object in space, as flat or round, centered or decentered, spectral or speck of dust, fated or forgotten in the grand scheme of the cosmos; and we may take a certain measure of relief in knowing that the world is far older than us, pre-dating the human condition and therefore housing this condition, calibrating our fundamental being-in-the-world as childlike and forgivably fallable. But if philosophy can be said to begin with the experience of the "thinkability" of the world, with an experience of the world as an object-event amenable to various philosophical positions, then the concept of world not only is as old as philosophy but also sparks philosophy into action and the activities of metaphysics into systematization. The spark is created by what I will call the friction of consciousness: the *self*-consciousness that we exist, and that our existence, while shared, is equally solitary and capable of further separation from the world into which we are, so to speak, thrown. Indeed, it is difficult to imagine philosophy's interest in the world as a whole without taking into account the wounds incurred from this "fall" into knowledge. The philosopher's lifelong passion in this regard is to piece consciousness back into a more natural relation with the world: the primal, blissful, and infinitely intimate "garden relation."

Since philosophy's great, monumental, all-encompassing or all-consuming object of study (the world, or the world as thinkable) may be taken to ground or even *found* the Western philosophical enterprise, I will approach the history of this concept as a series of attempts—some solid, others flimsy; some possessive, others responsive—to grasp the ungraspable. I also like to think of this series of views of the world as a multilayered history of world-view transformations. In other words, just when we thought we grasped something significant about the world that we did not hitherto know, the tides of history demonstrate—in a way no historical being can properly imagine without the luxurious leverage of retrospect—that only the world-view changes, and with it the way of life it secretly promotes or enforces. Our ideas about the world are always dependent (and, in a sense, historically contingent) on how it is being viewed, from where the view occurs, who is doing the viewing, various degrees of proximity and detachment, and above all on the inescapability of occupying a view of some kind despite common misunderstandings of objectivity, or, more specifically, the scientific method as a peculiar species of neutral "viewlessness." It's simple enough to say that a view of the world amounts to a worldview, but what does this entail exactly? A view of the world is a picture drawn with the well-founded or biased assumptions of epistemological striving; it is an angle, let's say, whose pointedness elucidates while simultaneously eclipsing—the psychology of philosophy would say "repressing"—other points of view no less tenable or hospitable to the pressures of human understanding. I would also stress that this particular perspective—the view that only the worldviews themselves are viewable—is a specifically modernist perspective in Western philosophy that holds a mirror to the history of ideas and bends the past to its will of self-consciousness, a newfound will fueled by the criticism or skepticism of philosophical egoism (the "I think" is diagnosed as pure "ivory tower" abstraction). Today, such philosophical self-consciousness can be found at work in virtually any field with some claim to authority, whether the source of that claim stems from the practitioners or the public; however, when it comes to the makeup of the meta-perspective itself—how it emerged, why it has taken root, what it reveals about humanity and the times—we may look no further than the title of Martin Heidegger's provocative essay, "The Age of the World Picture."[1]

World is both a figure of everyday speech and a fundamental concept of metaphysics. The world is often described as visible to us, thinkable by us, and infinitely communicable and negotiable amongst us—but, metaphysically speaking, we are bound to it and conditioned by it; in a sense, we are *made* for it. For everything that has been raised and ruined in its name, everything from the source of inner worlds to the stepping stone to afterworlds, one thing is for certain: the world is the omnipresent stage and sometimes primary agent—blocking or yielding paths to knowledge—in the great metaphysical show of Western philosophy. For centuries the world was portrayed as the grueling gauntlet and shining gateway to so many afterworlds, whereas today it functions (dysfunctions?) in a godless age where such a concept can be made self-aware, plural or exponential, thus raising the stakes of philosophy in an instant—especially in opposition to theology—by providing endless stores of fuel for our wildest dreams of world-making/unmaking. The autonomy, efficacy, transparency, and mobility of philosophy's world—indeed, all these qualities woven into the fabric of a single thought or spark of consciousness—is measured by the degree to which it epitomizes "the general," and to such an extent that what philosophy receives in return for its indiscriminate claim upon the world is a radical (and seemingly impossible) *particularization of the general.*

What I refer to as the particularization of the general licenses the largely psychological act of philosophical systematization at its most sweeping and robust; in this sense the acts of word-building which echo throughout the history of worldhood attest to what Stanley Cavell has called "the arrogation of philosophy."[2] Speaking of voice rather than speech, of the unreasonably authoritative tone of the philosopher regardless of the rationality of his or her train of thought—a voice stemming equally, it seems to me, from too much *and* too little knowledge, or the obsolescence of wisdom—we can imagine this unconditionally self-believing voice as growing from an indulgence in the abstractions of reason and the loftiest ivory-tower philosophy to speculate *ex nihilo* or fantasize the ultimate utopia for all. This embrace, to a certain extent unavoidable, of philosophical arrogance, may warrant the blunt accusation of greed, the near insatiable thirst of the rational instinct which forgoes the limits of the flesh and with it a more immediate experience of the laws of finitude. The great systematizers of philosophy typically regard the cooling of the passions as the triumph and not the downfall of reason. So it is that philosophy's world can be a cold and calculated place.

Systematic philosophy, as exemplified in the work of Descartes and Locke and Leibniz and Kant and Hegel, aspires in various and often competing ways to encompass the world in its totality and have each of its claims pertain to the world as a whole, the world we hold in common, the world as it has been with us since the beginning and—who knows?—perhaps before the beginning. Here is philosophy as the emancipated "bird's-eye" discipline, in flight over the world and seemingly unbeholden to a given object of study (even what philosophy calls "the given" can be dropped at will and exchanged for other metaphysical concepts). In response to this awesome yet ultimately burdensome pride, one could have cause to say that philosophy does indeed have an object and that it is called "world." Its object is *to reach out and objectify*, as a means of balancing what I described earlier as the thrown or flailing state of the human condition, which philosophy objectifies, hence empowers, as "subject." Reaching such a place of philosophical stability and peace requires a fixed worldview superseding a plural world, or a system of thought carefully maintained rather than picked apart. In a way, philosophy's "world" is as much an object of belief as one of knowledge.

With the world as philosophy's eternal, beloved, and often criticized object of faith/knowledge—whether it is conceptualized as outside the mind (for realists) or inside the mind (for idealists)—I have offered a view of modern philosophy in particular as the inexhaustible enterprise of forming views of the world, many of which desperately vie for the dominant view (sometimes viewing it from as many angles as possible), while others are content not to hold a view at all (sometimes breaking its view into shards of thought called fragments or aphorisms, beginning with pre-Socratic philosophy and exemplified in the work of Friedrich Nietzsche; or refracting itself through the prism of literature and poetry, again exemplified by Nietzsche's *Thus Spoke Zarathustra*). While the former approach strives to build a view of the world worthy of its complexity, plurality, beauty, cruelty, instability, habitability, and hospitality to our fundamental human situatedness, the latter seeks to destroy such logical scaffolding, acts of totality, or repressed longings for transcendence—a handy term for such a practice is "decreation"—by opposing philosophies that present their particular view(s) of the world for the world as it actually *is or ought to be*. One may build a philosophy in the hope of living in it, or by it, with integrity, or one may destroy a philosophy (ideally one's own) in the belief that truth is homeless. And so, with these two tendencies in mind, across this vast continuum of creation and destruction, philosophical metaphysics is exposed as a process of valuing and devaluing the world, one that begins in metaphysics, passes through epistemology, and ends, well, with the end of metaphysics as the closure of the Platonic or supersensory or noumenal or divinized realm (pick your poison). In the end, if we regard philosophy not just as a field or discipline but as the adoption of a certain type of attitude (for Nietzsche a hopelessly all-too-human one where the cache of knowledge dwarfs or altogether usurps the place of wisdom), we will see that the philosophical psyche is fundamentally split by the concept of world, and perhaps has been so throughout its historical striving to achieve abundant and better knowledge of the world. The philosophical psyche is as if pulled in two opposite directions with respect to the construction of views of the world: the pursuit of greater objective accuracy and transparency on the one hand, and the equally pressing push towards more elaborate forms of subjective substantiation and creativity, on the other. It is tempting to perceive the history of philosophy as progressing along a straight line from the former to the latter, if only the *personality* of philosophy did not clearly indicate the workings of *two* minds interlocked and at odds with each other.

As for the radical transformations of the concept of world throughout Western philosophy, from Descartes to Kant to Nietzsche to Heidegger to the analytical philosophers (many of whom would expunge the concept altogether if they could), such transformations at the conceptual level can be viewed as operating in stride with concrete social, political, and ideological revolutions. I take this to be the main point (if works of great ambition could ever be said to have "a point") of Thomas Kuhn's *The Structure of Scientific Revolutions*, a book in which changes in worldview, what he calls paradigm shifts, amount to or are identical with changes in the world itself.[3] Here the world matters only insofar as it *means*, and insofar as it already has meaning independently of what we ascribe or renounce, what we are then talking about is the world as we know it, which is typically the world as we inherit it (the epistemological givens of our day, entrenched in tradition, ideologically airborne). But the risk in seeing philosophy's transformations of the concept of world in light of transformations of the world we live in, along with the further suggestion or leap that philosophy's conceptual transformations are put into practice by our collective realizations, is that what philosophy calls world is bound by the timeframe of *today*. It is in this spirit, perhaps, that Ludwig Wittgenstein can suggest the following in his *Philosophical Investigations*: to destroy a philosophical worldview is not a cause for distress or tears, for that which is destroyed is provisional and, in his words, nothing more than "houses of cards."[4] The power of a house of thought lies not in its sturdiness or resiliency but rather in its sense of charm, seductive grandeur, and need for protection against threats from all sides. For Wittgenstein especially, the extent to which such edifices flee the ground of language on which they stand and press towards the stars is evident in the awestruck silence of the onlookers who dare not touch them.

The world may be a reverberating and neverending house of cards, insofar as it spurs the great totalizing efforts towards complete comprehension and intelligibility, even piecemeal efforts should they prove to harbor similar motives of exhaustion. What the philosopher seeks to know, or unknow, is in the palm of his hand, or so he believes, for in truth *he is in the palm of the world's hand*; philosopher or not, he is part of what he seeks to know—that is why we have been toiling in the desert for so long, going around in circles, duped by the horizon and its empty promise of an end in sight . . . Now when the metaphysical results of philosophy have been tallied and logged, when Descartes's methodology for clarity and distinctness through reason is juxtaposed alongside Kant's criteria for the categorical inaccessibility of the thing-in-itself, and when these two paradigms, one empowering and the other disempowering, are brought to bear in light of Heidegger's suggestion (not quite method or criteria) that our concern with "world" or "being" or "truth" is also a symptom of our growing estrangement from that which is most near, the temptation may lead us to conclude that the world is *just there* while pointing in just about any direction for proofs or invitations to participate. Who would deny it and what reason is there to expect anything *more* from a world whose existence precedes and outlasts our own?

To avoid generalizing a concept deemed to be one of the most general and lording of them all, and to avoid reducing the meaning (or "meaningful meaninglessness") of the concept of world to a totalitarian metaphysics bent on controlling the world picture from deep inside the discourses of philosophy, I would like to consider an insight from a particular mode of philosophy that regards itself as having awakened from the "bad dream" of metaphysics and into the world as *lived*—on the ground as opposed to in the trees or skies of philosophy—I mean the scientific, problem-solving nature, and highly logical orientation of analytical philosophy and the philosophy of language. The idea I wish to borrow is an extrapolation of this strand of philosophy's emphasis on the interrelation of language, logic, and context within what is called the everyday and which much of Western metaphysics has managed to obscure. The notion of picturing—mental or visual or linguistic pictures—is itself only a picture, as I have suggested, a meta-picture, as it were, whose basis or point of reference lies not in the world "out there" or the mind "in here" but in/through/as our language. Language is being rethought from a one-way street correspondence with the world to a complex and unstable network of streets, extending into a vast city or world in its own right. For many philosophers of language, specifically those who associate themselves with ordinary language philosophy, it is a grammatical, situational, and culturally relative process of picturing that delimits for speakers the terms under which a world can be inhabited. The linguistic world picture, however, is thrown into sharp relief only when speakers of a language use language to picture what is *outside* of language—philosophers are particularly adept at this—the result being not only bumps on the head, as per Wittgenstein's classic dramatization of human understanding running up against the limits of defamiliarized language (imagine the *low ceiling* of language), but also what strikes me as the speaker/picturer's self-portrait as a transgressive for whom the word as a measure of the world is simply not enough and is therefore stretched too thin.[5]

I will return to the perspective of the philosophy of language or ordinary language philosophy in more detail later on, but for now I will propose the following thought experiment for continuing to explore the complex resonance between world and worldview, thus preparing ourselves for the upcoming analysis in the second part of this chapter on cinematic viewlessness. What if we were to describe the history of Western philosophy in different terms, not as a chronological series of pictures of the world but rather as a multifarious nexus of subconscious self-portraits of the metaphysician in action? Should we proceed along these lines, what can be glimpsed straight away is that such a description will be forced to overturn, or at the very least double-check, the basic terms of reference in which philosophy has been understood since the time of the Greeks: philosophy as a community of individual thinkers, historical arch of ideas, stratified continuum of paradigmatic shifts, hierarchy of canonical and marginal texts, all revolving in one way or another around the moorings of metaphysics, questions of epistemology, and methods of representation—an inherited and perhaps instinctive system of thought patterns congealing into what Richard Rorty identifies or diagnoses as "the mirror of nature."[6] To better understand the value placed on the mirror of nature, I suggest that we picture philosophy not only as a way of picturing the world with greater accuracy and permanence (the clarity-and-distinctness criterion of Cartesian absolutism), but also as picturing the eclipsed path of picturing itself, and therefore ourselves as "picturers." The logic here is that if our goal in gaining an accurate representation of the world is ultimately an epistemological one, that is, to better understand the world we live in and share with others (and from which we will eventually pass away, leaving all others behind), then an emphasis on self-portraiture, what I am tempted to simply call "style," will foreground the thrust of the quest for knowledge to be not only never-ending but also self-fulfilling, if not self-fashioning. I like to think of this quest, foreseen in advance to be precisely and passionately and liberatingly without end, as philosophy's social-psychological *a priori*: the accumulation of knowledge throughout every aspect of human life is, upon closer inspection, a mosaic of agreements and disagreements; the world is riddled with possible worlds, which are also *necessary*; and you may discover this world best when you realize your own, as Emerson advised, finding your truth not out there in the world but rather, let's say, amongst friends. I believe this is what Nietzsche means when his Zarathustra declares to his followers, hence to the human instinct to merely follow, "This is *my* way; where is yours?"[7] The question is not exactly a rhetorical challenge from Zarathustra to his faithful disciples to become, like him, a way to the overman, but rather a genuinely curious glimpse into the will to power coursing through fledgling or malnourished souls. "Where is yours?" is a question whose answer is a way of life that Nietzsche interprets simply as *dancing*; it is a request from Zarathustra for compensation in dancing out his alleged "waylessness." He asks to be spared his wretched solitude by being, at last, on the receiving end of the will to power, reciprocated by his friends, the favor returned so that Zarathustra himself may be overcome. For every friend who shares your way lies an enemy who parts ways, ready to betray you for *their world*. For each *has a way*, indeed is *on the way*, although they might not yet know it or have the proper tools to show it; it is their *secret*.

Zarathustra's knowledge of the will to power, while undoubtedly a self-knowledge and a vital source of existential style, is also importantly a metaphysical knowledge about the world—an apparently counterintuitive claim that Heidegger makes with remarkable force in his essay "The Word of Nietzsche: 'God Is Dead'."[8] Here Nietzsche's great contradiction—that the experience of one's will is not, in fact, in one's sole possession; that to sit on the seat of one's will is to strip the will of all its power—is given its fair share of logic, I suppose the very logic of contradiction, and is therefore validated within its own terms without smoothing out the crucial clashing of terms. This peculiar "inverse" metaphysics as explored by Heidegger has astounding implications for the philosophical concept of world and can be expressed as follows: the power of will, a presumably psychological feat, derives its power from the will to power of Being itself. Only then can a particular being—for example, a human being—experience the power of his own will and use it for his own betterment and elation (and hopefully for the sake of others as well— say, by bringing out the overman in us all). As a result, Zarathustra can be said to know—which for him is to live by—these two contradictory aspects of the will to power. First, the will to power holds for all beings because it is germane to Being itself. Second, the human being is the being most suited to harnessing the will to power, affirming life in all its forms, *and* turning this will against itself (the will to powerlessness and death of spirit). What happens in Nietzsche that is pertinent here is the beginning of a view of the world that is not one of mind approaching matter but rather the endowment of mind *to* matter, a move which accomplishes the following decisive transformation: it nullifies the distinction between mind and matter.[9] This would seem to leave behind *only* matter (Nietzsche's word is "earth"); however, with the death of God on the verge of unleashing an unprecedented wave of disenchantment and nihilism ("the darkening of the world"), we can call matter mind again (Nietzsche's word is "spirit") and laugh where we would have previously managed only tears.

After Nietzsche and Heidegger, the desire to *know* the world slips, consciously or unconsciously, into the human capacity—what must be one of our greatest capacities—to create the world (Nietzsche) and dwell in the world poetically (Heidegger). As vital precursors of what Rorty calls "philosophies of edification," these thinkers almost singlehandedly cut the tools for postmodern self-fashioning and world-building. My understanding of philosophies of edification is that they are more interested in inspiring us with the possibility that philosophy can be *lived and breathed*, pressing us on the following points which are not to be memorized so much as kept like promises: in order to discover something about the world one must change it or contest it; to declare a proposition a fact one must express that proposition as a value; instead of grasping the world as a whole one may follow the whim of concrete particulars and subsist on the wholeness of those particulars alone;

and so on. Rising to the occasion of such a philosophy calls for *ingenuity*, or what I am calling "style." But the degree to which such styles are attuned to the complexities of the world, rather than imposed upon it in a sweep of solipsism or madness, endows a vital sense of plasticity and is a sign of strength, for one thing which is true of any style is that it inevitably changes over time as long as it is permitted to change *with the times*, lest it become obsolete. When something falls completely out of use, its beauty also fades; it may be interesting or curious (beaming from behind the glass casings of history) but rarely calls us into action.

Now if we take a moment to reflect on the consequences of the "style claim" on philosophy's most fundamental metaphysical concepts, we will be forced to the conclusion, or the recognition, that traditional metaphysics is an observational rather than a proximal practice. The concept of world (the primary concept in Heidegger's lecture course *The Fundamental Concepts of Metaphysics*) is based paradoxically *within* the world (or in the midst of this thing we call "world"—how could it be otherwise?), which means that metaphysics cannot reach out to the world as it exists independently of our reach, independently of ourselves. In the end, metaphysics is performed by intellectually ambitious or sometimes spiritually starved "physical" beings gazing deeply into the firmament of reason, for whom the act of "reaching out" can never reach far enough, can never escape being-in-the-world to the securing of a clear and distinct notion of the world-as-such. The sense of separation or, better yet, bifurcation belongs to the sense of sight and its influence on thought, so that a reach which fails to touch is merely sight in disguise—separateness being the price of knowledge manifesting visually as world. Beings *in* the world fancying themselves as privileged observers *of* the world is a picture (not without humor) that seems to me absolutely essential for understanding the history of the meanings ascribed to "world"—and perhaps the meaning that is common to all of them is that the world, while we may (do, must) live in it, can be known by us *as if we did not live in it*. This deep-seated tendency of Western philosophy points to the real purpose behind worldviews: *to protect us from the world*.

For Descartes, the inaugurator of modern philosophy, this sense of separation (subject from object, mind from body, reason from experience) is the first victory of the self over the threat of skepticism, a victory that, according to Cavell, is simultaneously and paradoxically a discovery or an unleashing of skepticism in light of the futility of absolute certainty and the potential pain such knowledge entails. For Heidegger, the critic of modern philosophy, this separation from the world as the key to our knowledge of it is built into the very fabric of Western thinking (a fabric woven, in large measure, by Cartesian pictures), such that the underlying meaning of the word Being is precisely our estrangement from "it"—the very "thing" which truly ought to go without saying. But it is the fate of the human condition that *nothing* goes without saying, and it is perhaps for this very simple reason that Heidegger can say, in his essay on language, "language speaks […] mortals live in the speaking of language."[10] In this sense the word "world," like Being, is charged with the loss of the unspeakable mystery of the world. And that, I believe, is why Wittgenstein can declare at the opening of the *Tractatus*—matter-of-factly and unmysteriously—"the world is all that is the case,"[11] suggesting that the only world we can know is the world as we actually know it (epistemologically—drawn by the limits of our language) and not as we *dream* of knowing it (metaphysically—in defiance of such limits, speaking in the space where we ought to remain silent). For that dream, as we now know, became the nightmare of metaphysics where truth was won at the expense of human finitude and our words, estranged from their propositional logic and everyday usage, no longer bore the sharp and familiar ring of truth (that is, meaning in a given context and for a particular purpose or cross-purpose). If, indeed, such a word as world finds its way meaningfully into our everyday speech and conversation with others, it may amount to no more and no less than a *daydream* that is sharable only by stepping inside it, as in stepping into somebody else's shoes.

By the time philosophy reaches the linguistic turn of the analytical philosophy movement from the early twentieth century, metaphysics as the pursuing and positing of "unshakable foundations" was forced to take stock of its modes of behavior and reflect on its transparent sense of style. For some, the self-consciousness of metaphysics was enough to bring metaphysics to an end, but it is worth our further reflection upon the basic methods, assumptions, and underlying motivations of the sweeping attacks of analytical philosophy, if for no other reason than as a safeguard against any over-zealousness or desperation to make philosophical progress by discarding all metaphysical propositions—which turn out, according to logical analysis, to be the great majority of philosophical propositions and philosophical greatness—as inherently nonsensical on the grounds that they exceed the limits of language by bending logic and grammar unrecognizably out of shape. A. J. Ayer in his book *Language, Truth and Logic*, which functions almost as a textbook for this relatively recent movement or counter-movement of thought, writes the following as an account of the methodological aims of what strikes me now as anti-metaphysical philosophy:

> [T]he validity of the analytic method is not dependent on any empirical, much less any metaphysical, presupposition about the nature of things. For the philosopher, as an analyst, is not directly concerned with the physical properties of things. He is concerned only with the way in which we speak about them.[12]

This distinction comes from a philosopher who believes that the new method has so completely transcended the ancient traditions of metaphysics and epistemology that he is no longer willing to even call himself a philosopher unless it is to quickly qualify his practice as one of pure analysis, the kind with scientific objectivity and a sense of psychoanalytic scrutiny or suspicion on its side, keeping a watchful eye over all the things one may be tempted to say about the nature of things but shouldn't. Under this harsh lamp of analysis—which opts to listen rather than speak, or speak in response to what we are inclined to say, on high alert for any slips of the tongue into the dark depths of philosophical nonsense—the only claims to be made are claims about what we can and cannot claim as speakers of a language. The latter criterion—speakers of a language—is also taken to be the most complete definition of the human being, for all other and competing definitions of what it means to be human are necessarily bound up in the possible meanings of a given language in a given context.

It is clear, however, that Ayer is not denying that there are things in the world, or a world of things; rather he is insisting that it can no longer be the business of philosophy to do metaphysics of any kind when philosophy is dependent on a language the use of which is directed towards other propositions (rather than, say, the hypothetical referents of our words) and the meaning of which is contingent upon everyday contexts (rather than, say, the ivory tower of epistemological inquiry and metaphysical abstraction). But I still want to ask, and for now only ask: what, at bottom, is responsible for this sudden and drastic shift in philosophy from metaphysical to linguistic questions which claim to have little to no connection with the traditions and commonplace intuitions of philosophical questioning? What motivates this shift from "contemplating the world" to "analyzing our wording of the world"? Does the history of philosophy "progress" along such a path, or is this a new pioneering path that may or may not be consistent with philosophy as such?

The seismic shift of philosophical habit, while not without precedent and influence, seems to occur rather abruptly and hastily, swerving away from the primary paths of metaphysics and epistemology in an act of dissent, if not a state of emergency which philosophy calls the death of God (a death out of which the philosophy of film is born). The movement says the time is now—an impulsive now, a better-late-than-never and future-looking now—where philosophy must summon the courage to look at itself in the mirror, a mirror tarnished with the faded dreams of philosophy to discover truth in all its forms and absolutize it under a divine seal. And what it sees in the light of its greatest disillusionment is also its greatest discovery. In the mirror of its self-criticism and intellectual conscience it accepts the truth that it, philosophy, is not what it thought it was—a mirror for the objective representation of immutable truth.

It stares at itself and all it has achieved and sees only words and their accompanying actions, a world of words and a universe of contexts for the evolving and embodied life of language. What it sees is what it says—*language*, the *reality* of language whose signs knead human existence into shape and make possible all claims to truth and falsity. This is an anti-ocular woldview which posits a public self immune to solipsism, exposing the fallacy that our propositions operate on the same page as our perceptions along with the general misconception that what we say about the world works in the same way as how we see the world as something which fronts us. As a mode of language that can gain an objective foothold on the uses and abuses of itself, the first insight of logical analysis is that if language is the last vestige of a mirror of nature, then it cannot reflect the way a mirror reflects: that is, outwardly, outward to what-is—to truth prior to all meaning, grounding all meaning, conditioning the possibility of all meaning.

Rorty crystallizes Ayer's position, thereby shattering philosophy as the mirroring of nature, with the following claim: "Once conversation replaces confrontation, the notion of the mind as Mirror of nature can be discarded. Then the notion of philosophy as the discipline which looks for privileged representations among those constituting the Mirror becomes unintelligible."[13] While I agree with many of Rorty's criticisms and take to heart his emancipatory enterprise, his acknowledgment of a lingering urge towards metaphysical thinking may carry more weight than the mere scratching of an insatiable itch. Later on he writes, "The urge to say that assertions and actions must not only cohere with other assertions and actions but 'correspond' to something apart from what people are saying and doing has some claim to be called *the* philosophical urge."[14] What I wish to suggest as a response, less as an objection than as a view from the other side, and as a provisional conclusion in need of patience, is that the urge to correspond—the great philosophical urge, as it is called, to face the otherness of the world and know what cannot be known once and for all—is not as becoming for us as it is for art, especially for film whose "world in its own image" bypasses correspondence. The urge to correspond can also be thought of as in itself a response to the address of the world, to our being affected by the world, which is to say by "something" for which there may be no ready at hand words and actions, or at least not yet. Wittgenstein famously concludes the *Tractatus* with the proposition, "What we cannot speak about we must pass over in silence,"[15] but the book doesn't end there—only language does. Its closure opens a new horizon where silence precedes speech, as if silence too can pass through the spirit of what we say. From this follows the even greater urge to speak by showing, or creating, and have our "language" be a part of the world—a highly dynamic and influential part. For silence is not just the absence of speech; it is—sounds like, resonates as—the presence of the world, the friction of being-in-the-world, the atmosphere in which speech sparks in all directions and formations.

As all philosophers know (or dread knowing), there is no such thing as complete and utter peace and quiet for philosophy, at least for philosophy defined or endured as the labor of *revision*. The truth that there is no end to the quest for truth, and no truth worthy of the name, is one of the great horrors of Western philosophy; and as a response to this horror, the history of philosophy has been known to think in the service of putting an *end* to thought. Metaphysical concepts are so many instances of philosophical finality. The irony or tragedy of this all-too-human phenomenon is that the desire to permanently satiate thought seems destined for disappointment or self-deception, for one thing that we can be sure of is *tomorrow's hunger*—the pleasure and pain of the flesh of thought. (Eastern thought seems to be more at ease with philosophical endlessness. Ancient thought in this area can be experienced as clearing rather than clarifying: or wise.) With practice, it may become possible to revise or completely release metaphysical questions before they burn at the hour of bewilderment. In general, though, the return of metaphysics in philosophy haunts philosophy, whereas in film this return is absolute and inaugural, as if it found its true home at the base of the ivory tower.

II. FILM IN THE WORLD'S PALM, OR THE WORLD IN ITS OWN IMAGE

In the Introduction and first chapter, I proposed that human consciousness represents the world through knowledge whereas cinema embodies a mechanical consciousness, or unconsciousness, that in principle allows the world to *represent itself*, bringing forth appearances which do not abide by the conditions of how the world appears to us. In this sense the cinema imagines the world from the perspective of the powerlessness or poverty of human consciousness. Now if a metaphysics of the moving image is found to be philosophically compelling in a way that most metaphysical systems (at least today) leave us wanting, it is because the latter's epistemological quest to *know the world* is interrupted by the former's ontological act of *letting the world be*. As to how this "letting-be" comes to pass to matter in films, ideally beyond those rare instances of sublime or fortuitous poetry, is something I am working towards and committed to working out, with a range of close readings in the book's second half being essential to any answer I could give. What I know for certain is that aesthetic positions such as Zen-like passivity, Warholian anonymity, the random courting of chance, or blind mechanical surveillance carry little weight and have a limited resonance in a metaphysical film style as I understand it. Whatever metaphysical value such techniques possess is inseparable from the *mere exemplification* of the values we seek.

In the first part of this chapter I tackled the admittedly daunting task of asking the question of what constitutes a world from the perspective of philosophy, questioning how philosophy asks the question and following the web of paths into which it has been led. In this second part my aim is to pose the question anew with respect to the medium of film and the discourse of film-philosophy, a discourse which represents the by no means arbitrary coming together of the two fields on this very question. At the outset I am again struck by the ironic reversal at the heart of this book: just as philosophy deems it necessary to substitute "worldview" for "world" (by making the rather difficult discovery that the value attributed to the concept of world implies a cut-off category of consciousness called "modern"), photographic and cinematic images of the world reassert the concept, a key concept in classical film theory that is described by various writers in somewhat post-human terms (even though such a dramatic term did not yet exist) as a form of what I will call *viewlessness*. For a metaphysician and phenomenologist like Heidegger, the world is something that humans think and must be thought responsibly, whereas for a metaphysician and phenomenologist of the image like André Bazin or, more recently, Stanley Cavell, it is the medium of cinema which "thinks" the world and prompts us into a rethinking of our place within it. While human consciousness is predisposed to constitute the world in its own image, mastering it through images of its own making, cinema reverses the tide of subject-oriented mastery and affords an encounter with the world "as a whole," with an image fit to bear away the familiar powers of human subjectivity. Whether viewers consent to this disempowerment or not, if nothing else we are given a *reminder* of how open to the world consciousness can be when unframed by the will (the cinematic frame, unlike painting, is in principle pure porousness). Reflecting on the intuitions governing this metaphysical perspective on film, Cavell writes:

> I have spoken of film as satisfying the wish for the magical reproduction of the world by enabling us to view it unseen. What we wish to see in this way is the world itself—that is to say, everything. Nothing less than that is what modern philosophy has told us (whether for Kant's reasons, or for Locke's, or Hume's) is metaphysically beyond our reach or (as Hegel or Marx or Kierkegaard or Nietzsche might put it) beyond our reach metaphysically.[16]

Film catches a glimpse of this "everything," realizing the ancient dream of metaphysics to know the world itself on the condition that the project of complete and perfect knowledge be stripped from our hands. The timing of this compensatory substitution seems to be more important for me than it is for Cavell: when modern philosophy discovers that views of the world are in fact worldviews, that only the worldviews themselves are viewable, cinematic representation presents a worldview of the world in its own image, which means the cinematic worldview is an embodiment or enactment of the viewless aspirations of metaphysics. This shift is as much a feat of historical circularity as medium specificity: the death of God and the birth of film, the end of metaphysics and the rise of ontology, automatism, and photo-realism in classical film theory are decisively and inextricably linked in time. The apparent coincidence has reciprocal properties in retrospect, as do all coincidences of a certain chemistry and magnitude. I am pressed to say that cinema's "viewless view" is the world's and not ours; it is a description of how the world views itself through film—how that which stands in excess of the concept of view as a measure of the human reach appears novel by *reaching out to us*. The "everything" at stake here can then be understood as the fullness and flesh of things ungrasped and, in this sense, freed. The viewless view of cinema opens itself up to object-oriented possibilities and perhaps even metaphysical "impossibilities" such as the materialization of the immaterial and the historicization of the eternal.

As far as analytical philosophy's critique of metaphysics is concerned, cinema's response or counter-argument to the linguistic turn of the twentieth century might be that the world in its own image is less a reiteration of the world than a *recreation* of it. The paradox of a mimetic reiteration which gives way to, or functions as the basis for, an ontological recreation is also Bazin's way of inflecting his notion of the world in its own image as a description of cinema's absolute, mythical, ultimately unrealizable form of realism. To fully appreciate the sense of cinema's being-in-the-world, one must be open to the idea of realism as an ontological condition and not just an aesthetic possibility, and furthermore as a mechanical, unconscious process rather than a percep-tual one guided by reason and convention. What follows is Bazin's account, from his essay "The Myth of Total Cinema," of the medium's participatory relationship with the world and some of the implications he draws from this unique and unprecedented relation:

> The guiding myth, then, inspiring the invention of cinema, is the accomplishment of that which dominated in a more or less vague fashion all the techniques of the mechanical reproduction of reality in the nineteenth century, from photography to the phonograph, namely an integral realism, a recreation of the world in its own image, an image unburdened by the freedom of interpretation of the artist or the irreversibility of time. If cinema in its cradle lacked all the attributes of the cinema to come, it was with reluc-tance and because its fairy guardians were unable to provide them however much they would have liked to.[17]

Cinematic realism, which is being developed in the historical context of the alternative and competing realisms of the preceding arts (painting, literature, theater), is described in this passage as being both specific to the photographic aspect of the medium of cinema and, somewhat para-doxically, as specific to the visible aspect of reality, if not a sense of reality itself. Cinema's innate propensity towards realism is such that reality can be construed the other way around as representing or calling forth the cinema. Cinema's nature is conceived as belonging to, sharing, or participating in nature itself, which it can do only insofar as its fundamental nature remains extrinsic to itself as the recording and undergoing *of* nature. But if that is the case, then it has no authentic nature of its own, an example in art of what John Keats called "negative capability."[18] In the process of its radical under-going, cinema loses the essential clarity and distinctness of its medium speci-ficity, for the medium in this case cannot be conceived independently of the world it mediates and mythologizes. In this sense we can better understand Bazin's romantic claim that photography, and by extension the photographic basis of film, affects us like a phenomenon in nature on the grounds that it, too, is so affected.[19] Cinema's world-affect, as it were, will only heighten as technologies improve, and yet, as technological progress guides the cinema towards more adequate and exemplary representations, they will always necessarily fall short of a mythical totality merely glimpsed as if into the land of plenty and promise. Cinematic representation, whether in its cradle or in full bloom, *symbolizes* the culmination of realism (that is, a total image of the world in the form of the world in its own image) such that the ontology of the moving image is always looking ahead to the day when the medium no longer matters because its matter will be the realization of the myth: cinema *is* the world, though by that time, should such a time ever come, it will not be called cinema anymore. What such a mythic perspective on cinematic realism does is epitomize realism by bringing its aesthetic discourse to its (il)logical conclusion in metaphysics.[20]

One of the things I find most intriguing about Bazin's ontology is the sense in which a creative dimension is attributed to cinema's mechanical mimesis. Why does Bazin speak of the world in its own image as a *recrea-tion* instead of a representation? We are not far from the theological idea of "incarnation": the photographic/cinematic image of the object is akin to its rebirth. The image of the world made by the world, the world's self-portrait, is obviously not a mere mimetic representation of it, or what we call mimesis does far more than represent, which is certainly true of the act of miming as one that entails an act of *becoming*, transformation being the criterion for what we call a good performance (not just an accurate one). In fact, the concept of creation implies that the world's self-portrait may be fundamentally painterly as well as photographic. While the representation's condition of possibility is non-human, like a fossil, at the same time human beings are the ones to have set up the conditions for an image to come to be by powers beyond their control and right to sole ownership, as if by virtue of the medium of film we secretly confess to our capacity for control impeding or altogether paralyzing the equal and certainly more valuable capacity to create. This emphasis on creation—representation interpreted in terms of recreation—also cannot help but bring to mind thoughts of *creationism* which may underlie Bazin's Catholicism. Whether or not the world is the work of a deity, and if beings come to be through evolution as opposed to creation, as our evidence suggests, what cinema does by fashioning the world in its own image is sidestep the temptation to fashion false idols depicting forces fundamentally alien to the earthly. The idea of the world in its own image reasserts the fact that human beings create not just through acts of will but also through acts of faith; the cinematic recreation of the world as world—*this* world, in all its beauty and terror—exemplifies faith because it embodies the human will to keep our hands tied, to move about gently and be patient or vigilant while standing on the various thresholds of encounter. This is what philosophy might call the ethical impulse. Naturally, to make a film—along with any act of making—is to free our hands, yet it is also possible to make a film—and read a film—by handling the medium with care and without "manhandling" its messaging capabilities, say, through a creative/critical process guided by an acknowledgment of the world's recreatedness on film.

Bazin's dramatic expression "the world in its own image" is linked with Cavell's more technical definition, "a succession of automatic world projections," the latter of which is slowly developed throughout the opening sections of *The World Viewed*.[21] While *The World Viewed* is notoriously short on references to film theory, in the Preface Cavell does cite Bazin's seminal essays, collected in the two volumes of *What Is Cinema?*, as among his few inspirations for the ensuing reflections on the ontology of film. The sign of inspiration as opposed to overt instruction comes in Cavell rarely referring to Bazin's ideas directly, but rather expanding upon and deepening that which lies at the heart of Bazin's own inspiration—the philosophical, perhaps specifically Heideggerian question of the being of film. This is a question which has much to offer the philosophy of art and, for me, the field of metaphysics, over and above the aesthetic question of what film can *do*. Contemplating what the "is" *does* is perhaps what philosophers do best and what philosophy itself ultimately is.[22] In any case, both definitions of cinema are working hypotheses based on the assumption that the medium to be specified is, for reasons discussed above, fundamentally non-specific. Taken together, cinema makes the world in its own image *make images*, and a world which makes images of itself *projects itself*, so that cinematic projection becomes a world projection. I also suggest that we read the succession of automatic world projections as the carrying over or relaying of world-light, an image of light unimpeded by the opacity or even the blindness of human consciousness. As autonomous self-manifestation under technological conditions, the world in its own image is the regaining of aura, of spirit, in the age of disenchantment.

But how do we know in the first place that the philosophy of cinematic technology is ontologically revelatory of the two decisive aspects of "world"—the world as it appears to us and the world as it escapes appearances because of our perceptual, cognitive, and linguistic limitations? On what grounds can we say that the world viewed on film constitutes a worldview in which the world exceeds or transcends the view, or where the world views itself? Dealing with such questions calls for a reading of two thinkers who wrestle with technologies of representation and therefore stand in dialogue with each other on the conditions of possibility for a techno-poetics: Heidegger's meditation on the nature of technology in his essay "The Question Concerning Technology," and a further return to Cavell's reflections on cinematic ontology in *The World Viewed*. The title of Cavell's book, by his own admission, is meant to resonate with Heidegger's essay "The Age of the World Picture" (which just so happens to appear in the same collection as the technology essay), an important and deeply perturbing work of philosophy in which, as I had cause to mention earlier, we find the bold thesis that the world in the modern age is experienced only through/as/in the form of worldviews.

In the technology essay, Heidegger cautions us—we moderns—against trusting even the slightest action or twitch of will towards the manifestation of the being of the world, a manifestation whose auratic purity or ideality appears doomed to concealment by the reign of representation within the age of the world picture and by the criteria of knowledge as a utilitarian and sometimes totalitarian mode of ordering. Heidegger's special name for this phenomenon (esoteric naming being a specialty of his) is "enframing":

> [E]nframing does not simply endanger man in his relationship to himself and to everything that is. As a destining, it banishes man into that kind of revealing that is an ordering. Where this ordering holds sway, it drives out every other possibility of revealing. Above all, Enframing conceals that revealing which, in the sense of poiesis, lets what presences come forth into appearance. As compared with that other revealing, the setting-upon that challenges forth thrusts man into a relation to that which is, that is at once antithetical and rigorously ordered. Where Enframing holds sway, regulating and searching of the standing-reserve mark all revealing. They no longer even let their own fundamental characteristic appear, namely, this revealing as such.[23]

Enframing is described here as a process of revealing whose technological ordering conceals the revelation of the world as presence. Its greatest limitation and danger is its own entrapment, hence perpetuation. The revealing of enframing is a concealing above all of itself, such that to be engaged in the mode of enframing, which happens whenever we objectify the world, is to be absent in this mode of engagement, an absence to which we give our consent by referring to ourselves agreeably as "subjects" and staying oblivious to the fact that to enframe is still to reveal, albeit poorly if not destructively.

Even though Heidegger's essay is a meditation on the pros and cons, progresses and regresses, openings and closings of technology as such, he remains characteristically abstract on the exact nature and workings of a revelation that is internal to concealment and a concealment that is internal to revelation. While the ancient Greek word *poiesis* is, according to Heidegger's translation, a "letting what presences come forth into appearance,"[24] it would seem that it can hardly accomplish this "letting"—indeed, such an *accomplishment* is a contradiction in terms—without the aid of *techne*. Technology becomes the necessary appendage for poetry; and poetry, in order for there to be an allowance or admittance or gathering of what is called revelation, must frame, enframe, order. In the seemingly paradoxical pursuit of truth as letting-happen (again, to call it a *pursuit* is a false start), the poet, condemned to the enframing configuration of the modern world picture and its governing subject, must try to reveal rather than profess or prove. This could mean an unmotivated revealing, or a searching without looking for (longing for) results. The poet is equipped with a medium, an instrument, a machine, albeit as an extension of the medium he or she already *is*—a conscious entity set up to set forth upon the world and take hold of it. Self as subject is something of a tool, a medium which reveals by way of ordering and orders by way of revelation, enacting subjectivity as the modern medium/machine of representation *par excellence*. If, however, the medium external to the self is being used as a means to an end, specifically *to reveal*, with the overt *intention* of revealing, my sense of what Heidegger is saying in the abstract—and which I would like to make concrete in relation to cinematic technologies of representing the world—is that it must conceal the very revealing it sets out to honor and acknowledge. But is this the destiny of technology in all cases? Is this ontological double-standard, backfiring, and Midas touch of modernity an absolute of entrapment from which there is no hope of escape?

Let's take a slight step back to the bigger picture of Heidegger's thinking on Being: modern man sets himself up as the sole setting for Being and in advance of Being. Now what Heidegger calls *Dasein* is still an inextricable and necessary part of Being, but this being who is *in* the world and *knows* it is culturally conditioned and biologically calibrated as well to present himself before it, to view it, use it, and occasionally to admire it, but primarily and above all to *master* it in some large or small way, in proportion to his will to power. Can this multidirectional predisposition towards control, extraction, mastery, and self-service ever find its way to openness, receptivity, carefulness, and respect? One of Heidegger's main concerns, in this essay and throughout the steady course of his philosophical enterprise, is that *Dasein* finds itself in a world—that is, a world of worldviews—which can no longer support beings, but rather only positions, coordinates of consciousness, if you will, thus confining *Dasein* to protective corners of planning and privacy from which the world is set into place and emerges as a representation, a product of what the will projects, the world *as* product. Since we are positioned inside ourselves and therefore outside the world, the world appears "framed up" by the self; the self is not unlike a sense—the sense of self-sufficiency, let's call it. "That the world becomes picture," writes Heidegger, "is one and the same event with the event of man's becoming *subiectum* [subject] in the midst of that which is."[25] With the concept of the subject understood as, say, the technologizing of consciousness into the mode of representation, Heidegger in the technology essay can define or rather find the essence of technology to be that of enframing, "which is nothing technological, nothing on the order of a machine. It is the way in which the real reveals itself as standing-reserve."[26]

Heidegger's most cherished philosophical objective here is to make us think more deeply about technology by suggesting that the anthropological or default way in which world appears is in its essence technological. At our complete and utter disposal in the modern age of rapid industrialization and globalization of means, the world lies ready and waiting for our encroachment as subjects and its appropriation into the status of object, revealing itself for a purpose alien to itself (perhaps revealing human beings as alien to this earth). But what if we were to reverse the terms of this analysis and say just the opposite: that enframing has *everything* to do with technology, particularly with technologies of representation; that it belongs to the order of the machine—for example, the camera machine. How does "world" reveal itself as standing-reserve to a machine modeled after man? Would it still present itself *in this way* to a machine designed to represent it in-itself rather than for-itself? Might the camera-machine not trigger a malfunction in the very order of representation?

Let's consider the example of the motion picture camera more closely and intimately—these mechanical "eyes" with sensitive "bodies" and impeccable "memories." I own a camera, as you probably do, maybe more than one (after all, your phone is a camera, or your camera is a phone …), and not infrequently I use it to record what I see (and hear, depending on the camera, but seeing comes first); and not infrequently it records what I did not see, wish to see again, refuse to see ever again. How does the thing work? I take my camera into the street or countryside. I watch the traffic go by or study the receding lines of the horizon or watch the trees spray their branches in all directions. I use the frame and focus to select, concentrate, think the visible, holding the rest of the world away; and when I like what I see, when I believe I have seen something of value, when what I see exceeds what I would normally see with my two naked eyes unsynchronized by any heightened awareness, I press the record button. Whether it was during those moments leading up to the capturing of a photograph or those moments during the recording of the motion picture, I hang on to what I see and the camera, for now, sees for me, sees and remembers without subjective distortion (technical malfunctions and celluloid decay notwithstanding). I know what I am seeing is stripped of a dimension—one of my eyes is shut, after all—and will be lacking this dimension as a mere two-dimensional image on paper or screen. Perhaps this lack will come at the expense of the world's dimensionality, just as music, when recorded, might be said to lose its unique timbre. (Many other things are lost or altered as well, from the concreteness of color to intangibles like the affects of perception, but the degree to which the sight has been transferred/transformed into something new distracts me from such losses.) Even though I am free to move the camera, I have settled upon a frame and keep it there; I do this, I tell myself, not for the sake of order and control but out of respect for the particulars—they are entitled to their duration, their being is a breathing, and the world beyond the frame seems to resonate in them: the world in a grain of sand, as they say (poets). Eventually, I stop recording and point the camera in a different direction. Or perhaps I have finished what I set out to do, had my fill of this strange little pastime, and head home. Or maybe I turn my back on the machine with senses sharpened, primed to experience the world through my own senses, such as they are, anew. But what exactly has taken place here? What do I hold in my hands, assuming I hold anything at all?

In the evening, I view the image for myself to see how it turned out, to see what I saw, to see what the camera "thought" I saw. Should anyone enter, say a child, and mistake it for the real thing, I should declare that what we have here is an *image*—nothing more, but nothing less either. The world is framed and ordered, albeit gently, such that no one could fail to recognize it. Does the world, or this aspect of it, have a "say" in its framing and ordering? Perhaps such a possibility introduces an element of chaos into an otherwise uninteresting and forgettable image, rendering mysterious its source and authorship. "What does it *mean*, though?" Well, I am tempted to say, given the circumstances of its casually improvised making, that it doesn't mean *anything*, or at least *not yet* (what you see is what you get). Its meaning is pending or suspended, awaiting the accompaniment of other images or text, or after-the-fact interpretations. In its raw infancy, may we confidently call such an image a micro-mystery, a pristine opaqueness, a plain view rendered abstract by viewlessness? These things, you see, in all their particularity, exist *now* as they did *then* when I saw them and no one else was around. They are present, again, these things of the world, this world of things—but does this photographic/cinematic image that you took with your camera show or reveal that presence? If Heidegger were in the room, he might say that it conceals it by bringing it forth technologically, and that the strength of the concealment may very well be proportional to the strength of what we take to be a genuine and meaningful revelation. But does it conceal it philosophically or technologically, in principle or on formal grounds? Well, what does the picture show of its showing, what are we looking *at* upon being invited to look *through*?—It *looks like* what it looks like, it appears to our eyes to be what it is. Cavell was right: objects, unlike sounds, are simply too close to their appearances (he calls them "sights") to give them up for mechanical reproduction.[27] But, on the other hand, he may be wrong to assume that what the camera-projector system does is posit objects in the first place, whereas our viewing them—in the modern condition of viewing—may turn out to harbor the greater power and practice of objectification. As for what it *is*—an image of the world, the world in its own image—shall we try closing our eyes and opening our minds? The ideal approach might be to *think with our eyes*.

These paradoxes of representation in which we find ourselves hopelessly entangled—where being and seeing are conflated yet in conflict with each other—belong to a distinction or limitation that philosophy has maintained in various ways throughout the ages, perhaps as a way of sorting out different domains or dispositions of representation and tempering the ocularcentrism of the West. I am referring primarily to the distinction between correctness and truth, which can be used to come to terms and even assess the concept of mechanical reproduction as adequate to the world or as facilitator of the world in its own image. For Heidegger it is possible for something to come to presence correctly but not necessarily truthfully; presence expressed in terms of correctness may amount to nothing more than what philosophers call "reality" and artists or aestheticians call "likeness." But if it is our plan and passion to summon Being itself to its rightful place within our midst, fully resonant in our thoughts and actions, then correctness may have nothing whatsoever to do with the condition of possibility for something *actually being* as opposed to merely seeming to be. To what extent, I then wonder, is this predicament or endangerment at work in the ontology of the moving image of the world? Is it the case not only that these representations of the world are correct in terms of their likeness to the world (true _of_ the world), but also that this correctness may come at the expense of their truthfulness (truth _as_ the world)? In asking what constitutes the truth or untruth of a moving image's unique verisimilitude, we acknowledge that the criterion of correctness is convincing enough, powerful enough, dramatic enough on its own, to at least make a _wager_ on truth.

All photographic/digital images of the world, whether they are static or moving (but the moving world is, I will say, privileged insofar as it takes space and adds time), are often correct in a technical sense but not necessarily truthful in a poetic sense.[28] This happens all the time: the objects represented, the people and places and things, have been gathered into a compositional form whose structure or purpose the objects themselves have no knowledge of or investment in. The result is the world's indifference to itself onscreen. In his _Notes on the Cinematograph_, Robert Bresson suggests that such indifference can be countered in the following enigmatic rule of thumb, the implementation of which is anyone's guess: "Make the objects look as if they want to be there."[29] For screen objects to exude a sense of presence, will, and interior life characteristic of human consciousness is for the camera machine to be able to see, listen, apprehend, and possibly think. Bresson wishes for objects to harbor the same attachment to existence as his human characters who tend to have as little control over their destinies. In Bresson's films, people and objects appear to have equal weight because the world itself feels weighted down by its own gravity—the engine of fate. The world, too, _wants to be there_, in other words, _elsewhere_, affirming itself in a realm completely foreign to itself: onscreen, in the dark, before an audience, with shadows full of light. While I will be exploring Bresson's complex film theory and aesthetics in depth in the next chapter, this sense of a _desiring world onscreen_ is more palpable in the early work of Terrence Malick.

III. METAPHYSICAL FIGURES IN _DAYS OF HEAVEN_

In the Foreword to the enlarged edition of _The World Viewed_, Cavell remarks almost in passing—yet, strangely enough, as one of a mere handful of analyses of actual films—that his experience watching _Days of Heaven_ (Malick, USA, 1978) brought to mind certain key passages from Heidegger's sustained meditation on the nature of Being, exemplified in a series of lectures entitled _What Is Called Thinking? Days of Heaven_ is a film set in nature (the wheat fields of the Texas Panhandle), in the past (early twentieth century, the age of early cinema), featuring a love triangle that ends in tragedy (Shakespearean), and is narrated by a young girl imaginatively open to the beauty and mystery of her surroundings (let's say Blakean). But it is the film's sublime realization of its images and sounds, realized in accordance with what Cavell describes as "the casual rounds of earth and sky,"[30] which sets the stage for this almost unprecedented collision between philosophy and film, one that scholars from both fields may see as untenable, if not completely farfetched. After all, what has beautiful cinematography to do with the truth of Being? ... Cavell worries too, but insists, after Emerson, on finding the right tuition for his intuition about the film. After viewing it (presumably only once, given Cavell's stated interest in memory over textuality and philosophy as autobiography),[31] his immediate impression is that Malick has indeed enacted the Heideggerian refrain to heed the call of Being, putting to the test Bresson's belief, mentioned at the end of the previous section, in the possibility of filling film objects with what I described as a desire to be onscreen. For Cavell, the natural world in *Days of Heaven* has been *made* to appear in this unique way: its power of presence—its desire to be—is marked by extreme beauty, an unbearable and unserviceable beauty. (Beauty is truth, truth beauty? Very well, but on what grounds? Through which criteria?)

Perhaps only someone who reads and writes philosophy could have such a spontaneous reaction to a film that is, after all, quite non-philosophical (and, in a sense, anti-intellectual). Cavell does well to remind us that Malick, many years ago, studied philosophy at Harvard, and even translated into English Heidegger's book *The Essence of Reason*. But Malick's departure from philosophy into filmmaking in the late 1960s should not necessarily be construed as an attempt to do philosophy through film in particular or through art in general.[32] Cavell's elaborate and challenging multireference to Heidegger in this atypical context—an introductory Foreword to a work of film theory—stems from an intuition that a profound affinity prevails between Heidegger's metaphysics and Malick's romanticism in light of what he perceives to be a mutual interest in, and subservience to, the question of Being. This is a risky interdisciplinary leap that continues to set the bar high for the philosophy of film.

Cavell's unanticipated plunge into the worldhood aesthetics of *Days of Heaven*, prompted by a signature series of remarks from Heidegger on the original Greek understanding/experience of Being, is worth sharing here in full. The block quote begins with Cavell's setup of the Malick–Heidegger comparison (interdisciplinary thinking is comparative, after all), and ends with an interpretation that never ceases to ignite my philosophical interest in film.

> The particular mode of beauty of these [*Days of Heaven*'s] images somehow invokes a formal radiance which strikes me as a realization of some sentences from Heidegger's *What Is Called Thinking?* (Harper Torchback, 1972).

When we say "Being," it means "Being of beings." When we say "beings," it means "beings in respect of Being." ... The duality is always a prior datum, for Parmenides as much as for Plato, Kant as much as Nietzsche. ... An interpretation decisive for Western thought is that given by Plato. ... Plato means to say: beings and Being are in different places. Particular beings and Being are differently located. (p. 227)

According to Plato, the idea constitutes the Being of a being. The idea is the face whereby a given something shows its form, looks at us, and thus appears, for instance, as this table. In this form, the thing looks at us. ... Now Plato designates the relation of a given being to its idea as participation. (p. 222)

The first service man can render is to give thought to the Being of beings. ... The word [being] says: presence of what is present. (p. 235)

The presence we described gathers itself in the continuance which causes a mountain, a sea, a house to endure and, by that duration, to lie before us among other things that are present. ... The Greeks experience such duration as a luminous appearance in the sense of illumined, radiant self-manifestation. (p. 237)

And now comes Cavell's epiphany, arguably the inspiration for *The World Viewed* and left undisclosed in the original edition:

If Malick has indeed found a way to transpose such thoughts for our meditation, he can have done it only, it seems to me, by having discovered, or discovered how to acknowledge, a fundamental fact of film's photographic basis: that objects participate in the photographic presence of themselves; they participate in the re-creation of themselves on film; they are essential in the making of their appearances. Objects projected on a screen are inherently reflexive, they occur as self-referential, reflecting upon their physical origins. Their presence refers to their absence, their location in another place. Then if in relation to objects capable of such self-manifestation human beings are reduced in significance, or crushed by the fact of beauty left vacant, perhaps this is because in trying to take dominion over the world, or in aestheticizing it (temptations inherent in the making of film, or of any art), they are refusing their participation with it.[33]

My reading of Cavell on Heidegger on Malick can be called Emersonian insofar as it seeks to provide the complete tuition for Cavell's original yet ultimately unfinished intuition. Cavell's return to Heidegger through Malick is no longer the improbable, esoteric gesture it once was in the early 1970s when Cavell was led outside of philosophy by film, into film, to reencounter old problematics such as skepticism as an ordinary language philosopher fascinated by cinematic ordinariness. And yet the gesture retains its novelty insofar as the capacity for movies to expose beings through the light of the world and invoke the Being of beings in the form, say, of formless overexposure and beauty, remains in constant conflict with the equal drive of the medium to offer a seemingly inexhaustible mode of *escape* from what concerns us most as earthbound beings—Being. This tension in our experience of film is one between contemplation and escapism, between the world in its own image and the world in our image (as I am so fond of saying), between the world *of* a film and the world *in* a film (less fond), between the participatory equality of beings onscreen and the human beings who substitute domination for participation, thus projecting their self-manifestation onto the world (my interpretation of Cavell's somewhat confounding assessment of the characters and creators of *Days of Heaven*).

In an attempt to recover ancient Greek thinking on the experience of primordial Being, Heidegger suggests in a revision of Plato that Being is "the illumined radiant self-manifestation of beings." This definition is useful only in a technical sense (what more could we ask from a definition?) and as a way of learning about the history of the meaning of Being (as something fit for a philosophy lecture), for in reality Being cannot be defined independently of a live encounter. But a live encounter with what, exactly? With "it"? Again, our words fall short or stand too tall. Heidegger's nostalgia for a past age of enchantment puts the onus on we moderns to *relearn* how to be in the world by listening for the call of Being and responding to it, as Heidegger says, "meditatively."[34] Presumably, the call of Being is constant and imperishable, hence the muffledness or murkiness of the call becomes a symptom of our remoteness from Being, our having become alien to it and ourselves. Since Being for Heidegger in modernity is a question and not a fact, a problem as opposed to a possibility, our estrangement from Being has made a mystery of the facts such that philosophy must start from scratch. (This is why every metaphysics begins at the beginning rather than from where a prior metaphysics concluded or stopped.) Now for Cavell, it is possible for a film to stir up the fundamental question of Being in Heidegger's unparalleled understanding of it. Apparently, this one film, a so-called narrative film directed towards a so-called general audience, not only brings all this philosophy to mind but does so in such a way that it brings it *to life*, raising its stakes, finding its forms, *enacting* it. Cavell does with *Days of Heaven* what Heidegger does with Van Gogh's *Shoes*. Through what he calls its "formal radiance," the film functions as a realization of what Heidegger believed was confined primarily, if not exclusively, to the province of language. The film does so precisely because Malick, despite knowing some philosophy (Heidegger above all), does not focus solely on formal radiance, remaining equally committed to storytelling and refusing to undertake the complex task of aesthetic realization *as* a philosopher or in the *name* of

philosophy. Cavell's inspiration here (the experience upon which his recollec-
tions of Heidegger's rarified meditations strike him out of the blue, or in the
majestic dark of the movie theater) is not directed towards anything particular
in the film either—that is why he calls his reading a "fragmentary reading of a
whole film, [...] a prescription of such a reading."[35] What Cavell is responding
to, and what his response suggests Malick is responding to, is the *particularity
of the medium of film itself as world-disclosure*, put to work within this particular film
called *Days of Heaven*. And by enabling or activating such a vitally fundamental
aspect of the medium (its capacity to view the world in its own image, to let
beings be, to participate in the self-manifestation of beings without discriminating against those human beings who prefer to watch), Cavell's "Malick"
discovers within the ontology of film a metaphysical orientation towards Being
by way of the particular beings whose singular appearance the medium of film
makes possible. The effortlessness with which cinematic objects participate
in themselves, derived from the almost animistic empowerment of cinematic
automatism, is crucial to the experience of images and sounds that show what
moving images of the world do, in fact, that is ontologically, *show*: the persisting presence of things into a form that Heidegger boldly refers to as "face."
Things on film, having come into their own presence, have faces. Humans are
all face. They are beings who both participate and dominate, beings set *into* the
world and *upon* the world. They are the image makers: directors of their own
lives and actors in the lives of others.

In *Days of Heaven*, the natural world—"the casual rounds of earth and
sky"—is the main *setting* in both senses of the word: noun and verb. Nature is
the setting (noun) and the setting (verb) of Being. The film follows a torrential
love triangle unfolding in nature, but as nature unfolds in circles through the
seasons, the chaos of human emotion becomes absorbed in larger rhythms
of life in which all beings are at home, and at ease. Malick's authorship carries
a significant degree of servility to the natural world, hence to the nature of
film, an aesthetic of servility that also aligns with trends in modernist art more
generally.[36] It is as if the film never ceases to set itself up and so set itself to
work, as if nature were a stage of sorts. Heidegger's metaphor for such a
gesture is "the clearing." While in art there is often an alluring, absorbing,
sometimes alienating "playing out" of events that court our attention, this
play onscreen (also known as *the screenplay*) does not appear staged so much
as set in the world through contemplative yet at the same time ephemeral
combinations of long, medium and close shots of human beings resituated
in nature (the experience of which depends, of course, on their respective socio-economic situations). More importantly, the narrative does not
undermine or overpower the world-stage itself—in this case the luminous,
radiant self-manifestation of the cinematic screen—rather it is fundamentally

inseparable from it; its structure reveals the world like a bridge joining remote land masses or like a river flowing through various communities of life. In theater, a stage is described as being set *for* a play. Even if the play is just the empty stage (imagine a theater inspired by the music of John Cage), the stage is still set for that purpose, for that particular—and no doubt peculiar—play. But in film there is no stage *per se*; the world is, or can be, the stage, and it is always set—never a dull moment. To activate the medium and perhaps trigger the development of his art (artful artlessness), the filmmaker swayed by this modernist impulse may opt to *do nothing*, as it were, setting the stage of the world through the medium of film by engaging the medium's revelatory automatisms, a method in defiance of using the medium on the dramatic terms established by more traditional artforms like theater or literature. And so, this "doing nothing" may require *doing everything*.[37] In "The Origin of the Work of Art" Heidegger insists, "[T]his 'letting' is nothing passive but a doing in the highest degree in the sense of *thesis*, a 'working' and 'willing' which … is characterized as the 'existing human being's entrance into and compliance with the unconcealedness of Being.'"[38] Cavell's (Heideggerian) philosophical interest in Malick's (Heideggerian) aesthetic investment in the ontology of film marks a mutual concern for the question of Being that is felt to be restated, at long last, by light itself (the form and material of Being); and this hermeneutic constellation can yield the discovery that every shot in a film, not just opening shots or wide shots, can be cultivated into an *establishing shot*. A film whose images are permitted to establish or reestablish the world along the spatial edges of the frame and the temporal edges of the cut, creating a succession of aesthetic world-makings, transform the grave and deadly word "world" from a noun into a butterfly verb—*worlding*.[39]

Malick's way to worlding lies in rescue: the rescue of things from objecthood, beings from subjecthood. A thing in the world which does not come to presence as an object, in part because there is no subject to reduce it to one, could be said to have a rare foreground importance on film: a thing with a face. Letting things be involves letting them go; letting beings be—human beings, that is—involves watching things and other beings let go of them the more they try to hold on. Letting be, no shot in the film feels *held*. No shot is taken from too close or far away, as closeups tend to imprison things and even faces into the role of signifiers, while wide shots risk losing the details of life in a painterly mist. The attempt to rescue the world from our clutches and let things be is also mirrored in the attempt to let the images be: they wash over us like waves. Perhaps the first and most important step in poetically rescuing the time and space of the world from the time and space of manmade action and event is to rescue the camera from a machine that records the world, treating it instead as a medium that creates the world by revealing it. The terms of this creation–revelation may ultimately feed into an act of *decreation*, the poetry of clearing, an aesthetics of establishment. I would then want to describe the camera—the mimetic machine which became a creative instrument— metaphorically as the "fresh start" of consciousness. The world is there *before* we begin to gaze upon it, a fact which the camera helps us to recall, training us to meet the world halfway—a crossroads at which the world becomes not only seen but *felt* within the mind's eye of camera consciousness.[40]

To conclude this chapter, I take Cavell's brief encounter with *Days of Heaven* as provocation for a close reading of the remarkable way in which the world comes to presence onscreen in the fullness of its otherness, as if eyes are being laid upon it for the first time. Again, I am interested in how the film is deeply immersed in its own setting—set in the world like a precious stone—and how the storyline is rendered cyclical as a consequence of that choice. The figures which mobilize the film's metaphysics are earth and sky, horizon and house, horizontality and verticality, the face-like presence of things, the thing-like sculptedness of faces.

Near the beginning of the film, migrant workers arrive at a farm marked by a monumental house and gate spread far apart, a "heavenly" world of golden wheat fields that will be their new temporary home **(Fig. 2.1)**. It is summertime and harvest time in the Texas Panhandle. The poor workers work, play, and sleep outside; the rich farmer (Sam Shepard) looks on dreamily from his towering house—he is both lucky and lonely for that. But the film is not so interested in exploring these social inequities in much depth; in fact, it seems largely indifferent to them. Rich or poor,

Figure 2.1 *Migrant workers arrive at a "heavenly" farm marked by house and gate:* Days of Heaven *(Terrence Malick, USA, 1978).*

protected from the elements or directly exposed to them, the film's sense of the world remains, in a word, "beautiful," regardless of the perspectives of the characters or the narrative circumstances in which they live and die. Except for the film's child narrator, both rich and poor strive to escape their respective worlds, only occasionally stopping to gaze upon the world which the film as a whole never ceases to bear witness to. This project of beautification, therefore, is not only aesthetic but ontological: the sights and sounds which strike us as beautiful—formally radiant in Cavell's terms—are the result or "fruit" of the world recreated in its own image, the principle of which I have already expressed as an aesthetic concentration upon the world *of* the film in addition to the world *in* the film. This concentration separates these two worlds and shows the former to belong to the medium of film rather than the discourse of fiction. The world in its own image is inherently beautiful insofar as it shatters the illusion of our separateness from the world or, what amounts to the same thing, the illusion of a world that is nothing more than an extension of our self-image—an illusion out of which metaphysical films light the way, even if it is to show that the shattering of this illusion may mean death for the characters.

It is important to note that the world of *Days of Heaven* does not begin heavenly beautiful. We open on an urban atmosphere defined by industry, competition, poverty, and environmental disaster: dingy, noisy, almost black and white. A tall smokestack asserts the vertical demeanor of human civilization and conquest; it resembles an oil derrick sucking up the life from the ground below, which looks almost swampy and certainly poisoned with chemical runoff. A heated altercation between Bill (Richard Gere) and the foreman of the steel mill, ironically drowned out by the brutal banging of an industry that stops for no one, erupts in a burst of violence from Bill that propels him to flee in panic towards a white light diffused by thick smoke, a foreshadowing of his grim fate of there being no place for him on this earth except the fantasy of *the next place*. As he sprints for the nearest exit, we hear the voiceover of his young sister, Linda (Linda Manz), speaking in the past tense—yet as if it were all still so present to her—of a romantic yet arduous life of searching about for things unnamed, for possibilities open to the poor and disenfranchised classes of society with nowhere to go except *on*. The next shot dramatically establishes the film's horizontal configuration with a train gliding across a bridge perfectly suspended against the clear blue sky with the land invisible on either side. This train hovering between worlds is reminiscent of the enchantments of the Polar Express or Charon's punt on the River Styx, spewing charming wisps of smoke that seem to adorn the sky in fine drapery while reminding us that the black storm clouds of human misery are all too portable. The striking beauty of this particular image is pitched high via counterpoint with what has come before (the suffocating ruin of vertical extraction and exploitation) and in anticipation of what lies ahead—a promising and precarious gateway to what will become the film's spontaneous, ecstatic retreat into nature, a circular or spiraling space which seems to be harmoniously ordered even if human relations remain fraught with dissatisfaction and deceit **(Figs 2.2, 2.3)**.

A Heideggerian teaching with which Malick is undoubtedly familiar is that dwelling in the world constitutes the making of a world. How does the presence of people onscreen turn an image into a world? There is a chemistry

Figures 2.2 and 2.3 *The film shifts from vertical urbanity to horizontal passage into nature:* Days of Heaven *(Terrence Malick, USA, 1978).*

between earth and sky that the act of human dwelling itself orchestrates, a chemistry which goes by the name "horizon" where earth and sky touch at infinity, the touch being the *finite* apprehension of the infinite for mortals. In *Days of Heaven*—days which refer to time spent on the farm, deep in the Panhandle, in a nature rendered habitable by the ancient practice of agriculture—the world in its own image yields *image-buildings* comprised of earth and sky, enclosed by the horizon, housing people and animals and insects. Out here, images are built from the bottom up: earth before sky, horizontality giving way to verticality, the latter seen most vividly in the figure of the farmer's house. And if we carefully examine the base of some of these frames, we can detect a thin and airy crest of tousled wheat rising quietly from the earth, gently scratching the very footing of the image's standing, suggesting that the firm ground of the earth has something sky-like or watery about it, that the very foundation of Being is rife with the activity of Becoming. As a metaphysical rule, so to speak, earth precedes sky and gives way to it, receding away *and* extending above, for human dwelling stands proudly rather than crawls helplessly on the earth—and this standing is a movement between body and mind, feet on the ground and head in the clouds until we lay to rest, in sleep or through death.

Almost every image in the film makes room for this relationship between earth and sky via the horizon's cleave. Rarely do we find an image of all earth or all sky. Rather, Malick and his team of cinematographers[41] rely on the horizon to determine where the two primordial planes should meet and give way to each other in a temporary—and also illusory—reconciliation of their permanent staying apart. We look down and see the earth, we look up and see the sky, we stare straight ahead and follow both receding away in an image of their mythical betrothal—the vanishing point—an endless movement towards a unity amidst the heavenly embrace of the infinite.

In the distant background of a scene I notice an anomaly in the "behavior" of the world: the earth touches the sky very close to the *top* of the frame. Bill and Abby (Brooke Adams), the lovers disguised as siblings, are playing in a field after a long day's work. In the fading twilight, Bill is lying down watching Abby perform a series of cartwheels. The camera follows her erratic movements by panning to the left. While panning, the visibility of the earth's exchange into sky at the top of the frame, very close to its edge, is carefully maintained like a tightrope act. The camera movement here also resembles a child studiously *tracing*—panning as tracing. We can attribute this panning action to the flat form of the earth's presence on the prairie plains, where space is spread out across the horizontality of its opened expanse. In adherence to the shape of space, the camera receives the fullness of the world's horizontal character by tracing or perhaps measuring the topographical dimensions of the environment. If, for instance, Malick had chosen to frame the image *below* the horizon, thus square *upon* the earth, we would not be mistaken in identifying Abby's right-to-left movement to be the reference point for the corresponding movement of the camera. Even with the horizon deliberately framed, the almost indiscernible thinness of it relative to the imposing mass of the earth makes the image appear as if the motions of the camera were conceived entirely with respect to Abby and not the horizon. Yet if we examine the relational structure of this image more closely, we may find ourselves wanting to ask why the filmmakers visually insist on preserving the frame of the horizon so close to the upper limit of the film frame, creating a kind of rhyme between horizon line and frame line. Let's see what happens by keeping our attention firmly fixed on the outer limits of the diegesis, moving quietly with the camera along the rails of this erratic sliver of a traced horizon.[42]

During the course of Abby's first pair of cartwheels with Bill looking on, the camera can be seen tracing a line across the horizon while following the horizontal movements of the vertically oriented being **(Figs 2.4, 2.5, 2.6)**. This is, again, significant because horizontality and verticality constitute the film's most fundamental metaphysical motifs. Together they are architectural harmony, as in post and lintel or the bridge over water, and primordial strife, as between participation and domination, going with the flow and against the grain of life. The human being emblematizes *both* directionalities: a pointy rock of consciousness jutting out of the stream of life, and a piece of driftwood at one with the stream itself.

Figures 2.4–2.6   *A visual (almost imperceptible) rhyme between the horizon line and the film's frame line:* Days of Heaven *(Terrence Malick, USA, 1978).*

At this point we can assume that Abby's centered position in the shot, determined by her central character subjectivity in the story and vertical prowess in the composition, is in control of the camera and its generally anthropocentric angle of vision. But in the midst of her third and final cartwheel, the camera, while following her, hits a bump in the landscape's horizontal or "horizonal" flow in the background—the gradual beginnings of a slight drop in the horizon's linear trajectory. Interestingly (to me and for our purposes), it is near this exact spatial moment that Abby suddenly veers off from her path of play, away from the camera and further into the depths of the image. Both shifts in line—human and horizon, vertical and horizontal—make subtle yet separate claims on camera consciousness, which means an act of *reframing* (rethinking?) is likely to occur in response to one of these pictorial claims. So far and without surprise, it is the character of Abby who presents the more persuasive diegetic case, and if the filmmakers were to continue being convinced of this, we would see the image of her movements adjust to her adjustment and remain more or less bound to the pivotal line of human affairs commanding the stage of the world. In other words, with Abby's slight swerving action we could expect a quick counter-adjustment from the camera, a reframing and refocusing, a reaction of following and adherence, a storytelling response to persons in the form of a sharp upward tilt of the camera mind.[43] However, such a camera-reply is not forthcoming and Abby is not *adhered to* the way human agents typically dictate camera movement in the movies. Instead, the very opposite occurs: a sharp *downward* tilt seemingly without motivation or justification. Of what, we may ask, is the camera conscious in this case? The answer begins with cinematic events of which viewers are likely to be *unconscious*: the horizonal line of the world in its own image, the soft claim of the lowering land, the succession of vanishing points in the distance which mark the retreat of earth and sky while measuring the contours of the world's elemental enclosure. During Abby's third and final cartwheel, the horizon spills down, opening the sky and challenging the earth. The lip of sky above the land is the bare minimum needed to constitute the upper half of the horizon's straight line. It is not the sky *per se* that is filmed so much as the sky-in-horizon or sky-in-transition, the hinge between earth and sky. This near imperceptible downward camera move is by no means trivial: such a micro-gesture returns the role of the horizon in the image to one of maintaining the perceptual legibility of the world, a sense of enclosure or intimacy outdoors, and even a metaphysical homeostasis as a holding together of the elements in space and time. In adhering to the horizon rather than the human, Malick acknowledges a fundamental fact of the metaphysics of film: earth and sky are object-planes that, as part of the story of their self-manifestation, recede to a point in the distance which cannot be objectified—the vanishing point where a sense of the infinite pervades—meeting in the presence of a disappearance which also thematizes the presence of absence onscreen. And without the standing verticality of human beings to dig into and divert the flow of earth and sky, the self-manifesting story of the horizon babbles on about infinity while teasing us with the possibility of resisting an endlessly rotating world.

As mentioned at the beginning of this analysis, at the center of the film's recreation of the world in its own image stands, alone in nature, the farmer's monumental and impeccable house. Once Bill, Abby, and Linda leave Chicago and reach the open fields of the Texas Panhandle by train (an expressive figure of the horizontal world they are about to enter), it seems to me that without the *vertical* structure of the house—this sprout of civilization, symbol of cultivation, heart of human domesticity and dignity—the primary and peripheral characters in the film would remain in a nomadic state, forever meandering along wide ranges of horizonal flatness, and perhaps the film itself would dissolve into a stream of impressions, wandering aimlessly in search of its subject matter. Without the *Days of Heaven* house, the exposed open-air dwelling of nature would remain unchecked, directionless, friction-less; the horizon's smooth waltz between earth and sky would have nothing to pivot against or sing to; and without such enclosures—vertical breaks or buoys in the swell of space—human beings scatter like fireflies and the social fabric misses its most vital stitch **(Fig. 2.7)**.[44]

There would also be no wheat fields without the house, for the wheat has been grown in the same way as the house has been built—again, vertically. Politically, the house (and the equally solitary and presiding gate which filters

Figure 2.7   *The metaphysical anchor of the house:* Days of Heaven *(Terrence Malick, USA, 1978).*

the outside world) turns this piece of land into personal property, a territory, an industrial operation, a protective if alienating home for the rich and a *plein air* barracks for the poor. Ontologically, as if holding the world in/of the film in place, the house strikes me as a footbridge between humans and nature, a primary coordinate of what we call "culture." Aesthetically, it functions as an axis for the camera to orient itself in space, setting up the film's metaphysical perspective and providing the characters, not to mention the filmmakers and viewers, with a logical light, as it were, by which to frame, set forth, venture into life. Time and again, we see it looming in the depths of the background as a reminder of how these people, mostly strangers to each other, have gathered together in the house of nature, and why the house of nature, for humans, cannot go completely astray from civilization. The togetherness of house and nature is so symbiotic that if you removed *that* house, the film would go dark, and so I am tempted to say that the house makes possible the making of images, illuminates the world of the film like a blaze burning in the middle of nowhere. The film's camera-consciousness obsessively seeks out the house like the north star, leans toward it with hands outstretched to what is most familiar, building frame after frame (image houses) so that the world of the film may stand tall and true. Sown into the horizon and thrown into sharp relief with walls and roof vividly silhouetted, the house shines forth like a sun, radiating its own metaphysical light by day *and* by night.

In the following example from the film, to remove *this* house would be to remove *this* image. As in the previous example of earth, sky, and horizon, I ask you to consider the significance of a completely minor detail, crucial yet bound to be overlooked. Linda is splashing water onto a man in black who leans hunched over a washing station set up for the workers to strip off the dirt and sweat of the day. There are barrels flanking the right side of the frame with some slanting inwards, obscuring the landscape except for a patch of clear blue sky in the top-left corner. As a giggling Linda eagerly departs the station, the camera follows or rather accompanies her into the open field, thus opening the field and with it an intense swarm of people young and old frolicking and lazing away in the piercing yet fading rays of the setting sun. This place of rest in the open plains is ruled by the unspoken fellowship of human beings, the sense of togetherness perfectly insulated against the cool draft of loneliness and exhaustion. Meeting Linda in this outside gathering space is Abby, who asks if her hands are clean before enjoying the hard-earned meal. Behind them a man without a shirt towels his body dry. An off-white trailer tinged yellow by the hot sunset has its front door wide open. Children run after each other within a vague circle of adults. Two men, side by side, get to know one another. Open umbrellas stand in the ground and emerge out of the tall golden grass like giant mushrooms. Plates in hand, Abby leads

Linda into this sedated swarm of famished workers. They enter as Bill exits, and while crossing paths Bill gestures offscreen towards some place quiet to have their supper. Moving now with Bill, from behind the trailer appears the farmer's house, alone in the distance, cut off from the melodious clamor, looking on, a non-mythological Xanadu which holds up its guard with sheer distinctness and remoteness as opposed to ironclad gates. From this perspective it appears so small that one could pick it up like a snow globe, and yet its unassuming presence exudes the eerie command of a lighthouse. It enters the background of this tracking shot seemingly by accident, but as soon as it states its presence it's as if it begins to gaze upon the action, justifying—if not possessing—the image as a whole. There stirs a strange sense onscreen of a fundamental yet tangential source to all that we've been given to see and hear throughout this scene—the house as the "sun" of the film's global topography that we cannot afford to lose track of. In focusing almost exclusively on the actual, we forget what makes the actual *possible*. Things could be otherwise than they are, but they are what they are for a reason. The presence of the house on the horizon turns out to be a *necessary condition* for this dense and gently rippling scene of quiet human ordeal and fleeting reprieve to emerge as it does. Nucleic and sentient-like in the distance (like the open window eyes of a house at night), the farmer's house tills cinematic being-in-the-world, spreading a quilt of consciousness over a natural world previously untutored, anonymous, unmapped, and still largely indifferent to all claims of ownership **(Figs 2.8, 2.9, 2.10. 2.11, 2.12)**.

The steady vigil of the manmade structure within unmade nature also brings to mind similar occasions in the film where the house *bears witness* to many essential happenings and most of the events of the narrative. The house makes a strict background appearance starting with the couple's arrival on the farm, when Abby questions the foreman about the owner of the house, and again quite strikingly when Bill and Abby rest by a haystack gently carpeted with snow, licking their wounds after an excruciatingly hard day's work **(Fig. 2.13)**. The house in these instances is more deliberately composed in the background, lodged to one side and illuminated from within in warm tungsten tones, looking ever so inviting and thus amplifying the hardships of the homeless, whereas in the tracking shot described above the figure of the house *slips into the image*, bare or as it is, stripped of its customary pictorial gravity and grandeur. Specifically in Figures 2.10–2.12, the sudden appearance of the house in the distance is a necessary intrusion on the frame, calling for spontaneous *reframing* from the camera operator. For once, the film's pristine mise-en-scène looks a bit taxed and disheveled as the shot becomes occupied with the dual task of following both the human and metaphysical narratives of the film.

Figures 2.8–2.12   *A tracking shot finds its bearings when the house appears in the background:* Days of Heaven *(Terrence Malick, USA, 1978). *Black circles have been inserted for added clarity.*

Let's briefly return to this intricate tracking shot, whose specific unfolding becomes subject to the guardianship of the onlooking house. The casual persistence of Bill's forward movement keeps the house in the distance scrolling along comfortably. To let the house slip off the frame-edge at this point would be the equivalent of bringing it down, and with it the image-as-house. Consciously or unconsciously, the filmmakers respond to the confrontation between Bill and another worker with an apprehension that infects the composition. Moments before the heated argument ensues, the camera notices Bill's walk increase in intensity and responds accordingly, keeping the house on the far-right side of the image background as if anticipating the reaction delay such a spontaneous collision may impose. When the man finally delivers his suspicious insult regarding the perceived intimacy between Bill and Abby (who pose as siblings), an incensed Bill stops abruptly in his tracks, causing the camera to acknowledge his action while simultaneously keeping visible—keeping in mind—the house, without which, to put it strongly, there

Figure 2.13   *Bill and Abby rest by a haystack, the house looking on:* Days of Heaven *(Terrence Malick, USA, 1978).*

is no film. During the confrontation, the house, which moments before stood far to the right, now stands on the far-left side of the shot, teetering on the edge of the frame, half-erased. If the image is slowed down at this point, as Bill continues his aggressive stretch towards the man, coaxing the camera to stretch with him, it is possible to detect the camera's apprehension in the encroaching disappearance of the house into the void offscreen. The closest the house comes to being cut off by the narrative framing and disappearing completely is about the one-quarter mark, at which point the filmmakers, in a sure act of intuitive or magnetic allegiance to it, nudge the camera ever so slightly to the left, reestablishing the house in full and making practical use of the sky as a strip of insulation to hold it in place. As a filmmaker equally committed to the metaphysical logic of the world in its own image as to the dramatic logic of the scene, Malick insists on keeping the house in the background and in so doing *keeps its keep*, reconciling the house *in* the image with the house *of* the image and the people in the film with the people watching it.

The relatively lengthy tracking shot comes to a rest only when the presence of the house is rendered permanent. I have said that without the house this scene and to a certain extent the entire film occurs without a place, that is, hypothetically and solely in terms of the narrative, with the audience forced to immerse themselves in the fictional space in order to give it the feeling of fact. There are established conventions, some so strong and binding as to function almost as aesthetic algorithms (for example, continuity editing), by which screen space is legitimated in the absence of adequate buttressing from the world in its own image. We sometimes say that works of art should be built to last, but quite independently of their content and style, a criterion of their lasting is also their (meta)physical ability *to stand*, to display a sense of architectural integrity along with artistic quality, which remains subjective. Films which honor their own metaphysical conditions of possibility are in good structural condition, allowing fictions to rest on foundations and the foundations to permeate the fictions with facts. The seeded and tended world on film sprouts through the fine cracks in our consciousness, forming a garden of light welcoming our return.

CHAPTER THREE

Paradise Exposed: Psychic Automatism in Film

> Kleist wrote somewhere that what the poet would most of all like to be able to do would be to convey thoughts by themselves without words. (What a strange admission.)
>
> — Ludwig Wittgenstein, *Culture and Value*

> I try to be a true attendant upon grace. Perhaps it will come—perhaps it will not come. Perhaps this quiet yet unquiet waiting is the harbinger of grace, or perhaps it is grace itself. I do not know. But that does not disturb me. In the meantime I—have my friends with my ignorance.
>
> — Franz Kafka, with Gustav Janouch, *Conversations with Kafka*

PRIMER: "WHILE THE WILL IS OFF ITS WATCH"

What sort of being dreams of being a non-being? The human being. The human may be the only being for which being is a blockage. Imagine someone who is borne away by his speech yet cannot bear the sound of his own voice. Someone who speaks in the present yet hears his voice as if from the past, abhorring the sound he makes and cannot not make—for, just like an animal, this is his sound. He wants to sound like somebody else or something else, not out of any thirst for conformity or fantasy but because he does not know how else to lose the knowledge, the false knowledge, that reduces his self-knowledge into a habit or at best a rhyme. The problem is that he wants to change, but wanting this, unfortunately, is not how change happens; change forces itself like a storm, whereas it stands before him as yet another feat of strength, a great boulder that he may very well budge, or even move about with tremendous exertion and pain, only to find that the boulder never takes off of its own accord.

This being I am sketching in broad strokes and who seems frightfully unhappy, let's call him "fully formed," perhaps a tad "overripe." He knows all too well who he is mainly by being attached to what he is; people recognize him on the street and honor him by the simple act of remembering his name. Naturally, he is nothing without the trial and error of an experiment no human being can avoid or opt out of: that of personality formation and all the contingencies which go into its making. And yet, here he is, staring at his own reflection, struggling to surprise himself, trying in vain to do "something" that will not reinforce the image he sees before him, staring him down from the watchtower at the center of his court of consciousness. Can he finally open his ears and hear the lost lullaby of his childhood, translated into music seeping through the vents above his head? Will he ever open his eyes and see with the eyes of his first love, gold-beaded and serpent-swirling eyes? It's simple, is it not? All you have to do is turn on the tap, as you do every morning and throughout the day. You wouldn't suck the water out of the pipes when you could easily let it flow, so why are you so afraid to let yourself go? A slight rephrasing of the question: when was the last time you were afraid of yourself? Your courage is perhaps nothing more than a profound sense of acclimatization. And now you want to open the window and disturb the finely tuned tepidness? If you are still awake, a breath of fresh air may require more courage than you have mustered in a long time. If you are still enough awake, then you may be forced to the unbearable conclusion that what you call your self-knowledge is actually the hibernation of the self. Breathing is automatic, whereas taking a deep breath is an act of will. The will is just too strong not to intervene, and indeed the will, once discovered, is pure strength. Once discovered, it teaches you, the "I", that it has survived all your transformations, and perhaps it insists that you would not have survived them either without the will to carry you along and keep your precious head above water.

So, you have been led by your will, willed by your will, onward and onward to this very moment. And so here you are, again, the "willer" of your will, you will your will, and with that the will drops you to the floor upon which you land on your feet—your feet, they willed you along splendidly, because you told them to and they move as one. You will them, they move like so; they move like that because you willed them—did you not? You don't remember doing any willing, but if you didn't will them, they wouldn't have moved like that and you would hesitate or come to a standstill. Such an expert willer you are that you need not will your will anymore; it takes care of itself, happens all by itself, like a machine that works at full capacity as long as you do not give it a second thought or gum up its gears with impractical self-consciousness.

Well, that is how it is with our poor seeker of selflessness: the mountain is too high to climb because the mountain is him. But at night he shall sleep and dream and awaken soaked in dreams only a fraction of which are remembered and whose remembrance, very often, dries them up in a flash. And while he struggles to remember his dreams, and if to remember is also to forget, he at least knows that last night and every night henceforth hold dreams that no human being can consciously experience. For dreams are the events that take place when the will is off its watch. In dreams, the will—comically, tragically, at long last—is fair game.

The point is that we know we do in fact let go, and that this letting-go cannot be known any more than dreams can be processed by excising the dreamer. The point, if you will, is that we know that knowing reduces us to a point—from here everything is possible, but from here, also, possibility can come to lose all its currency and what is longed for is the pure gold of grace. The gold within the mountain, locked in darkness, surrounded by worm-rich earth and completely and utterly raw; the gold that is worth nothing, that retains its secret and whispers its splendor and goes completely unnoticed in the marketplace. Grace will always be in high demand for beings whose nature is one of partial or total exile, and perhaps the only way to reclaim it is by stumbling back into it, backwards, as if preparing to be caught off guard. In taking back what's left of ourselves we see that our hands are tied and pockets sealed. All articles are to be left at the door.

I. THE MECHANICAL GARDEN

We once doubted that photography and film could be legitimate artforms on the grounds that they are mechanical mediums and as such cannot be artistically generative without being, first and foremost, mimetically repetitive. How wrong we were: the machines at the heart of these artforms became ideal for all manner of humanistic and aesthetic expression. While the meaningfulness of the mimetic arts is now beyond question, the inherent automaticity of photography and film—not to mention technologies of digital capture—still remains a counterintuitive and philosophically problematic candidate for the arts. If the likeness between photograph and referent makes Stanley Cavell "ontologically restless," then the apparent clash between automaticity and creativity is a cause for *aesthetic restlessness*. Regardless of the commonplace ubiquity of photographic and cinematic representation alongside various other technologies which have been admitted into the realm of the aesthetic, it seems to me that the following line of questioning does not disappear with our skepticism but is rather begged all the more forcefully.—What does it mean to say that photography and film are, were, and perhaps always will be *mechanical artforms?* What does it mean to say, or to recall, that photography and film were not—could not have been—for this very reason thought of *as* artforms when they wished to be regarded as such? What does it mean to say, as Cavell has said, that cinema knew this about itself from the beginning, that it "[arose] out of magic; from *below* the world,"[1] in contrast with the mythical genealogy of the preceding arts which came to us as if from above, from the heavens, like gifts from the gods? What sort of "soul" does such an artform possess if human beings have called upon machines in the creation of art, machines the logic of which automatically produces the very images that constitute a series of photographs or go into the making of a film? As we have seen throughout this book, the contradictions with which the philosophy of art must continually wrestle in thinking the status of (re)presentations warp the criteria of clarity and distinctness that philosophers rely upon in finding their way through darkness and despair.

Since the middle of the nineteenth century with photography, and perhaps as early as the late eighteenth century with the phantasmagoria, theorists and practitioners have made a strong appeal to the unique abilities of machines in the making of art.[2] What the recording–projecting continuum of the cinematic apparatus in particular embodies as a vehicle for our contemplation is something far less aesthetic (existential or psychological are more apt terms) hibernating at the very intersection of mechanical reproduction and artistic creation: an immaculate automatism in the meaningful representation of a reality that appears readymade despite being perpetually formed and deformed by the manmade; a mindless, technically sophisticated, remarkably unflappable automatism through which an image of the world is realized independently of us, even if the content and formal configuration of that image are invariably an extension of us. The concept of automatism in this context is therefore not reducible to the camera machine's automatic recording of the world; rather it frames the cinema's recording–projecting of the world in its own image as a human valuation of mechanical revelation, hence a valuing of the non-human, one which equally extends to forms of immanence in matters of the processual (for example, creative fluidity or biological homeostasis) and to forms of transcendence such as human mediums and what we call magic. But at this stage of our investigation, what an automatic image on its own makes manifest and how a "self-manifesting image" comes into being in the first place strike me as less important than the human inclination to regard the *non-human* as the embodiment of innocence and perfection—and redemption.

As a condition for the redemption of the human condition's burden of knowledge, steep climb to faith, and condemnation to consciousness as a relentless self-imaging of the world, another word for the perfection or purity of automatism would be *grace*. While I will be exploring the relationship between grace and cinematic automatism in more detail later on, suffice it to say that when external conditions for perfection are met without being the object of conscious striving, then theology's disparagement of the human condition as fundamentally fallen (immune to perfection) is in effect.[3] Such "perfection" also becomes justifiable not merely in mechanical terms as scientifically sound (exemplary of the true) but equally in artistic terms as poetically revelatory (exemplary of the beautiful). This radical form of representation (call it mechanical, automatic, non-human) will be accused of lacking the ground upon which human beings stand as perceivers of value, perceivers of their own passions and prejudices; but because the spirit of automatism "believes in the world" first and foremost, it frees the world of beliefs for how it might be or ought to be—beliefs which belittle the world. In this sense, automatism opens a way for human consciousness to model the credulity and hospitality of mechanical consciousness in its "ontological selflessness." We are being carried (away) to a decisive moment in the history of ideas where the disappointments of metaphysics, the disenchantment of the world, and theology's consignment of spirit to the ineffable and otherworldly (as a response to what is deemed most unredeemable in the human condition) find relief—if not redemption—in the automatism of cinema as specter of grace and paradise exposed.

With these preliminary speculative remarks on automatism, I will be embarking on a prismatic reading of the phenomenon of cinematic automatism in particular that acknowledges the mechanical apparatus of the medium as harboring significant implications for human consciousness and the assumptions underlying our self-understanding as "human." The theoretical, aesthetic, psychoanalytic, religious, and sometimes ethical value ascribed to automatism, most notably within the metaphysical strains of classical film theory's various realisms, suggests that the conscious interest in or unconscious participation with this form of mechanization implies the medium's inherent or ontological grace—that sublime quality best known to cinephiles in which the mechanization of the medium is perceived or felt to be humanized, or where automatism is spiritualized without warning in the melding together of medium and mind. Cinematic automatism as a subliming of representation makes it possible to accept the world like an abiding child for whom adult logic is virtually absolute—yet to accept it *imaginatively*. This investment in the automatic is again a matter of the psychology of cinematic ontology: for the world in its own image to appear as in a dream, it is not enough for man to disappear (as Bazin thought) but to be *beside* himself. The cinematic apparatus is a radical displacement as opposed to an effacement of human consciousness.

Enacted by mechanical processes that see without thinking or sense senselessly, the paradoxical and in some sense mystical value of automatism can be described, simply enough, as "that which happens by itself," and those who value it above all else (above formalism *and* realism) as "seekers of grace." They are believers in the power of cinema to redeem the ills of human consciousness, restore the wonders of childhood infancy without the accompanying falsities and fears overlooked by nostalgia, and diagram an inventory of luminous material fragments of paradise which gleam in the wake of the death of God. They see the possibility for an innocence of human experience to emerge as the fruit of knowledge, hence the possibility of emancipation within a modern disenchanted world (a post-metaphysical world) in which the moving image projects the last light (the twilight) of metaphysics. If cinematic automatism can be said to recall traces of the prelapsarian world, it does so by channeling the concept of revelation from theology/spirituality and into technology/aesthetics, or from the domain of the miraculous to the mundane where the self-manifesting spirit of divine enchantment pulses without pretense of otherworldliness.

While automatism is briefly explored by classical film theorists who are enchanted by the realist configuration of the apparatus, and is epitomized by Cavell's (the late classical film theorist's) partial definition of the ontology of film as "a succession of automatic world projections,"[4] this lesser-known sense of automatism—the psychic sense, or the psychological logic of mechanization—is relatively absent from theories of cinematic ontology, in part because it originates from surrealist discourses that are ultimately suspicious of film's hegemonizing of vision and ordering of representation. An important task here is not only to rectify this gap but to gain some insight into its persistence and avoidance. The psychological appeal but also repression of cinematic automatism as a theory, practice, and aesthetic may be less a result of abandoned metaphysical thinking than one of valuing art that appears *unmade* or better yet *self-made*. We can think of this as art in which the human touch has permanently landed or cast a spell, manifesting in the precision and transparency unique to the mechanical and culminating in the uncanny efficacy of the passage between intention and expression—a passage to be navigated by map or whim until it runs of its own volition and into a realization of the artform on terms alien to the artist's personal taste. (Incidentally, one of the exemplary aspects of automatism will always remain tied to the self-discovering spirit of modernism in twentieth-century art and culture.)

Classical film theory's realist proponents, or new metaphysicians as I have been calling them, are often guilty of perpetuating an old theoretical habit by which automatism is linked solely to the mechanical recording functions and alleged representational objectivity of the camera, microphone, and other image-making aspects of film, regrettably reducing the automatic to the merely technological and yielding a rather superficial reading that strips automatism of its various incarnations throughout the arts, particularly automatic writing and drawing, not to mention the theory of psychoanalysis (those famous Freudian slips) and the psycho-geography of modernism (the paradigmatic arrival of the autonomous subject). By granting automatism a more complete range of associations, film theory can move past the medium specificities and limitations which have dominated its discussion. Beginning as a literal description of purely mechanical processes in the audiovisual representation of the world, automatism becomes an essentially human or possibly more-human-than-human (a superhuman) activity, that is, once humanity and mechanicity are finally (and carefully) reconciled. On the one hand, automatism strives to reach beyond the realm of the human altogether—beyond culture, history, and ideology, outside our unique and finite form of life, a "beyond" that the camera-eye is pictured as privy to, gazing as if into another world. But on the other hand, automatism is found to reside within the human condition itself as a paradoxical condition in which a positively dehumanizing force seeks to cut the strings of consciousness and shatter the mirror of self-consciousness.

This line of thinking returns us to the moral of automatism, over and above its somewhat irrational logic, as the most modern incarnation (and possible redemption) of the biblical myth of the Fall.[5] But the difference with the Fall as told by the mechanical arts, in a variation of the Old Testament theme of our irrevocable entry into knowledge, is that the former's post-metaphysical rendition of the myth locates the possibility of redemption *on earth* and *from within the self*, in what amounts to a complete inversion of the properly religious orchestration of messianic redemption. Yet paradise, regardless of the route, is never as we imagine it to be, for the cinematic redemption of physical reality as described by Kracauer, when raised to the level of metaphysics, suggests that the Garden of Eden still exists but only through a mechanical vision of the world, a vision that lies buried within the un- or non-conscious, to be cultivated at the intersection between movies and dreams or perhaps via the waking dreams of surrealist experiments with automatic writing and drawing. But the failure—or rather, I should say, the disappointment—of many of these surrealist experiments attests to how the chaotic monstrosities of the liberated unconscious diverge so drastically from the orderly naturalness of the mechanical *non*-conscious. The discipline of cinematic automatism is indicative of the pressure to perform the correct maneuver of dehumanization (a mechanical eye buried within the human "I") in luring the return of the primordial state of grace as the key to reenter the "knowledge-produced innocence" of "the mechanical garden" and be free (from ourselves). Mythologically speaking, the machine in us all—the body that Adam and Eve covered up in shame—is yet to be discovered. If we continue (as we must) to cover up the body, with clothes as a metaphor for self-consciousness, it is perhaps because there is no way to completely clothe this consciousness of self, no way to conceal the revelation of ourselves to ourselves. What the automatism of cinematic representation makes possible is the *nakedness* of a world projection oblivious to the Fall, a world in which it is still possible for grace to exist without hanging in the balance of a moral duel between good and evil, either sanctioned by divine blessing or sabotaged by devilish curses.

In order to carefully mine these depths of automatism and come to a greater appreciation of the value it holds for a metaphysical conception of film, I look towards two very different texts from different centuries yet bound by similar themes and passions: "On the Marionette Theater," an essay by the German novelist and playwright Heinrich von Kleist, first published in 1810, and *Notes on the Cinematograph*, a short book by the French filmmaker Robert Bresson, first published in 1975, his only written work as far as I am aware.[6] Kleist's essay is a casual dialogue that swerves into monumental philosophical seriousness; Bresson's book is a collection of diaristic fragments that sound from the depths of tireless discipline and solitude. I am inclined to describe the general tenor of these texts as eccentric or divergent or esoteric or even homeless within their respective genres: "On the Marionette Theater" encompasses literature, philosophy, and dance, while *Notes on the Cinematograph* drifts on the margins of film theory and practice. Both are complex yet candid works in that they are openly driven by what strikes me as a mystical inquisitiveness organized eschatologically. Enigmatic yet highly rigorous at the same time, each offers a philosophy of automatism informed by the biblical myth of man's fall from grace, suggesting that a mechanical as opposed to a spiritual perspective on ourselves can reenchant the human condition dimmed by consciousness or paralyzed by self-consciousness. For Kleist automatism is a corporeal reentry into paradise, for Bresson it is a cinematic exposure of paradise. Both take leaps of faith.

In these works, Kleist and Bresson offer insight into the limitations and general narrowness of human consciousness as it pertains to the arts, speculating on a possible integration into the human condition of that which appears to necessarily fall outside the domain of consciousness—grace—located, say, at the point where the metaphysical and the unconscious meet. The speculative journeys of these two texts, despite their radical differences in form and field, are ignited by a feeling or fear that human nature—or something about the way humans tend to define their own nature—is *unnatural*, and the prophylactic belief that any attempt to redeem the human condition from haunting cycles of error and disgrace calls for supreme tact over talent in art. For both writers such a belief leads to a skepticism of the artmaking instinct along with the classic repertoire which has intention precede/predict expression. Formulas of intention and expression patterned by consciousness can make for interesting and appreciable art, no doubt, but according to this skepticism such a pattern is not a true reflection of how we think, act, or create. Despite these inescapable limitations or poverties in consciousness, and far from advocating a passive or thoughtless aesthetic practice, Kleist and Bresson remain committed to finding *loopholes* into/out of consciousness, a term I find useful but which neither writer explicitly invokes. By "loophole" I have in mind a set of practical but also paradoxical techniques for transforming instead of exerting thought and overcoming the pitfalls of adult reason, artistic self-indulgence, and the siege-like temptations of cliché. Here, even the slightest trace of didacticism and dishonesty raises a red flag in the circuitous search for grace through art, grace being analogous to the Holy Grail of the human condition. Through a dialogue between these two writers (representing literature and cinema respectively), followed by an exploration of the links and tensions between Bresson's theories and films, a metaphysics of automatism will establish conditions for an *aesthetics* rooted in the mediums whose secrets they serve (the marionette theater and the cinematic apparatus). The common goal becomes not so much the conditions under which unconventional or avant-garde artworks can emerge, but some sort of alternative to, or ideally a purification of, the fact of being human, in the process overcoming any recourse to describe such a fact as a *fate*—this being a basis for artworks of great and enduring interest to us. Importantly, neither Kleist nor Bresson can be said to offer any instructions other than riddles for realizing such an aesthetic, assuming anyone would want to try their hand at it.

II. HEINRICH VON KLEIST'S MARIONETTE THEATER

As glimpsed in the chapter's "Primer," the philosophy of automatism is esoteric and its grammar elliptic, ever winding and tightening in circles of paradox like the following: human beings conditioned by consciousness act on the strange feeling that they are also conditioned to want to *escape* consciousness, to find loopholes out of it yet by means of it, ways around the total eclipse of grace, even if tearing it apart is in order (and sometimes the meaning of our words becomes torn in the process). The paradox, so familiar to the Surrealists, of using thought as a way out of thought, specifically out of thought's confounding or paralysis of action, generates a philosophical wormhole through a dimension of thinking characterized by the tragedy of the Cartesian "I think, therefore I am"—a tragedy which hits home all the more forcefully when one has experienced for oneself that thinking need not necessarily precede being or stand in opposition to being. The whole scenario—tragedy *and* comedy—of trying to think one's way out of thought itself is brought to rambunctious life in Kleist's "On the Marionette Theater." Paving the way for Friedrich Nietzsche's experiments with irony and parable, Kleist's voice, attuned to philosophy yet untrained in philosophy (unlike Nietzsche in this respect), never assumes that the darker or more debilitating aspects of the human condition can only be overcome through anarchic critique or sheer will power. On the contrary, Kleist does not arm himself with concepts of this size and scope; and in being a writer of novels and plays first and foremost, he is completely and perhaps strategically ill-equipped here as a thinker of philosophical ideas. It is, then, quite fitting that Kleist casts himself in this piece as an openminded novice of the art of dance and the marionette theater, with no hint of a philosophical agenda and no desire to bring to bear any preconceptions on the subject. Instead of beginning and ending with philosophy's self-centered "I think," Kleist questions the integrity of this philosophical muscle perpetually flexed by recounting the details of what appears to be a life-changing conversation with a professional dancer in awe of marionettes. This unexpected encounter leads Kleist to the edge of reason, a limit-point absent from philosophical works that hope to sway us with solid yet sterile claims of truth, or from philosophical systems that fail to generate what we call an "epiphany."[7]

Kleist's short essay offers a direct path into a metaphysics of automatism, with pertinent links to cinematic automatism, because it documents a prescient displacement of the Anthropocene—accompanied by the tones of exhilaration and despair that such a displacement would have likely stirred at the time—while bringing to light the "consciousness" of inanimate non-conscious life. The narrator, for all intents and purposes Kleist himself, shares a very simple story—deceivingly simple, like much of Kleist's fiction—about an encounter with a professional dancer and passionate advocate of the puppet theater, an art which Kleist, a devout man of letters, has never given much thought to until now and may have dismissed as mere child's play. The dancer character surprises Kleist with the conviction that the art of dance is not only epitomized by the marionette but modelled after it—the mere model that the marionette is—while human dancers strive in desperation for a perfection so utterly alien to their imperfect nature. Why wait for a moment of mind–body harmony and, should it come, give credit for it, when we can enjoy a continuous display of grace from (non)beings fundamentally incapable of doing otherwise? The dancer not only insists that the grace of movement in which mind and body are unified—a state eternally sought after by the art of dance—is actually the province of the puppet on strings, but what is more, the puppet sets the standard for the poetry of movement, occupying a permanent state of grace—and all this in spite of the human being who maneuvers the puppet, masterfully or crudely, from behind the scenes, bringing life to an otherwise dead object. So even though it is a human being who makes the puppet dance (dancing his own dance offstage), and of course some will do it better than others (this is, after all, an entirely distinct artform, a full-bodied expression involving complex feats of coordination and finesse), the radical claim is put forth that the great puppeteer controls the movements of the marionette and reaches a perfection of the dance not through virtuosities of touch, timing, and skill, but rather in a manner analogous to everyday acts such as switching a light or turning a faucet, setting into motion what turns out to be a completely self-sufficient process. The puppeteer's veiled performance—relatively free of personal expression, hovering between directing and being directed, tethered to the puppet in a strange reversal of authorship—pursues not a new form of art so much as a new *form of life*. The pinnacle of this art is the recalibration of the conditions of life as inherently artistic, without the need of an artist.

An awakening wrapped in a confession forces Kleist, via the compelling reasoning of his interlocutor, to reconsider his conscience instead of his craft and give up his previous belief, itself the fruit of morality's labor, that what stands to redeem the human condition as "fallen" is art as a sacred site of *human* expression and dignity in the face of the tragedies of history. In the marionette theater, however, it is not the puppeteer who attains grace but rather the puppet itself, the puppet which is in no position to act with intention and pursue any kind of self-expression, not to mention a virtue as supremely pure and ineffable as what we call "grace." When human dancers pursue grace and are judged accordingly, they are described by the interlocutor as lunging awkwardly into poses where grace is gripped and caged like a bird. Such a tragic correlation between intention and expression, action and event, is evident in the fraught micro-movements of human striving, which more often than not throw off the center of gravity in an effort to relocate it to the next transitional point or stoppage (an unwavering center of gravity being the most vital organ of the artform in question). Mobilized and splayed all too suddenly, vulnerably towards various joints in the body and unto the extremities of hands and feet, the guidance of conscious or learned intention and an overall sense of purpose mixes precariously with the maneuvering of the movements themselves, which congeal into knotted muscles full of tension and tenacity, muscles which, in flexing, risk trembling and giving way—whereas effortlessness and even a sense of relaxation are the ideal. An excess of mental and physical energy on top of years of trial-and-error experience are required to do something which ought to feel and appear completely natural and automatic—a situation that can be described not only as difficult but as working against all odds. The dancer *knows* what he has to do, and does it to a tee, though he also knows that too much knowledge can become a liability; he wants to do it great, and oversteps, for his share in greatness is to come *undone*, like the precious crack in the opera singer's voice; the dancer— watch him closely—moves like the wind and is on the verge of bringing a movement full circle, but before he can spiral into the next movement he must release the pose, the picture he has made of himself onstage, the period he has struck by taking a deep breath—and nothing is more difficult than doing two things at once. As for a truly gifted dancer who makes the hardest of feats look incredibly easy, the impression I get from the interlocutor's speech is that a sublime display of grace may be just that: *a display*. The most compelling performers are equally skilled at putting on airs for the sake of a good show and to win the respect of an audience. After all, who could blame the dancer for wanting to take a bow at the end? Humans were not born to fly, and masterful moments of levity (aided, always, by a touch of luck) are surely worth some heartfelt applause.

The main obstacle to the perspicuous fluidity of movement and the sublime embodiment of grace through dance—that sense of complete and utter naturalness and self-possession, ironically possessed by the unnatural and selfless puppet—is the force of gravity itself. The marionette uses the ground for everything but rest, of which it obviously has no need, gliding about with a fairytale lightness. The decisive moment comes when the puppeteer releases the string, bringing the wooden foot to the floor and discovering that the puppet lands rather than falls, receiving the ground rather than returning to it, like we do, as denizens. We belong to the ground the way spent adults recline on a park bench while their children play or sit beside them on edge, bouncing, their feet unable to touch the very ground that mother and father use to plant themselves like rocks. Or we belong to it in that hilariously pitiable moment when the iconic cartoon coyote, hurtling recklessly through desert expanses in pursuit of his roadrunner kill, plummets to the earth when his face fills with the blinding awareness that hubris is a poor substitute for wings. Regarding this beloved pop culture reference, it is significant that when Wiley Coyote realizes his doomed transgression he turns to face us, the viewers, as if to tell us, or warn us, that we too will fall and hit the ground if consciousness and its skepticism are permitted to ensnare our wildest flights of fancy at the very moment in which they are put to the test. The moral shared in laughter is that fear of falling comes from the same impulse as the longing to ascend—and consciousness presides voyeuristically to curse the former and bless the latter. Kleist, through his interlocutor, seems to be saying something similar about our ties to the earth: the marionette, like the roadrunner perhaps, is subject like anything else to the forces of gravity, whereas the human being, in his knowledge or surface awareness of what happens when he jumps, is subjected to these forces *as law*. The law of gravity can trigger a desire to transgress it—take Icarus—or master it—take aviation and astronautics. Whatever the case may be, the experience of gravity as force-of-law rather than force-of-fact can bring about a deeper, heavier, more traumatic fall, the meaning of which is analogous to the biblical notion of "the fall from grace." A knowledge of gravity, compliance with causality, adherence to patterns of the probable when the possible seems within reach—such things turn gravity against us, causing it to pull us down rather than keep us level. A small difference that makes all the difference in the world: beings lodged between earth and sky yet disposed towards longings for flight are fueled by the knowledge that they are fated to return to the earth, for that is where they find themselves restless instead of at peace; whereas non-beings made in the image of human beings (Kleist's marionette) can no more covet the heights than fear the depths, and if they seem to float through space and embody grace it is because they are unconsciously *of the earth*—like trees dancing in the wind or thick clouds assuming images so vivid that even the best of painters gaze aghast.

The marionette's movements are ontologically effortless; they are automatic—automatism is the criterion and seal of their grace. The thoughtlessness of the marionette is not a lack, but rather its truth. Such a phenomenon throws into sharp relief our contrived and pathetic *attempts* at grace. For us the path to grace is intensely uphill and fraught with peril because grace is a state that no longer comes naturally to the human condition (if it ever did). A stab at grace is a foolhardy performance, backfiring into an illustration or commemoration of the Fall, for what an inanimate yet animated object possesses is precisely the *absence* of what allows us to perceive grace in something unperceiving (like a puppet) or seemingly unperceiving (like an inspired musician with his or her eyes firmly shut). As beings in the condition of this kind of consciousness, our access to grace must always pass through the knowledge that we are fundamentally at odds with ourselves, for to be at one with ourselves is a unity instantly contradicted by the term "our self." What "I" know and am is what I cannot "be," for one must be *in* a state of grace, hence know nothing of it; to know *about* grace is to be outside of where we want to be and looking in, gazing onto a land of milk and honey and going no further; and short of a birthright here, no approach or appeal to grace is sufficient that does not make room for the miraculous. To acknowledge the presence of grace in the movements of the marionette is to extrapolate the myth of our eating from the tree of knowledge and consequent exile from the Garden of Eden, as this is ultimately a story about leaving nature in order to take possession of nature, and in the process losing touch with nature forever. The beauty, sheer simplicity, and inimitable perfection of the puppet theater is, for Kleist, a reminder that paradise does indeed exist *but not for us*, at least not as we stand. Here is Kleist on regaining admittance: "[P]aradise is locked and the cherubim behind us; we have to travel around the world to see if it is perhaps open again somewhere at the back."[8]

Recovery from the Fall calls for existential ingenuity against all odds: locating a backdoor of the world to paradise lost, a backdoor that could lead straight into hell.[9] On the possibility of embodying the spirit of the marionette's movement so as to glide gracefully through the world—speaking without the possibility of stammering, acting without the possibility of hesitating, and reentering ourselves without becoming, like poor Samsa, hopelessly alien to ourselves and to others, pure at last but without place—Kleist poses a partly rhetorical question to the dancer–interlocutor, a Sphinx-type question in response to the criterion of the backdoor to paradise: "We would have to eat again from the Tree of Knowledge in order to return to the state of innocence?"[10] The dancer's reply is equal parts astonishment and assurance: "Quite right. And that's the last chapter in the history of the world."[11] At the threshold of a new yet unapproachable beginning, the oldest and most enduring Western myth comes full circle to reverse the spell of original sin by paradoxically repeating it. But what does this mean exactly, eating again from the tree of knowledge as the circuitous sidle into some form of primordial innocence—grace, perfection, or happiness? Is such a notion not completely senseless—*more* knowledge as the way to cancel or overcome the burden and errancy of knowledge? Or will this bite be different, knowing what we know about the foulness of the first bite? Is there a new knowledge premised on "non-knowledge," a new knowledge that will help us *unlearn* what we know?

In addressing these questions, let's consider more detailed story-based evidence from Kleist regarding the impoverishment of the human condition when compared with conditions organized according to automatism. Aside from the rather eccentric theories of a dancer who sees his art perfected in the mechanical movements of marionettes, what is Kleist's evidence for the human condition's fundamental fallenness and paradoxical proximity to grace via automatism? What *is* the human condition such that the mechanical is perceived as natural and grace as the province of the unconscious or preconscious interval of innocence? Kleist offers two revealing and somewhat comical anecdotes from outside the inanimate realm of marionettes, one related by the dancer and the other by the narrator. Both anecdotes are strange enough that we may doubt whether they actually took place, though I welcome the possibility that Kleist experienced both with his own eyes, bringing the secrets of the marionette theater to bear on them. Whether real or imagined, the anecdotes are reminiscent of parables, the lessons of which are easily grasped yet nonetheless call for constant repetition, lest we forget what we already know.

The dancer also happens to be an experienced fencer. He relates to Kleist a peculiar incident where he found himself challenged by a group of friends to test his exceptional sword skills against a new kind of adversary. After defeating his friends one by one and emerging as clearly the best fencer, it is proposed that he now face a chained bear in a duel—an apparently lopsided contest favoring not only the unfettered but the more "intelligent" of the two. Indeed, what sort of step up is this? Wouldn't a novice fare just as well in these circumstances? What is the theory underlying such an odd experiment? The top fencer, heedlessly confident that the bear could never be his equal in fencing, is astonished to learn that the animal, even while chained, possesses a remarkable, inexplicable proficiency in self-defense. The bear, not knowing how to fence and, what is more, not being capable of such knowledge in the first place (or so it would seem), will surely succumb to the big-brained being with supple hands instead of brutish paws. But the bear proves to be incredibly fast, cunning, and uncannily prescient in its defenses. The dancer/fencer describes the extraordinary and disorienting feeling of being accurately anticipated by the bear at every turn, outmatched not only in terms of strength, which is a given, but also in terms of rational intelligence and a global sense of dexterity. The bear is able to counter the stealthiest moves with great ease: that is, *automatically*. The experiment shows that what we call "intelligence" is incredibly advanced and varied in its manifestations, by no means reducible to the scope of reason or the capacity to learn. "Reason" is our name for the distinction of human intelligence in particular, an intelligence diagnosed by the experiment as expert above all in *making distinctions*, which are often self-serving and turn out to be rather embarrassing. Now great players are always worth challenging at their chosen sport because they *can* be broken and will *eventually* fall to someone like them with plenty of youth, zeal, or fearlessness, basically a version of their former self—but when it comes to this bear (and let's not forget that the bear in this story is *chained*) the dancer/fencer quickly realizes that it is useless to continue against such an exemplary master. Such forces of nature, by virtue of the lack of self-consciousness, or by virtue of the lack of a self about which to be conscious (when there are more important things to be conscious of), lack nothing of value in this context: they are at one with themselves, or so we say, we who speak in such strange ways . . . Whatever the case may be, it is clear that reason and knowledge are of value only ironically, that is, for *imprisoning* the bear, but even then nature finds itself at no disadvantage, adding salt to the surprise and humiliation of the so-called expert fencer who can hardly be called "free" anymore.

The second anecdote, related by Kleist himself (and which may be autobiographical), shifts decisively from the animal to the human realm with a scene involving a handsome young man at the baths. With Kleist looking on, the young man unintentionally strikes a pose reminiscent of a sublime piece of classical statuary that he had been admiring earlier that day with Kleist. The slipped-into pose is reflected in a mirror in which the two friends catch a glimpse of its uncanny perfection—but only a glimpse, for the perfect pose is fleeting and leaves the young man wanting to claim it as his own. Convinced by the bravado of youth and impressed by what he believes to be the great accomplishment of life imitating art, the young man is certain that he can repeat the pose at will so as to prove it was no accident, that in that moment grace naturally became him and still does. Kleist is also in awe of the pose and at first is unopposed to his friend's proposition, though at the same time he is not so quick to credit the alleged author, for he believes so graceful a gesture can only be achieved non-consciously or automatically—say, in the spirit of an artwork having freed itself from the intentions of its maker (and if we know anything about Kleist's highly principled, almost religious approach to literary practice, the work of art cleansed of vanity and born of suffering is the backdoor to paradise).[12] With ferocious obstinacy the young man proceeds to enter and reenter the pose, each time descending deeper into self-parody, seeing for himself the warped results reflected within the mirror and yet too proud to admit defeat, to concede that it is precisely *he* who thwarts the endeavor like a diabolically vengeful double. Now Kleist can hardly contain his laughter, and what was once a sign of perfection in man has been sullied by youthful pretense and foolhardy stubbornness. Rather than salvage what remains of his dignity (to say nothing of grace), the youth collapses into the pool of his vanity and sinks to the bottom where, we may imagine, innocence is forever lost.

What Kleist saw in the sadness of his laughter was that the young man might never regain that part of himself (or was it a flash of the whole of himself?) that channeled the divine inspiration embodied by the statue, which moved him so deeply such that it allowed him to slip into a state of grace undetected. Kleist observes not only the youth's failure to consciously display the grace which showed itself so powerfully and poetically in his person, but a literal fall from grace in the effort to possess it and parade it in public. When the young man made that graceful gesture at the baths, he was caught unawares by it, as was Kleist. Logically, then, the gesture is not really his; he did not make it; *it happened*, this gesture, inexplicably, and jaws dropped bearing witness. His beauty could occur and speak for itself, a private paradise to be lived and not known, and it helps to be beautiful—but alas, all innocence died the moment he started speaking for his beauty. There is a strange conclusion which Kleist succinctly draws from these two stories that, if true, delivers an alarming, defeating, yet potentially emancipatory verdict for conscious creatures enlightened by reason: "We see that in the organic world, as reflection grows darker and weaker, grace emerges more brilliantly and commandingly."[13] While this may strike us today as a highly Romantic if not spiritual notion, the snares of reason are as familiar to us as the clouds of coincidence. How is it that acts of grace are sometimes the least intended, the most automatic in their unfolding, purity outweighing the profound? I am sure we can all supply our own anecdotes.

The irrevocable consequences of original sin could not be more plain: we got reflection in return, knowledge of the world in the palm of our hand, like the apple we bit into. Yet how is it that the reflecting self—thinking and knowing, grasping and discriminating—has come to value modes of being in opposition to reflection and not readily reducible to the register of what we call knowledge (for example, grace or faith or love or even the everyday)—forms of non-knowledge about which nothing can be known in any traditional sense and where the goal is to overcome the condition of knowledge or, perhaps, to *be* overcome, to *feel* knowledge? Why does our knowledge, which we mythologically chose and keep on practically choosing, draw us towards metaphysical unknowables? Is this the case with grace? The unknown can in principle become known, whereas grace promises to redeem knowledge itself and open some sort of "afterlife" of the whole of knowledge.

Kleist continues the slippery spiral of thought with the possibility that the transcendental powers of grace need not necessarily come at the expense of the more rational underpinnings of our thinking, indeed *cannot* come at our own expense if grace is to be recovered amongst the fallen. He writes in what is the essay's conceptual equivalent to paintings of the Passion if drawn by Escher:

> But just as the section drawn through two lines suddenly appears on the other side of a point after passing through infinity, or just as the image in a concave mirror turns up before us again after having moved off into the endless distance, so too grace itself returns when knowledge has gone through an infinity. Grace appears purest in that human form which has either no consciousness or an infinite one, that is, in a puppet or in a god.[14]

How to navigate so complex and compressed a passage teeming with geometrical metaphors and spatial loopholes, paranormal flights and black hole-type thresholds and eerie points of no return? I find it fitting that the puppet and the god are described as potentially human forms, for it suggests that human consciousness not only gives form to life but also takes different forms, thus *lacks* a unique form of life to call its own. In this sense the properly human form of life lies stranded and misshapen between the two automatic purities of grace: "puppet" and "god." Perhaps the puppet's absence of consciousness and the god's infinite consciousness amount to the same thing, the same power, reaching a fundamentally elusive destination in the transcendence of consciousness by opposite means. For Kleist, knowledge must go through an infinity, then we might cease to know grace and actually become graceful. Rather than posit beings, knowledge stages a *becoming*—the black hole of philosophy into which beings reunite with the dimension of Being. We can think of this as knowledge ceasing to amass and exhaust, giving back the world its dignity. While the logic of knowledge tells us that grace is something we ought to be able to reach through action as opposed to mere accident, perhaps you cannot have one without the other. Is there an "action of accident"? Is that what automatism is? Can we become more rather than less human, inheriting traits from the puppet and the god, by cultivating the inherent and repressed mechanicity of the human? The humanist denial of the mechanical forsakes an entire realm, the realm of paradise.

III. Robert Bresson's Filmic Models

With Kleist's meditation on the marionette theater, I am approaching the question of cinematic automatism through his backdoor metaphor in what is, to my knowledge, an unexplored affinity between the automatist principles behind the movement of the marionette and the world in its own moving image, one which hinges more on surrealist and theological critiques of consciousness than any inherent predestination of a given artistic medium to stage a possible reentry into the lost paradise of grace. That the world on film is not that of the puppet theater is obvious enough, and that this resemblance is most palpable in the art of animation, particularly stop-motion animation, and not the automatic world projections of cinema, is deserving of its own investigation and does not detract from the ontological resemblance at stake here. Cinematic recordings of the world in its own image and the autonomous dancing of the marionette both have the same condition of possibility, and, what is more, this condition of possibility—automatism—can be put into practice through artistic methods best described as avant-garde.

Now I would like to bring this backdoor metaphor to bear on director Robert Bresson's theory of automatism as presented, or rather scattered about, in his *Notes on the Cinematograph*, composed between the years 1950 and 1974. The highly piecemeal theory resists any systematization I could offer, yet I believe it can be seen to revolve around three domains of filmmaking (what Bresson prefers to call "cinematography"):

1. The intuitive act of filming the world in a spirit of discovery.
2. The organic and open-ended editing of images and sounds around moments of truth.
3. The orchestration of screen performances designed to withstand the penetrating gaze of the camera and microphone instead of appease the critical gaze of the viewer in search of familiarity. This third automatism is the most important for Bresson and so I will give it a name: "automatic acting."

Bresson is best known for formally austere, eccentrically modernist, existentially tragic yet quietly transcendental narrative films. They are deceptively simple stories expressed through the universally concrete yet fragmentary vernacular of everyday life, in a vision of humanity as clear as it is cryptic. The films feature unassuming and often self-isolating protagonists who undergo identifiable forms of physical and emotional ardor, a gamut of existential gravities from the minor (like walking) to the immense (like dying), but in doing so seem to lack a common sense consciousness or certain basic anthropocentric familiarities in their everyday responses to the harsh demands and occasional reprieves of life. To the best of my knowledge, not a single Bresson character ever "properly" emotes the way the average film or theater actor/character releases an emotion from the inside out. Instead, Bresson has powerful and precise emotions sweep across the face and body of his characters: the corners of a mouth rise and fall as if a curtain were being drawn, drops of water run down from the eyes like a leaky faucet, a hand trembles like a placid lake stirred by the occasional air pocket or fish-flop. (If you know Bresson, you know hands have faces and feet sing when they walk.)

The trembling monotone, fragile flatness, gnarled woodenness of the acting experiment begins with *Diary of a Country Priest* (France, 1951), a film featuring for the first time in the filmmaker's career a completely non-professional actor by the name of Claude Laydu. Laydu plays a young priest who writes in his diary at the beginning of the film that he intends to record his humble life daily without justification or embellishment, for the religious life, according to him, is not just a spiritual quest so much as an endurance test in which faith and exhaustion are linked **(Figs 3.1, 3.2)**. Such a process of "selfless self-examination" can be described as taking stock of the contents of one's life without the immediate payoffs of a psychological or philosophical insight that would unify the wreckage of matter and spirit in constant strife. It is an absolute modesty which protects itself from the lurking threat of falsity by virtue of a steady vigil of anonymity. The priest's facial expressions and verbal intonations—stiffened by poor health, by physical as much as spiritual pain—are almost (but not completely) drained of the upward gazing, supplicating demeanor of Renée Falconetti's legendary performance as Joan of Arc from *The Passion of Joan of Arc* (Dreyer, France, 1928).[15] And unlike Ingmar Bergman's priest character, as performed by Gunnar Björnstrand in *Winter Light* (Sweden, 1963), Bresson's priest is not faced with a crisis of belief when nihilism suddenly makes perfect sense in a world fraught with evil and unanswered suffering. Instead, such a crisis is exactly what the newly appointed

Figures 3.1 and 3.2 *Bresson's priest—spiritual living in a world of spiritless matter:* Journal d'un curé de campagne *(*Diary of a Country Priest, *Robert Bresson, France, 1951).*

priest expects to wrestle with—in others and in himself—on any given day. Crises of faith along with brutal feelings of inadequacy before God are part of the labor of being a believer as a mere finite mortal in a world innundated with temptation. But for Bresson, the ordeal of a life of the spirit is waged outside rather than inside the self, in a world of spiritless matter at the mercy of gravity and contingency, in a body whose incessant demands for satisfaction and preservation reward its possessor with illusions of contentment and fires of the heart. And it is precisely "outside the self" where Bresson positions his actors in relation to their characters, a position from which an actor cannot *play* a character in any conventional sense of the term, as it is a position reserved exclusively for non-actors "to act." This is why Bresson, throughout the *Notes on the Cinematograph*, insists on the term *model* instead of actor, a term which combines the indexicality of photography as theorized by Bazin with the vacant stoicism of painting or fashion models. To call an actor a model is to cut all ties between cinema and the theater where actors project to an audience, and no less between cinema and canned theater where actors project to the camera—the all-seeing audience.[16]

The radically decentered and somewhat behaviorist construction of film characters in Bresson prevents them from directly eliciting our emotional sympathy, if not our basic spectatorial compass of identification, thereby preventing us from coming to terms (the usual terms) with who they are and what they believe in or refuse to believe, what they live for and are prepared to die for. We are denied this legible sense of interiority by which to navigate and make sense of the web of contingencies ensnaring their everyday actions, as if the muscle of free will has atrophied, flexing only when oppressed in a last-ditch effort at defiance. The great majority of conventional patterns of identification in film are blocked in an almost systematic way by this anti-psychological disaffectedness and strangely monosyllabic mechanicalness of the performance style, which is often criticized for being "wooden" (the organic variant of the mechanical) when compared to styles of acting regarded as more psychologically "real" (fantasy absconding with reality), leaving many viewers feeling puzzled, alienated, and often disoriented. However, these familiar patterns of identification are largely governed by escapist illusions of the human being as a cathartic circuit of motives and actions effortlessly passing the baton, as it were, and are themselves blockages to *new paths* of spectator engagement with onscreen persons which Bresson aspires to forge. With time and patience—along with something I am tempted to describe as aesthetically occult—these unrecognizable, virtually unrelatable characters emerge from the fog of anonymity to win us over with an indefatigable sense of authenticity and presentness. It is difficult to pin down precisely how this happens, if and when it does. Skeptics of

Bresson's experimental approach to acting can undergo a kind of "conversion" process, after which a rational account for why a seemingly poor or amateurish performance is now preferable to a soundly scripted, reassuringly "dramatic" one becomes impossible or unconvincing, that is, should one become *convinced* by the use of a model over an actor as the basis for a film character. Bresson therefore writes of the qualitative measure of acting not in terms of good or bad, real or fake, but in the *moral sense of right and wrong*: Does this person *fit* this character? Does this character know of *no other face*? If so, the model *is* the character and all the rest are doomed to fraudulence.[17]

The lead in *Pickpocket* (France, 1959), Martin LaSalle, at first lacks the hallmark intensity and desperation of the petty thief, Michel, but as soon as his hands acquire the necessary suppleness, as he calls it, to pick pockets with diabolical grace, he starts carrying himself with the assuredness of a tightrope walker destined to reach the other side. All of a sudden, he looks much more at ease and at home in his oversized suit, as if the model has succeeded in filling the character to the brim of his being. Without psychologizing the remote and quietly arrogant disposition of the character of Michel, the film appears to document the transformation of LaSalle from actor into model as he gradually fuses with the character. The decisive moment occurs before our very eyes when LaSalle (not necessarily us) becomes convinced of the reality of the character immediately after Michel's first successful theft, for now his eyes start to swell with the drunken power of those who have permanently turned their backs on morality **(Figs 3.3, 3.4)**. The aspect change (in a Wittgensteinian sense, if you like) can be attributed to the sense in which the character enters full presentness when he begins behaving in the actor's sleep, as it were.

To refer back to Kleist, perhaps those who believe in the truth of such "marionette-like" performances do not know if they are witnessing in these human figures onscreen the workings of a puppet or a god: the agency at

Figures 3.3 and 3.4   *The pickpocket's sudden sense of self-belief:* Pickpocket *(Robert Bresson, France, 1959).*

work here seems somewhat inhuman yet anything but monstrous—a strange (albeit kempt, never grotesque) combination of the mechanical and the spiritual. The micro-endurances of daily life, pleasure and ardor being of equal weight, along with the macro-flickers of fate, whose burden is challenged by dignity rather than destiny, require for their realization not only a complete lack of performance self-consciousness but also a stripping of the "overconsciousness" of the traditional actor's tendency to focus the minutiae of presence through the prism of representation. (For stars, the prism of representation is even more beveled with the personas they carry from film to film.) When phrased in these terms, familiar to us from Chapter One, we can see Bresson as developing a metaphysical approach to the representation of personhood in activating the ontological basis of cinematic automatism through the surrealist charge of psychic automatism. The result is an aesthetic of non-acting, what I referred to above as automatic acting, the primary tenet of which Bresson simply calls "intuition."

Even if Bresson strives to redeem his characters at the end of their sufferings (be it through a second chance at life, or death as an escape from a world of chance), their disposition during such threshold moments remains unwaveringly resolute, statuesque, and, I feel like saying, *circumstantial*. But if Bresson's characters are victims of circumstance, his models are the *vehicles* of it—their free will transformed (not altogether sacrificed) into the expressive mouthpiece of necessity. As vehicles of circumstance, their life-paths are the mechanical inscribers of the brute laws of a world from which the divine has retreated from the metaphysical to the physical, squeezed out or left twitching in everyday banalities made all the more enigmatic by their fragmentary relation to each other—as if everyday life, with its remarkable recurrences and indissoluble gravities, sends shockwaves through the singularity of the divine, dismembering it into a million moments of a muffled, gasping revelation, into a sea of minuscule, residual miracles crashing quietly on the shores of consciousness. The death of God manifesting as the birth of the everyday is most evident, not without surprise, in Bresson's films with overt religious subject matter that I have already mentioned (*Country Priest* and *Joan of Arc*), however such a reversal can also be seen in all of his films starting with *Country Priest*, where grace supplants transcendence as the key spiritual value that cannot be consciously aimed for except through death (a phenomenon I will discuss in some detail later on). Grace becomes possible only when the disheveled grayness and painful injustice of the world are left open for the possibility of redemption, which is not of a moral so much as a metaphysical nature, marked by a character accepting rather than choosing his fate. But on second thought, for characters who have been modeled under Bresson's program, it would be more accurate to say that they have *accepted fate itself*, embracing the dissolution of the autonomous subject into the necessity embodied by contingent objects and life-fragments, a necessity which may hold the secret of a new subjectivity the interior of which is left a mystery. It is why key moments from a character's life are left to dangle unassimilated by the consciousness of that character. It is why the human face is equally grafted onto the hands and feet, tools of touch which "speak" through resilient walking and doorknob-turning, often amplified in closeups reminiscent now of the art of Dreyer. Such headless hand-and-foot actions become all but unmotivated by a clear sense of agency in the world of plans, making the everyday life of human existence resemble the propelled dance of marionettes (sleepwalking is a kind of dancing). Bound for untimely deaths of their own self-destructive design, their legs carry them along a windblown course through the abyss of time, turning every corner without trepidation and sinking deeper into the dream-like aspects of their so-called waking life. As for grace, it happens, if at all, on the condition that the model is kept void, that the temptation of consciousness to awaken to itself for the purpose of knowledge and power is finally overcome.

Bresson memorably records the essence of this daydream in the *Notes* when describing a street scene that he appears to have directly observed and which could have served as inspiration for any number of scenes from his films: "The people I pass in the Avenue des Champs-Élysées appear to me like marble figures moved forward by springs. But let their eyes meet mine, and at once these walking and gazing statues become human."[18] This passage is remarkable in showing how everyday awareness of the real and surreal (waking life and dream life) can merge in a fragile moment of perceptual clarity. Here, humans are perceived with the humanity proper to them when they are perceived as *machines* (or components in the machine of life) whose organic clockwork and marble grace function best when their consciousness remains dispersed and undisturbed. The act of consciousness that is paradoxically required to witness such a scene, without necessarily excluding itself from it, cannot be caught in the act, as it were, lest the delicate balance of moving parts come crashing down. To avoid such a scare of consciousness, those street gestures which are performed so innocently, so thoughtfully yet also thoughtlessly—or better yet collectively—cannot be roused out of the slumber of automatism without immediate *en garde* reprisal, so penetrating and potentially paralyzing is Bresson's gaze that self-consciousness amongst members of the crowd can be sparked more quickly and potently than by any other sense, like flint on metal. Eye contact.[19]

This vision of human beings moving about like the marionettes described by Kleist comes to full fruition in what is without a doubt Bresson's most experimental and eccentric film, *Lancelot du Lac* (France, 1974). Bresson's rendition of the classic medieval tale interestingly avoids explicit religious or spiritual content by beginning after a failed attempt by Lancelot (Luc Simon) and his knights to locate the Holy Grail. What follows instead is an account of the corrosion of comradery to a higher calling—a corrosion of spirit which manifests, with uncharacteristic expressionism from Bresson, in the grotesque exaggeration of the metallic sights and sounds of *armor*. Such a heightened degree of attention, even obsession, is directed towards these enveloping pieces of equipment—especially on the soundtrack, which registers every chink and chaff—that it is sometimes difficult for the viewer to even concentrate on the narrative events. It is almost impossible to imagine the knights ever removing their armor for any reason, say, when going to the bathroom or retiring for the night. This emphasis on full body garb is how a climactic (though Bresson does not exactly deal in climaxes, or resolutions for that matter) tournament sequence—the joust—becomes drawn out to the point of parody and rendered so abstract as to become almost incomprehensible. Here Lancelot and the knights compete in a jousting event on horseback, their concealment under armor preventing us from clearly distinguishing the opposing sides, blurring any binary affects of "us and them" (hence the diffusing of climactic tension). As viewers, we are deprived of the predictable yet pleasurable suspense sensation of high-stakes competition with the plight of the film's main characters hanging in the balance. Bresson goes so far as to (de)construct the sequence in a spirit of mechanicity and anonymity established by the armor and reminiscent, once again, of the marionette theater. It is also noteworthy that Lancelot chooses to compete anonymously, his identity revealed to his fellow knights only by defeating all his opponents with the intrepid skill for which he is known. In this scene of serial and faceless jousting, Bresson is far more interested in tracing the smooth vectors of collision, juxtaposing the polar oncoming forces through a highly rigid system of symmetrical, almost algorithmic editing. Medium shots just of the galloping legs of horses alternate back and forth like wheels of fur-flesh moving with equal and ramping velocity, evoking a collision point which is never shown but loudly heard offscreen over a group shot of the knights stationed in the gallery, rotating their heads as if to the swinging pendulum of a tennis match. The repeated emphasis on the galloping horse legs suggests that the knights are not the ones driving the horses; rather the implication is that they are the ones *being driven*. According to the structure/ grammar of Bresson's montage, the fully clad knights are extensions of the horses—medieval incarnations of mythical satyrs. While the jousting faceoffs repeat mechanically, always with the same outcome, and as the closeups shift from horse legs to lance-tips to shields, always with the same abstract rhythm, the point-of-view of the players becomes increasingly if not absurdly undetectable, buried beneath so many impenetrable sheets of opacity that we may wonder if the transparency and continuity of consciousness hasn't completely suffocated. Eventually, the speeding lance-tips and wall-like shields become, for Bresson, substitute hands or even second heads growing from these odd metal-clad figures on horseback who dance their own destruction **(Figs 3.5, 3.6, 3.7)**.

The automatist articulation of the armored bodies of the knights is further amplified by what occurs *in between* each joust: a series of antiquated flags unreadable to the untrained eye are raised up a flagpole, presumably to indicate the battle colors of the players and the nationalist underpinnings of the war known as sport. As we might expect by now, Bresson does little to enliven the link between individual and group. Instead, the flags serve to further subvert such a bond into a parody of patriotism by rendering arbitrary these patterns, colors, and symbols of prideful belonging flapping in the wind. But since Bresson's primary objectives are not reducible to nationalist or any other politics, we may wonder why he insists on showing the raising of a new flag in between each spar, holding fast to the diagram of the tournament sequence whose organizational rigor promises expositions of identity and continuities of event yet delivers only a spiralling mosaic of narrative abstraction.

I suggest we turn to the soundtrack for a possible explanation behind this abstract parade of flags, serializing what is already a mystifyingly modernist sequence. The individual flags are raised to a musical theme played

Figures 3.5–3.7 *Horse, lance, and shield appendages:* Lancelot du Lac *(Lancelot of the Lake, Robert Bresson, France, 1974).*

on the bagpipes, a simple enough announcement prompting a new set of tournament players. But if we listen carefully to what we are seeing—when the buzzy wheezing sound of the instrument being primed is heard against the image of the flags moving up the pole without any sign of a flagpole operator—it appears as if this integral component or gear of the "tournament machine" serves a more fundamental purpose in *winding the spring* of each joust **(Figs 3.8, 3.9)**. Upon reaching the apex, the bag-piped flags indicate not so much a birthplace, the honor of which a particular player competes for, but rather a phenomenon entirely indifferent to the politics of sport: the *metaphysics* of sport. The fully torqued spring-flag sets up the variables of play and locks them tightly into position, like a mechanical starting gate holding a field of racing horses fairly aligned at the post. And when the jousters are released upon each other by the tournament machine, what ensues is a dynamic display of physics in which chance too has its place—a violent yet venial clash of forces that completely nullifies nationalist sentiments and medieval heroics.

While it is counterintuitive to think that Lancelot's presence as a variable in this game is arbitrary and that he wins all his spars by chance, Bresson never indicates that he does so because he is the strongest and most clever; put simply, this is because Bresson abstracts the character of Lancelot, leaving us in the dark about his true identity, a darkness shared by his fellow knights, who are, it would seem, interchangeable. Based on the perfect symmetry of the opposing forces thrown by the release of the tournament machine's "spring-flag," it is conceivable that any of the contests could have resulted in Lancelot being catapulted or impaled, assuming we care enough about him to root for him or fear for his life (Bresson isn't interested in *making us* care). Perhaps the metaphor of the racehorse ought to be taken more literally: when a horse crosses the finish line first, we cannot assume that it understands its victory or takes pride in it. This is not because the horse cannot know it (who knows what it knows?); rather, it is because it is a piece in a game, the rules of which have been established from without. If the horse, in its own individual and mysterious way, comes to know of its success, it will most likely be through the reactions of those in control of the game or who have something at stake in it; but again, there is no guarantee that the horse will understand or care about these reactions. (I think it is safe to say that no first-place thoroughbred has ever posed or smiled for any of the photographs taken of it in the winner's box.) What matters, then, is not that Lancelot wins the tournament but that the tournament produces Lancelot as a winner, spits him out as the last one standing, albeit badly wounded by the machine. Those whom he beat were beaten by "him": by the Lancelot-horse, by fortune, by the collapse of space and the breakneck speed of time, by the automatic ritual of the

Figures 3.8 and 3.9 *Winding the spring-flag of the tournament machine:* Lancelot du Lac *(*Lancelot of the Lake, *Robert Bresson, France, 1974).*

joust. The result is antithetical to glory and defeat, as winners walk away and losers are carried away—all pieces in a game (or a puzzle) until a new game commences and all is forgotten.

In the final scene of *Lancelot*, set in a gloomy forest where the knights are inexplicably attacked from above without warning, picked off one by one by a contingent enemy with bow and arrow reminiscent of a bird of prey,

Bresson purposely returns us to the undifferentiated cloaking of the armor and four-legged horse-bottoms of the knights to hide their faces and avert the eyes of the viewer from identifying these figures by name or sympathizing with their plight. This scene recalls the opening of the film *in medias res* where men in armor, fueled by senseless carnage, impale each other with frightening ease as if metal assumed the permeability of skin. Here a thoroughly encased knight is quickly decapitated, releasing a thin spurt of blood in the air. Save for the blood, there is no sense of flesh and bone beneath the metal, and so we could just as well call the lush red substance "oil" **(Fig. 3.10)**. Since these figures lack the elements of a more recognizably human form of life, what stops the headless knight from crawling on the ground like a ripped segment of worm? This image of headlessness is a cue from Bresson for the viewer to expand his horizon of experience *beyond the head* so as to *facialize the entire body*, in the process deconstructing the false hierarchy which has the body merely supporting the head. Now to come back to the final scene, also *in medias res*, of a horse racing through the forest, its rider presumably struck down, a similar sense of headless anonymity is evoked insofar as a knight-in-armor riding atop a horse constitutes some sort of fused lifeform, what I previously described as a medieval satyr-like being **(Fig. 3.11)**. The headless horse, as it were, runs freely, gracefully, on a forest path of unknown origin and destination, a path overseen by the archers stationed in the trees. I must have compromised when I described these perched archers as resembling birds, for what are they but the bows themselves? They seem to have no purpose other than the mechanical releasing of arrows. They are headless too ... **(Fig. 3.12)**. We can't be too careful in our descriptions of such "exquisite corpse" abstractions, for too hasty or convenient a response may lapse into an overly legible—let's say headier—version of human agency as the sole pilot of cause and effect and the turning of the world.

Bresson's epiphany while walking the Champs-Élysées contains a clue as to why the characters in this film are so difficult to identify, not to mention identify *with*: the filmmaker is constantly attending to how every section and hinge of armor isolates a body part, atomizes it and renders it autonomous; and he attends to the abstract faces of these parts, the insect-like segmentation of the whole, by emphasizing the peculiar extremities of the body and brewing a sonic stew of metal, set into motion by the organic electricity of walking, running, and horseback-riding. Even when the knights remove their helmets to engage in conversation, the pervasive sound of their armor, which rarely settles down to complete silence, becomes a part of their discourse; and even the very manner in which they speak—the disaffected monotony of their speech—comes across as deeply shaped by a lifetime of communicating while masked. Indeed, the armor's metallic and mechanical mold, its rigid

Figures 3.10–3.12   *Headless knight, riderless horse, bow-and-arrow beings:* Lancelot du Lac (Lancelot of the Lake, *Robert Bresson, France, 1974*).

and cumbersome segmentation (in contrast to the smooth flow of organic or synthetic fabric whose sounds resemble the perishable softness of the flesh), blocks the spell-breaking eye contact described by Bresson, so that this "dream we call human life" goes undisturbed by the nightmare of consciousness as a fixed point around which everything is made to revolve.[20]

In general, Bresson's unorthodox hypothesis is that a film director, if he is to succeed in creating genuinely novel and truthful images that expand onto each other and resonate long after they have left the screen, must learn how to wield the great powers of conscious intention and systematization above all to *thwart* the dominance of intentionality and its micromanagement of ideas. I believe this is what Bresson means, or partly means, when he states near the beginning of the *Notes*, in a mood reminiscent of Ralph Waldo Emerson's essay on self-reliance: "The point is not to direct someone, but to direct oneself."[21] Bresson takes seriously the fact that his image of human bustle as a swarm of figures who move along as if by clockwork is not one that he sought out or *intends to perceive* in an otherwise routine environment. Rather it is something he has happened to notice, an experience to be submitted for reflection and further empirical or aesthetic testing; it has struck him and filled him with wonder, a feeling made fragile by the locking of gazes which, in dreams, so often signals the moment of awakening; and if he were to allow himself to indulge the temptation to know *how or why* moving bodies are suddenly appearing to him under this unusual aspect, the fear is that *any* answer would affirm the very consciousness whose temporary and magical suspension makes possible the harmonious flow of life. As individuals they are on their way, from places and towards places like targeted satellites traveling through the vast in-betweenness of space, but as a whole these individuals are just faceless bodies moving about like an organism without head or tail. To search for causes here would be to ruin the effect of the whole, of the dream. And so, the act of looking into the eyes of members of the crowd as a humanist search for inner life turns out to be misguided, piercing the veil that Walter Benjamin attributed to crowds in general, for such soul-gazing presumes that the eye is a window to the invisible rooms of interiority where human beings are thought to reside in their purest form.[22] But that is just a myth, for the eye is only ever window-like during those moments of mutual understanding; yet such moments of eye contact are as brief as they are rare, as the curtains are drawn just as fast with a blink or sideways glance. For the most part, eye contact is eye *conflict*. Perhaps the eye and the "I" are too much alike, such that looking into someone's eyes is to seek out a soul in the wrong place. (It is the right place only where it concerns the right person.)

Repeated insistence in the *Notes* on the moral–aesthetic dangers of the excavating intelligence stems from a skepticism towards an excessively cerebral or calculated artistic process incapable of genuine discovery. Bresson's concern, on my reading, is that one's intelligence, even one's mind, may not be the most valuable or trustworthy tool for creativity in the cinema; knowing too well what a scene or shot is supposed to mean, or why a character must behave *this way*—understanding one's subject in exclusively rational and therefore speakable terms which one then proceeds to implement—can have a compromising or altogether negating effect on the openness of the senses, leading to a mistrust of the blindfolded sense of intuition for what/why/how things ought to be in the finished film. This must be the reason behind Bresson's beloved dictum that screenplays are written not as a definite plan to be followed but in order to be destroyed or transformed by the shooting and editing phases of the filmmaking process where the film itself undergoes multiple lives, for each phase or dimension of the process introduces not only new possibilities but new *terminologies* and even *physiologies* of artistic labor. Yet Bresson remains fully cognizant of the paradox in championing intuition *over* intelligence as a creative method, for doing so requires thinking his way through and out of thought—an intellectual feat if there ever was one—and we see him coach/coax himself with a daring reversal of received biblical wisdom: "Practice the precept: find without seeking."[23] While it would be interesting to know how Bresson actually practiced this strange precept, it can be read as an attempt to relax the rote, intention-bound, bruising hand of directorial imposition, which tends to conform to habits derived from other artistic cultures and perpetuate the Hollywood studio system myth that power (over others, over oneself) produces poetry. Regarding the inherent capacity of the medium of cinema itself to aid in the tempering of the negative or ill-suited aspects of creative intelligence, Bresson has this to say—or pray—in what is the book's final note: "DIVINATION—how can one not associate that name with the two sublime machines I use for my work? Camera and tape recorder carry me far away from the intelligence which complicates everything."[24] Find without seeking?—The two "cameras" (motion picture and sound) are means for being carried away and becoming lost.

If one were to use Bresson's epiphany in the street as inspiration for a film scene, it would most likely result in the contrived imposition of preconceived ideas and metaphors, the meaning of which "states x" rather than reveals something previously unknown. A scene that is *about* human beings appearing mechanized or somnambulistic internally structures the vital ambiguities and contingencies of a real event; in a word, such overwrought conceptualizations of form and content will yield the *cliché* of humans going about their business, pretending to be machines or otherwise presented as automated. How to find the truth of *this* image without seeking it out? Bresson's answer is to let the medium itself seek it out as much as possible. The automatism of the camera (and the audio recorder, which Bresson insists should never be excluded from discussions about the cinematic image), deriving its powers of perception from recording reality scrupulously yet indifferently, is calibrated to represent humans mechanically, not exactly as machines but as forms of life—moving, breathing, thinking objects, autonomous yet automatic, bound between an erratic self-sufficiency and a complete dependency on rote.[25] But activating this automatism is not so simple, for the audiovisual camera is equally fated to look these spiritualized machines in the eye, in part because the camera-eye in cinematographic practice is still a surrogate for a human eye. As such, it is just as capable of summoning consciousness into self-consciousness—the antediluvian fall into consciousness that made us all at once completely unfit for life in paradise because we knew we were being watched, and by none other than ourselves.[26]

The metaphysical problem of reconciling the human and the mechanical within the cinematic apparatus is handled by Bresson in the following way: "Your camera catches not only physical movements that are inapprehensible by pencil, brush or pen, but also certain states of soul recognizable by indices which it alone can reveal."[27] As a technological incarnation of the principle of automatism, the camera is presumably privy to these indices of spirit, what I would call metaphysical indices, catching like a butterfly net the human and non-human gestures of the world unawares. However, it is not obvious at all

from Bresson's note—nor from any of the other notes concerning the cinematic apparatus—*exactly how* the camera in particular can be made to reveal
the world in this way. For a concrete methodology or technique, specifically
an aesthetic tailored to the metaphysic of cinematic automatism, we must
turn back to the conceptual centerpiece of the book which has already figured
in my interpretation of Bresson more than once: *the model*. Throughout the
unfolding of the *Notes*, the cinematic apparatus becomes a source of both
revelatory and redemptive power when its automatism is activated above
all through the medium of the Bressonian model—the primary object of
the camera's eye and the microphone's ear. Paradoxically, the two cinematic
senses reveal "soul" only to the extent that the model hides "self."

Bresson's use of the term "model" is an anthropocentric variation of
André Bazin's usage from his essay "The Ontology of the Photographic
Image," in which model comes to stand for the radically causal identity
between photograph and referent. While Bresson's models are occasionally
as stoic and silent as the models who pose for paintings, it would be more
accurate to read his concept through Bazin's essentially metaphysical claim
that the photograph not only represents the model but *is* the model.[28] Both
theorists appear to advocate for a kind of religious transubstantiation in
which the idea of the model, as photograph or actor, *embodies* that which it
represents, as in the Eucharist ritual where bread and wine become the body
and blood of Christ. Model actors (properly *un*trained) are like photographs
of their characters. The criterion for a good performance becomes that of
solid, luminous presence. An aesthetic extrapolation of Bazin's model theory
of photographic ontology that is specific to the art of performance can be
glimpsed in Bresson's anti-representational approach to indexical embodiment as the principle for a (non-)acting style rooted in the metaphysics
of film. Two notes, despite being enigmatic and leaving much unsaid, are
worth singling out here: "Cinematography, the art, with images, of *representing*
nothing," and earlier in the text, "To your models: 'One must not act either
somebody else or oneself. One must not act *anybody*.'"[29] Like the model of a
photograph which becomes the photograph by virtue of being what it is and
being allowed to be what it is by virtue of the medium, Bresson's models must
also be permitted to display their being by coming to presence as opposed to
delivering a performance. In what sounds very simple yet must be very difficult to do (finding the backdoor into oneself . . .), the models must not act,
they must not think as actors think about playing a role; they must *be*—not
another being or their own being, not anybody but *nobody*: only then can
they become models of the characters and not representations of them. As
models, they *are* the characters in the same way as the photographic representation *is* the model.[30] The term "model" for both Bresson and Bazin points

to the collapse of representation, of the very space of reference, suggesting that the act of representing something in a photographic or performative way allows for what I described in Chapter One as presence overriding representation and entering the realm of signification on its own terms. But since properly photographic/painterly models pose rather than perform, the idea of a cinematic model complicates matters significantly for Bresson. The act of filming may be as automatic as that of being, yet the likelihood of filming a being acting another being, or even his own being, is a constant threat. You can hear the filmmaker's conscience whisper to itself: "The camera and microphone are letting-be types of technology, so I am set up or ensnared to let be this being who pretends, this most strange and unusual being being other than himself, this being who is quite uneducated about what it means solely to be by giving all being a meaning. A result no doubt of his training as an actor, not to mention his background as an adult versed in duplicity. I must find fresh ways to steer clear of this setup and precarious pitfall, such that I let-be only what-is—and no less within an environment conditioned by theatricality, spectacle, and commerce to bringing-forth what-is-not. But you know you're on the right path (the path of truth in art) when the odds are stacked against you."

I do believe that Bresson is aspiring to a kind of metaphysics of performance here, insisting that models be "true" first and foremost so that when they are projected onscreen as images and sounds they will not project beyond their nature or in excess of their actual aura. Ideally, they should project in concert with the inanimate objects that cannot be otherwise than they are (though for objects, being is simple and straightforward, is it not?). For an example of how strict Bresson is on this issue, consider the following direction for what should *not* be done: "To your models: 'Don't think what you're saying, don't think what you're doing.' And also: 'Don't think *about* what you say, don't think *about* what you do.'"[31] Bresson's rule—don't think!—assumes that his models, as conscious beings, *will* think and *will* inevitably act for the camera unless he can somehow rid them of this will. (Kleist's solution, as we have seen, is to get rid of the human being entirely and replace him with a puppet or god. Except for the armored knights in *Lancelot du Lac* and the donkey in *Au hasard Balthazar*, Bresson is committed to, or, like Dostoevsky, has resigned himself to, human beings.) Of course, all actors have some form of training or experience and in varying degrees strive to think before and as they act, which is why Bresson simply refuses to cast them in his films. It is always for the sake of being as opposed to seeming-to-be—even if being is far less interesting or dramatic than appearance—that Bresson declares that filmmakers, at least those beholden to a medium-specific mode of film performance, should "radically suppress *intentions* in [their] models."[32] This is because the concept of intention creates a separation between actor and character that, once exploited, can never be mended. For someone like Bresson, who believes that most of human behavior—and all authentic behavior—is unintended, hence automatic, the concept of intentionality will therefore govern human action primarily in retrospect, in an attempt to ascertain why someone—or oneself—behaved in a certain way that may not be officially (that is, morally) endorsed by that person. The world is not a stage for how we would have *liked to act*; it is not a stage for actors but a *staging of actions*. To that end, Bresson's direction will consist in setting up the ideal conditions for what is usually a directorial fantasy by rethinking the character in terms of the mind and body of the person who shall not act because they will have no need to act; they simply do what they are told to do, as if puppeted, and as long as they comply—and have no reason not to comply with their own nature—they will perform in their own unique way that neither they nor Bresson could have foreseen. They will also present, as opposed to re-present, a character who is, as a rule, absent onscreen (as far as the camera is concerned, and perhaps for viewers as well, the actor is the character). In this way and if all goes "according to plan," models are made to forget, through a cultivation of their behavioral automatisms, that they are actually "acting" in front of a camera; they are made to become their character not from the inside out but rather from the outside in, which amounts to saying that they have no inside separate from outside—their "outside" stretches and staggers across their entire person. They are what they are, such that *what* they are becomes *who* they are. This path to personhood constitutes a rug-pulling eradication of any *a priori* conception of the human, an exchange of spirit for what I would call "raw material."

The automatism of the camera is not only instrumental in capturing and recording the automatism of models; it is also the condition of possibility for a human being onscreen freeing himself from the prison-like inauthenticity of self-consciousness and becoming as automatic, if not as graceful, as a marionette. Two remarks from the *Notes* are worth isolating in this respect: "Model. It is his non-rational, non-logical 'I' that your camera records"[33]; and "Models mechanized externally, internally free. On their faces nothing willful. *The constant, the eternal beneath the accidental.*"[34] Like many classical film theorists, albeit with greater subtlety, Bresson plays with the analogy between the "I" of the model and the camera-eye. I would also point out that these definitions of the model are specific to the cinema's recording functions—there is no separation between model and medium, just as there is no separation between actor and star. The first definition is concerned with what the camera and not the viewer sees, or rather that the camera does not so much see as records the model as he is and not as he sees himself. The second definition is more complex in suggesting that the camera's automatism is instrumental in automating the behavior of the model by focusing (not exactly in an optical sense) on the accidental surfaces of the world. The implication is that if the surfaces of faces in particular are shaped by underlying forces like the will, then the camera will *see through* those surfaces, imprisoning those faces. The cinematic apparatus, which represents reality non-consciously, approaches human personality at the ruling threshold of its anonymity. Now anonymity here does not refer to the absence of an "I" but rather to the mechanization of the "I" as expressed in the second note, an outward mechanization that in principle frees the "I" from the inside (consciousness) to the outside (the face). This face is a complex field of moving parts, a contingent dispersion of gestures organized according to mechanized habit rather than human-ized motivation or intentionality, a "system" that shatters the illusion of a stable, rational, accessible pinpoint of interiority where consciousness looks out from behind the face. While such a face is thrown into an anarchy of the accidental, Bresson insists somewhat paradoxically on the presence of something constant and eternal *beneath* the contingency of the face. But the word "beneath" is also misleading insofar as it draws yet another line between inside and outside, setting the stage for the return of the will and its engine of purposeful yet doomed consciousness. What is needed to over-come these incommensurable binaries—particularly the opposition between outward mechanization and inner freedom—is what I described earlier as a movement from automatism to autonomy, a transformation of the former into the latter. However, the condition for such a transformation is that the autonomy which results from automatism will be metaphysical (constant and eternal) instead of psychological. One way in which Bresson attempts this transformation is by making his models repeat lines and actions inces-santly until they lose all meaning *for* the model so as to take on a life of their own as part of the model's being.[35] If Bresson were Kleist in the anecdote about the young man's cursed vanity, he would have him repeat the graceful antiquity gesture past the point of parody and into sterility, a path destined for the uncanny realm of total mechanicalness—the backdoor of the human condition—which may have the power to reenchant the gesture or at least rule out false gestures. There can be no guarantee that the repetitions of mechanization (automatism) will spark the light of grace (autonomy): "If, on the screen, the mechanism disappears and the phrases you have made them say, the gestures you have made them make, have become one with your models, with your film, with you—then a miracle."[36]

In my experience, the model theory of acting is most fully realized in *Mouchette* (France, 1967), particularly in two scenes where the young female protagonist (Nadine Nortier), forced prematurely into survivalist adult-hood by poverty, unfit parentage, and lack of love, engages awkwardly and enigmatically in acts of what we might call "play." Having been deprived of a childhood phase in life when play is practiced with some regularity and care-freeness, for Mouchette the energies released by play have accumulated to such an extent that they have become warped into seemingly violent impulses towards sex and death. In the first scene I wish to discuss, Mouchette is shown wandering by herself at a carnival, looking characteristically dour and forlorn, unapproachable and bizarrely out of place. She makes her way to the bumper cars and stands helplessly in front of the ride, inviting the pity of a woman in the crowd who gives her the necessary coins to enter. Shortly after the ride begins, Mouchette is hit from behind by a man nearly twice her age who seems to be drawn to her stoically concealed vulnerability. In an enclosed environment framed by play, the man pursues Mouchette amidst the clutter and chaos of bumper cars, ramming the back of her car with increasing ferocity. At first Mouchette half-smiles at the excitement aroused by the heated hit-or-be-hit game, especially when she finally manages to land a bumper blow on her pursuer, but as she continues to be struck more force-fully (and passionately) by the man, Bresson catches her face in a moment of uncontrollable release, a gaping expression of agony combined with ecstasy **(Fig. 3.13)**.

I use the word "catch" very deliberately as a description of Bresson's filming technique when his models manage to deliver the correct automatic gestures without any trace of intention behind their expression, for when this

Figure 3.13   *Bresson catches Mouchette's automatic gasp of pleasure/pain:* Mouchette *(Robert Bresson, France, 1967)*.

happens it must be quite unpredictable and yet the filmmaker must, as they say, expect the unexpected by keeping the "camera net" ready at opportune times. And the potential for a revelatory act of automatism is opportune here because the mechanical and contact-sport nature of the bumper-car ride mechanizes Mouchette externally, setting up ideal conditions for the emergence and capture of gestural automatisms which are not willed but seem to embody the will of her locked-up libidinal energies. As we follow Mouchette and relish her brief reprieve from chronic dissatisfaction with her life, it might dawn on us during this "play scene" that we do not know enough about her *inner life* to know if she wants or is able to release these energies herself or if she needs someone else to help release them for her. With an increasing sense of thrill-laced frustration, we watch her struggle to navigate her bumper car away from the flirtatious barrage and ideally into a position of attack, yet with each jerk of the wheel she finds herself on the "losing" end, faced with a wall or further enmired in a car-clump as the man resumes control. The pinball nature of the ride prevents us from determining what exactly her intentions are here; the ride sets her body into motion, out-running her inhibitions, electrifying her with a desire she does not properly understand and appears to be feeling for the first time in her young—but also old—life. When the ride stops (as abruptly as it started), she emerges from the car as if still dreaming and, like a sleepwalker, continues the dream of desire by approaching the man in a desperate yet surprisingly assertive way, reciprocating his implied courtship by finally getting the upper hand on him. Pursuing her pursuer outside the automatic space of play, that is, in all seriousness and *for real*, her father intercedes by blunting her gesture of desire with one of coldest cruelty—a slap across the face that brings her back down to a loveless earth.

The second related scene also involves a sublimation game, yet this one Mouchette is intent on putting into motion herself. Since the scene comes at the end of the film, it requires some setting up. First, she is shown walking along a dirt road by an open field. The setting here is all peace and tranquility, crystallizing this present moment in time, this clear horizon of possibility and newness that, for a moment, might offset her unforgiving troubles: bullied by schoolchildren, surrounded by poverty, oppressed by a negligent father, abandoned by an invalid mother (who loves her but, tragically, lacks the necessary physical strength for love), and victimized (ambiguously) by rape, resulting in her being scorned by the community. She is the product of a suffocating accumulation of brutal experiences (some of which approach the pearly gates of love, only to be turned away), leaving her understandably brimming with a generalized resentment towards the world, a nihilist anger which consumes her even when receiving rare acts of kindness; and yet, despite that heavy burden, on the shining surface of the here and now she is still a child exploring the garden that is the world. It is like a great fork in the road, but in order for her to inhabit this "garden life" she too must be nurtured in some way. As we scan with her the wide-open panorama of aloneness and abandonment, there seems to be no imaginable place or person for her to reach out to for support, emotional fulfilment, ideally love, and a chance at some shred of happiness. After the death of her mother, some of the local townspeople do extend hospitable hands, suggesting that the world is not *all* selfishness and cruelty, but Mouchette turns them all aside in bursts of rage—it is a kindness deformed by pity, not to mention extreme tardiness, for it is far too late for her to become softened by these or any other gestures of consolation. As she walks alone, carrying beneath her arm a bundle of dresses and a funeral shroud given to her by an elderly woman enthralled by the dead, the overcast sky of her face continues to darken and block any access to the beauty of her surroundings. And this beauty, like that of Mouchette herself, is quickly crushed by the sound of gunshots as she witnesses a series of hunters stationed in the trees prey on wild rabbits racing for their lives. Much like the archers in the treetops in *Lancelot du Lac*, these hunters fire their guns at the rabbits in automatist fashion, like tall waves crashing on a beach or lightning strikes in broad daylight. Lacking a recognizable motivation other than *power*, the hunters are as much mechanical as human forms—call them killing machines—firing shots one after the other, with the camera shots of their gunshots appearing in uncanny unison. Here Mouchette bears witness to the reign of the strong over the weak, experience over innocence, life as that which plucks its own fruit. And yet (despite that heavy burden of truth), she does not run for cover or so much as flinch at the poor rabbits before moving along, more assured of the logic of her entrapment than ever before: "This is the way of the world and my place in it. I am tired of being abused. I am tempted to run away or become my own worst enemy. But I despise all of it—all of *them*. Is there no other world?" **(Figs 3.14, 3.15, 3.16)**.

Now she is near a river and lies down on the grass, not to gaze questioningly into the heavens but to play another game. She grabs hold of one of the fine dresses given to her, only to discover that it is being held back by the earth, torn up by the sharp branches of a claw-like bush. With the dress permanently marred, she finds another use for it, rolling herself up into a ball, a game ball, so she can roll down the riverbank like a boulder or a log. While Mouchette may be thinking of her fleeting sense of freedom when riding the bumper cars, I am instead reminded of the pinball scene from *Pickpocket* where the hypnotic metal sphere is shown bouncing around at the top of the playing board, going this way and that, completely at the mercy of chance forces after only one initial release from the so-called player set the ball into

Figures 3.14–3.16 *Mouchette bears witness to a mechanical law of nature—the strong trump the weak:* Mouchette *(Robert Bresson, France, 1967).*

motion. What a strange game for Mouchette to be playing, and even stranger timing for play. The object of her game is still a mystery because, in child-like fashion, she seems to be making it up as she goes along. What is clear to me is that she has succeeded to turn herself from player to *plaything*, or from agent to object, paradoxically freer as a game ball than as the will which powers it. The first roll (of the dice of her life) down the bank fails, the momentum of her automatism running out due to friction. She stands up in defeat. Then she notices, in reachable distance, someone (familiar?) driving a tractor along a dirt road, and impulsively raises her arm in a vague half-wave that fades away into the ether **(Figs 3.17, 3.18)**. Considering the fact that the tractor driver is facing away from her (though he does briefly look back over his shoulder), the gesture is a weak visual signal of distress, a voiceless yet spirited squeak in the wind, a final reaching out to others, including enemies, which shoots out of her seemingly against her will, like the whiplash gasp of pleasure–pain on the bumper cars. Nothing save for a loud cry for help could span the great barrier of communication, but no such cry is forthcoming, for a cry at this point simply requires too much will, and she is in the process of *relinquishing* her will through this game she has invented. The ineffectual half-wave gesture derives its authenticity, power, and "rightness" (to use Bresson's term) by not being fully formed and directed outward as a clear call for help, for if it were so intended, then we as viewers would *know* that Mouchette is calling for help; but Mouchette does not quite "call for help," which is one reason why the tractor driver so quickly turns away to resume his business. She is not prepared to fully submit to anyone's will expect her own will to die. So, she does what she does in Figure 3.17. It is an almost illegible gesture: she hesitates to call out while surprising herself that she *would* call out after deciding definitively to leave this world behind. But as we have seen, she cannot carry out this decision by her own will alone ... It is a fruitless endeavor to psychologize Mouchette, or anyone on the brink of suicide for that matter.

Figures 3.17 and 3.18   *Mouchette's cryptic call for help:* Mouchette *(Robert Bresson, France, 1967).*

Not noticeably disappointed by her abandonment, Mouchette walks back to the starting position of the game and resets herself as the ball. The second roll collides with a bush in which the already torn white dress becomes irrevocably caught—the symbol of femininity, marriage, and class consciousness exfoliated like snakeskin—and she leaves it there to wither, drained of all value, as if, in the context of the game, it is now considered legally "out of bounds." The third roll, the start of which is shown yet not followed through by Bresson's camera, terminates in the river with a loud splash heard off-screen. Success. Bresson cuts to his preferred view of an event: the aftermath. The rippling surface of the water. As the ripples stirred by the suicidal plunge peter out and give way to undulations, if you look closely you can see something extraordinary happening on the surface of the water: the filmmaker joins Mouchette's game by reciprocating her supplicating gesture ignored by the tractor driver. Bresson very subtly manipulates these undulations on the water's surface so that they appear to retract or implode, not all the way back to Mouchette's entry point in the water (what's done is done) but near the moment of her descent to the bottom of the river and her final resting place within the small black hole of the pinball game of her life. He reaches out and gently pulls the strings of redemption, granting a micro-miracle intended to go unnoticed, I think, or just scrape by our consciousness—the very sort of miracle which Bresson claimed can occur when a model becomes one with the film and one with the filmmaker **(Figs 3.19, 3.20, 3.21)**.

What I find compelling in these scenes as illuminators of the model theory of acting is that the more Mouchette becomes an object of circumstance and figure of automatism, the more expressively "herself" she becomes. Through automatism she undergoes both overripe sexual desire and existential despair, emotions which are "mechanized outwardly but internally free." Bresson knows that Mouchette's fate by the river is not in the hands of a benevolent deity, and yet, in watching her give up her will to live and roll down the bank towards her doom, as the creator of *this* world on film he intercedes by saving her, in a certain sense. During the third and final death roll, the camera can only look on and record the event as a bystander, perhaps waiting for the world to introduce another counterforce to Mouchette's obstinate gravity. While the camera-as-net can't/won't catch her before she falls into the river, it can avert its eyes, as we have seen, and open them on the aftermath in what Paul Schrader calls an image of stasis suggestive of the transcendent.[37] But I would say Bresson's treatment of Mouchette's implied death goes further than transcendence: it *animates* it, and quite literally. Of all his characters, something about Mouchette's tragic fate compels him to break his own rule of restraint to "empty the pond to get the fish."[38] *He goes fishing*: editing and optical processing techniques are subtly deployed to catch something that

Figures 3.19–3.21   *Mouchette plays a life-and-death game with herself as "the ball":* Mouchette
(Robert Bresson, France, 1967).

really cannot be caught, halting the forward indifference of time and looping
the film's final frames of the young girl's dissipation into the void—the visual
equivalent of a breath—about six or seven times before fading to black. With
the looping of the fading ripples, Bresson stops looking and listening passively from above the water and starts to *think over* the water's surface and *hold
onto* Mouchette, blessing her death with chords from Claudio Monteverdi's
Magnificat, which bear witness to the grace of her mechanical resiliency
through unbearable—and unjust—hardship. Her abiding, perspiring persistence through life is matched only by Balthazar the donkey in Bresson's
subsequent film, *Au hasard Balthazar*, at the end of which the director tries
to redeem a dying animal by orchestrating the mysterious brotherhood of
beasts. In his final moments, Balthazar, the beast of burden, finds himself
surrounded by a herd of sheep, the beasts of dreams: swathed in a blanket of
sheep, a swirling cloud-herd of sheep, a cocooning vigil of concentric "sheep
ripples" washing over his body in silent solidarity **(Fig. 3.22)**.[39] As awe-
inspiring as this scene is, it does not take the risk of *Mouchette's* more extreme
formal liberties with time and space, which flirt with fantasies of stopping or
turning back time yet fall for neither in the quest for redemption. The spinning motion of the film loop, especially during the final fadeout, continues
forever Mouchette's spinning motion down the bank, and shows Bresson
relieving her in her game just as she is about to lose. He may be trying to save
her soul, but that's not for me to say. Whatever the case may be, this is divine

Figure 3.22 *A blanket of sheep on Balthazar's deathbed:* Au hasard Balthazar *(Robert Bresson, France, 1966).*

intervention as performed by the creator of *this* world, the world of *Mouchette*, and whose powers flow from the metaphysical properties of a medium he holds sacred.

Many of Bresson's films end with the death of the main character, hence with the death of the model, a death undergone in the depths of despair yet expressed in terms of emancipation and gesturing towards grace. But what on earth could be graceful about death? Why must his characters meet such an end in order for their sacrificial suffering to be made redeemable? And how is redemption even possible here without the clear promise of an afterlife? ... It is the *manner* in which his characters/models perish that is significant as a condition of possibility for the emergence of grace in Kleist's understanding of the term. According to Kleist, what stands in our way to grace is—simply, tragically—ourselves. What better way to enter a state of grace than by losing oneself, shedding layers of consciousness, whittling the ego down to a humble nub, carving out the moment when one can die with unassuming dignity, with the breezy effortlessness of letting go. But is the self actually capable of giving itself up? If the self is not prepared to die, it is then that death as we know it, fear it, *comes*, always unannounced and unwelcome in any form but relief. The self, by nature, is unfit for death and for the same reason that it is unfit for grace. Death amplifies the self at the very moment when it ought to yield, just as the artistic impulse amplifies the self—making the self conscious of itself—when it ought to be at its most open and responsive to forces greater than it. Now as we have seen, Bresson's characters, who are often destined to die, are portrayed not through the lens of selfhood but rather through the lens of automatism. Whether they are killed or commit suicide, the self is lost automatically because their sense of self is not centered but radically dispersed. Therefore, Bresson's main characters do not meet their end so much as *come to an end*: that is, when the film ends and, perhaps, *because* the film ends—because the film has no reason to exist without the existence of its primary model, which for Bresson is akin to its soul. (And the same goes for Bazin with respect to photography: without the model there is no photograph whatsoever to speak of. To describe a photograph as a mere depiction of its model is to deny the *shared or plural* ontology of photography; it is, in fact, to describe something else entirely.)

Those characters who do not perish at the conclusion of a Bresson film will typically face death's counterpart: rebirth. Either way, Bresson's models reach some sort of limit point by the end. In claiming that the film and model share the same ending, I mean that if the death of the character is also the death of the model, then the completion of the film is also the completion of the model's lifespan in film as such. At least in theory, Bresson's plan is to both discover a model and prevent the possibility of the model becoming an actor, playing different characters across different films and developing a persona. That being said, many of his models did go on to have substantial careers as film actors (Claude Laydu, Marika Green, Anne Wiazemsky), and in the case of Dominique Sanda of *A Gentle Woman* (France, 1969), a rather illustrious one. They were free to do so, but they were not free to become actors in the first place when Bresson, as was his way, plucked them out of their everyday lives and dropped them inside his films, discovering them when they were not necessarily looking to be discovered.[40] Leading a model to his or her untimely death or rebirth was perhaps Bresson's way of returning the model as found object back to "its" natural habitat. On the one hand, Bresson's characters die with dignity, but on the other hand he deliberately kills them off, taking them by the hand to the end of their life not just in *this* film but in the future of film as a whole. He sets out to do this by casting a non-professional first-time actor, breaking down the instinct to act, using the remains of the model to give birth to the character, ending his films with the death of the character (a death which logically implicates the model), and finally never casting that person again in subsequent films. The realization of the full lifespan—birth and death—of the model within a film is also indicated by the fact that *some* of the models never did perform again onscreen. While it was likely Bresson's preference that the models not be viewed through the prism of the recurring or star actor, he could hardly have taken formal measures to make sure of it, though the radical differences in the way the actors performed "post-death" when invited by other directors to act—to put their experience as actors to use, to play rather than model a part—suggest a clear break between model and actor phases. At least we should not be surprised by those models who abstained from acting, given that models are trained not to act and, most importantly, are put to work in such a way that they cannot model a character *other than the one* to which they have permanently bonded with. These leads shall go by their real *and* character names: François Leterrier/Fontaine of *A Man Escaped* (France, 1956), Nadine Nortier/Mouchette of *Mouchette*, Guillaume des Forêts/Jacques of *Four Nights of a Dreamer* (France, 1971), and Antoine Monnier/Charles of *The Devil Probably* (France, 1977), with Luc Simon/Lancelot of *Lancelot du Lac* appearing in only one subsequent film, a TV movie, in what appears to be a very minor role. (Ironically, the precursor for all of them is an actor *par excellence*: Renée Jeanne Falconetti/Jeanne d'Arc from Dreyer's *The Passion of Joan of Arc*—the woman who embodied an iconic historical figure who perished in martyrdom and, as if having perished with her, never appeared onscreen again, though not without having displayed the full range of her acting abilities, the heights of which still remain out of reach for most actors. As a sign of Bresson's many problems with a film he obviously respected a great deal, the director decided to make his own minimalist version of the Joan of Arc story, casting a relative non-professional, Florence Delay, who, unlike Falconetti, remains emotionally withdrawn throughout and unable or unwilling to explicitly channel her faith/doubt in God to anyone but herself. Delay rarely appeared again in films, and Falconetti, as we all know, disappeared completely. Once in a blue moon, stars are born and die in a single role, a single film in which the bond between actor, role, and film is of purest monogamy, what I will call "poetic monogamy.")

Of all Bresson's variations on the theme of death, it is the suicides of his youths which are the most pertinent to the themes of this chapter.[41] While the principle of suicide can be generalized as a conscious act of self-destruction, a self stripping the self away from itself, in Bresson suicides occur in a more peculiar and less decisive way where conscious intention, passion/desperation, and detailed planning are indiscernible from a sense of anonymity and contingency. We have already seen this at work in Mouchette's death scene, in which a seemingly innocent act of play results in her drowning. It should be obvious by now that I would hesitate to say that she drowns *herself*, and not only because we are not shown her entering the water nor any trace of her body lying at the bottom of the river. The roll-down-the-hill game besets the forces of gravity and chance with the task of carrying her away. Suicide is set into motion and then occurs as if by itself. It is not exactly *committed*. She spins like a log only to sink like a stone. She gives up and goes down quietly, her death a departure from the world of the film in a state of selflessness or, perhaps, grace.

Another ambiguous suicide occurs at the end of *The Devil Probably*. A deeply disillusioned and troubled young man, Charles, bearing a nihilism that rejects even the anarchy of destruction, contemplates his own death while admitting to an analyst that he is unable to imagine himself actually taking his own life. He longs to die as the logical conclusion to this extreme form of nihilism, but at the same time his nihilism prohibits the committing of so bold and affirmative an act. His thoughts are as clear as they are contradictory: he confesses to holding life in contempt, only to go on to say that he despises death even more. He admits to having conducted some suicidal experiments in his bathtub by keeping his head below water, only to realize that the life coursing through his body wants none of it. From this he concludes that he does not abhor life at all; in fact, he is very much attached to the rhythm of human experience—of seeing, hearing, and thinking the world—and cannot imagine a world *without* the refractions of consciousness and fluctuations of sensation. Hopelessly mired in the contradictions of suicide, the psychologist responds to Charles casually, almost dismissively, yet with hints of frustration when he declares off the record that the solution of the ancient Romans was assisted suicide. What is a mere historical fact for the psychologist, an opportunity to be worthy of the long rows of books presiding behind him, turns out to be deadly for Charles. The sequence of actions Charles performs upon leaving the psychologist's office all seem to point to the arrangement of an assisted suicide: stealing a handful of bills from the desk of one of his lovers, asking a friend to purchase a gun by the Seine, awakening his best friend, Valentin (Nicolas Deguy), in the middle of the night, who agrees to do his bidding in exchange for the stolen money. It is important to note that Charles never verbalizes this plan to anyone and, in true Bressonian fashion, performs each of these tasks in a mechanical way devoid of transparent or otherwise readable motivations. Given these subtle yet significant circumstances leading up to the suicide, the grammar of intentionality must be checked at the door of language: Charles *takes* the money as if it does not belong to anyone, *gives* some bills to his friend, who then *returns* with a loaded gun, asks Valentin to do *something* in exchange for handsome compensation, refusing to say *what*, still always thinking about "the what" while taking all the steps of "the how."

Like Mouchette, it is not obvious that Charles intends to commit suicide; for one thing, the very idea of assisted suicide, which is also an accurate description, I think, of Mouchette's suicide via play, clouds the self-motivated willfulness of the suicidal impulse, contradicting the contradiction that is suicide itself. If Charles can be said to have a motivation or plan in place, it could only be described in contradictory terms: as the desire to commit suicide by being murdered. It is important to him that *he* not be the one to take his own life; he wishes not to die but simply to cease to exist in the world, or rather in *this* world which he experiences as politically uninhabitable and irrevocably damaged by the powers that be. His fear in taking his own life may stand in the way of a possible world where life would be worth living, for Charles a mechanically moral world of universal nonattachment that generates justice daily like sugar or wine. However, in this tragic spirit—his tousled cloud-head of nihilistic thinking at war with a virile body and sprightly feet—he leads Valentin to a cemetery, hands him the gun and walks ahead, leaving his back exposed **(Figs 3.23, 3.24)**. It is yet another ambiguous gesture, for Charles's walk resembles a casual stroll or contemplative pacing as much as a death march down the green mile. Executing while improvising "the plan," still immersed in thinking about letting someone do what he cannot do himself, Charles does not physically brace himself at this point, nor does he provide any sort of cue for Valentin to pull the trigger. The plan for the assisted suicide itself has not been discussed, worked out, or so much as acknowledged by either one. Instead, the plan is encrypted in a series of actions which suggest competing wills towards life and death. Charles remains, strangely enough, partially oblivious to the situation in which his fate is wrapped. He regrets not having more sublime thoughts to think and share at such a time, a sentiment implying that he might need *more time*. His disappointment at himself for lacking more romantically inclined thoughts could also be taken as a sign from him that his time has indeed come, that his ability to ascribe value to things, including death, is dead. But this confession is immediately followed by the spark of a new thought and a reaching out to his friend with what may be a final epiphany, the one he was looking for: "Do you know what? You know, it just occurred to me …"

Figures 3.23 and 3.24 *Charles exposes (intentionally? inadvertently? half-invitingly?) his back to the armed Valentin:* Le Diable probablement *(The Devil Probably, Robert Bresson, France, 1977).*

Perhaps Charles's death walk sows the seeds for a new spiritual life. We will never know. What we can say is that at this particular moment, *the* moment of his life, the act of suicide may be on his mind but is not in his heart, and just as he starts speaking in the unmistakable tones of truth, he is cut off with a gunshot to the back—shot mid-sentence, or mid-life—completely unaware of his decision to die. In this sense he commits suicide not only indirectly through Valentin but unconsciously, with and without his consent. He is killed while thinking, and so the impact of the shot is as sudden and instantaneous as being accidentally hit by a truck or struck down by lightning. This is also due to the fact that Valentin, after initially holding the gun loosely and timidly, turns out in this moment—also *the* moment of his life—to be empowered by the gun, hence to be a murderer when asked to be a savior, to harbor the destructive impulse of murder regardless of what motivates him (money or friendship or both). Valentin discovers that he *can* kill. Charles chose wisely in this respect, but he failed to appreciate that killers are fundamentally impulsive and, lacking a protocol, will act before conscience awakens and intervenes. Another possible reading of this ambiguous scene is that Valentin pulls the trigger prematurely out of a deep understanding of the task which he has been saddled with, an understanding deeper than Charles ever realized. By shooting his friend without waiting for authorization, in the back while walking and talking, he catches Charles in a moment of innocence and incomprehension, relieving him of the burden of contradiction that is suicide. He helps him to completely sidestep the violent exercising of his will at the very moment when the soul seeks the nothingness of grace for its untimely departure.

The Devil Probably begins with two newspaper headlines that anticipate the cryptic actions of Charles and Valentin: "Young man commits suicide in Père Lachaise," followed by "Père Lachaise 'suicide' was murder." The film then jumps back six months into the past, effectively presenting itself as a tracing of events leading up to the mysterious death of Charles and a possible resolution of what actually took place. However, as we have seen from the preceding analysis of the final section, both headlines psychologically and grammatically oversimplify what are ultimately very complex automatisms irreducible to the rational institutions of the media and police.

A Gentle Woman, made eight years prior in 1969, operates according to a similar structural principle of reexamining the indecipherable facts surrounding a suicide, and in this sense is a companion piece to *The Devil Probably*. The film opens with the immediate aftermath of the apparent suicide of Elle (Dominique Sanda), presented through a haiku-like series of audiovisual resonances describing a fatal leap from the balcony: the blank stare of a housekeeper, a rocking chair in motion next to a table tipping over on the terrace, a white scarf floating down to the street where the body of the woman is found dead. As in *The Devil Probably*, the death of the main character spurs a shift into the past, yet here the shift occurs without an explicit demarcation of time. It is also filtered through a particular subjective perspective, that of Elle's husband, Luc (Guy Frangin), working its way back to her suicide in an attempt to comprehend her unsuspected motives.

When the film comes full circle, returning to the moments right before Elle leaps to her death, there is no verbal suggestion of suicide exchanged between her and the maid, Anne (Jeanne Lobre). On the contrary, Elle tells Anne that she is "happy," a confession which turns out not to be a lie; and like Charles, her actions leading up to the deed are performed mechanically, without clear premeditation or emotional inflection. In representations of suicide, it is always tempting to look for a line separating action and inaction, courage and fear, yes and no, which the sufferer treads as if on a tightrope. But as with the previous examples, no such line can be comfortably drawn. Just when Elle seems prepared to willfully cross the line, grabbing the handles of the French doors to the terrace and opening them with sheer conviction, she hesitates, almost angrily, before shutting the doors and throwing her back hard against them. She then returns to her seat at a desk where she had been toying with a figure of the Crucifixion—hardly a minor detail yet not exactly a master key to her mental state at this juncture—and cracks a half-smile (not unlike Mouchette's half-wave) before gazing up at her reflection in a mirror hanging above her on the wall **(Figs 3.25, 3.26)**. A quick shot of her reflection is followed by a cut back to her gaze, now filled with a strong sense of purpose: she stands up from the desk, walks towards the window of the terrace, and in an extreme closeup—rare for Bresson—looks through the glass with cold, animal-like ferocity before leaping to her death offscreen. But why did she smile like that? Why did she suddenly gaze at her own reflection? Why did these gestures precede/propel her suicide? These are unanswerable questions, hence poor questions, but I believe we can productively pause over the change which occurs in Elle—and in the film—when she catches her reflection: it is as if her image of herself in the mirror performs the deed, an image she may not recognize in the slightest, an image that she has *become*, and so she can "safely" commit suicide by lacking the very self which suicide would destroy. It is perhaps for this reason that Bresson does not show her leap off the terrace, focusing instead on the aftermath of object ripples, for an image of her *in the act* would imply that she is fully conscious of her actions, whereas, according to the silent exchange with herself in the mirror, she is not necessarily in possession of herself at all. Images of "her" would falsify the intentionless automatism of her mirror-image self, the paradoxical agency of selflessness, which lends her death a tragic innocence—say, the tragedy of a child's death—while elevating it into

Figures 3.25 and 3.26　*Elle cracks a half-smile at her reflection before leaping to her death:* Une Femme douce *(A Gentle Woman, Robert Bresson, France, 1969).*

the transcendent realm of grace, particularly through Bresson's emphasis on the bird-like flapping of Elle's white scarf, which follows behind her and floats gently down to earth, becoming in the film's final image the coffin's white sheet, beneath which she rests in peace yet upon which Luc projects restlessly his guilt and confusion.

If one looks closely, the ethereal movement of Elle's white scarf in the air is followed in the next scene by the brief billowing of her white burial shroud.

The metaphorical juxtaposition of these two fluttering fabrics carries a meta-physical charge similar to that of the final image of *Mouchette*. The cut from the scarf to the shroud causes the latter, stiffened by the corpse it covers, to shift and very slightly deflate, indicating that Elle's body just became a touch lighter. These "effects" (I don't know what else to call them) are so inconspicuous that one wonders if Bresson intended for them to be consciously registered at all by the viewer. It begs the question as to whether Bresson himself was fully conscious of making such choices. I believe this is less a matter of aesthetics than *belief*, but at the same time what I mean by belief here is not religious or spiritual but purely aesthetic: with the repetitive loops at the end of *Mouchette* and the cut at the end of *A Gentle Woman*, Bresson forges links with the spiritual world just as the brutality of the material world has finished its rounds, culminating in death. The end of a life, timed with the end of a film, inspires him to give viewers something to *believe in*. For film that means something *to see*—the very image of belief itself.

———

Notes on the Cinematograph is filled with paradoxical descriptions of the model technique of acting, a term which I have been understanding as pertaining to actors who are led to the spirit of the character via an accidental embodiment of their own true nature, made to stumble upon themselves in the process of being someone else or, in being denied the chance to become someone else, having to *find themselves*—and this "finding" is what Bresson aspires to document in his fictions. But at some point along the way his models are told, or they realize for themselves, that their so-called "true nature" is measured not by what they know about themselves but rather by what they do not (perhaps cannot) know about themselves. This non-knowledge might hinge on the discovery that one's core movements and gestures are, in fact, *signatures*, and that these signatures constitute the inimitable poetry of our everyday actions, the very fabric of our lives. They are uniquely ours and sum us up from the outside. These signatures of self may add up to a sense of self, or imply one, but only after the fact—they are, as it were, *unsigned*. They are not to be taken as expressions made on behalf of a self that is posited *a priori*. Near the end of the *Notes*, Bresson quotes Montaigne's optimistically behaviorist picture of human life before offering his own qualification or correction in automatist terms: "*Every movement reveals us* (Montaigne). But it only reveals us if it is automatic (not commanded, not willed)."[42] This note stands apart as a dialogue or miniature debate with Montaigne, who, in acknowledging the perspicacity of our everyday gestures and implying that the struggle to know the self will be epic if every movement reveals the self, does not fully affirm what for

Bresson is the revelatory spirit of automatism: the perpetual motion machine of human expressivity.

It is no accident that the more we try to know Bresson's characters by humanizing their behavioral machinations through psychological concepts like the will, intentionality, or desire, the more their actions will strike us as contradictory or devoid of sense. These characters, as we have seen, lack the requisite degree of identity—and identifiability—necessary for us to question whether what they say and do is typical of them or completely uncharacteristic. This is because their humanity—that is to say, their freedom—is not to be found *inside* them; it is not to be found *anywhere*. Rather it is, as Wittgenstein said of the meaning of our words, public and in plain view. That many viewers and critics of Bresson have felt aversion or mistrust towards the mechanized/wooden (marionette-like) characters attests to the human desire to see ourselves as fully in charge of ourselves, lodged comfortably and confidently within our bodies, ideally positioned to speak through our mouths and act as if every twitch were a conscious choice. While we may feel that we come to know less about Lancelot and Mouchette and Charles and Elle over time and that may be frustrating, is there not some truth in it? When we question the actions of someone we know by saying "That isn't like you at all," the felt response, whether voiced or not, is "Well, who am I anyway?"

The Bressonian model is an attempt to make a puppet out of a human being, an attempt to sedate the irrepressible surges of consciousness and dilute the will throughout every corner and crevice of the body. And if we grant credence to the possibility that the mechanically automatic form of life constitutes a purification rather than an eradication of the human spirit, then the seemingly spiritless woodenness of the Bressonian model can be seen as a discovery of the poetics of the marionette theater *within* the cinema. It is well known that Bresson called for a cinema in opposition to the histrionic artifice of the live theater; a significant portion of these particular notes, for which a separate analysis/critique may be in order, are spirited attacks against the explicit or residual presence of the theatrical within the cinematic. But Kleist's puppet theater of grace turns out to resonate with Bresson's vision of cinema as a pure artform, certainly a metaphysical artform, which activates the automatisms of people as well as things. The puppet theater and its spirit of automatism is the backdoor to a cinematic paradise in which the world itself is on strings.

Nature, Whose Death Shines a Light: Exteriority and Overexposure in The Thin Red Line

> Have mountains, and waves, and skies, no significance but what we consciously give them, when we employ them as emblems of our thoughts? The world is emblematic.
>
> — Ralph Waldo Emerson, *Nature*

> From time to time I was afraid. That is the fault of a false view of life.
> — Ludwig Wittgenstein, diary entry, May 6, 1916
> (from an observational post during World War I)

I. INTRODUCTION

In this chapter (the last of this scope) I turn my attention to the narrativizing of the world in its own image through the metaphysical figure of *nature*. My aim is to find the numerous threads and analyze the intricate workings of this figure as it unfolds throughout an entire film, *The Thin Red Line* (Malick, USA, 1998). To know what to look out for in this case and how to read the various permutations of this complex figure will require the lenses of theory (including those theories which I have developed up to this point) in addition to the vision of philosophy, one that sees film as doing philosophy—otherwise the metaphysics of nature can go no further than the poetics of "wind in the trees."

The figure of nature functions in films which are, of course, set in nature but, more than that, are set on sending us *back* to nature through paradise's backdoor. This is nature understood not only as the beauty or poetry of the world in its own image, but the poignancy of the world in its own *past* image—the way the world *was*. Here the world of the film has gone on retreat, modern technology is packed and sent away, civilization is left in its own dust. From this perspective, even the city is riddled with cracks through which nature comes back to reclaim it, making the cinematic city into a montage of mud and cement, trees and buildings, sky and smog, green and gray colors. Of course, this return to nature still takes a view of nature that risks dominating it the way humans have always dominated it. Such views are often spellbound by the filmmaker as gazer or stargazer, if you will, who turns to nature as a gateway to the cosmic and is struck all over again by the ancient dualisms of good and evil or god and devil, dualisms which mask the simultaneity of order, beauty, and terror in nature as it stands. Nature's moral ambiguity in film is one of its most powerful features, marked by a sense of distance or remoteness from human affairs and an inassimilable rock-like recalcitrance towards cinematic narrativization. But, no matter how indifferent nature may seem, it is *human nature* to ascribe meaning to it, even if this is to say that it has no meaning, or lacks the meaning it once had, or hides all meaning behind its many masks.

This investigation into the cinematic site of nature is provoked by the following line of questioning.—How does nature express itself on film? Why do filmmakers committed to camera consciousness take an interest in something like nature when it is really *culture* that is at stake in film or any art? Nature may make for nice pictures, as in the photography of Ansel Adams, but does it make for interesting stories, themes, and filmic events? If narrative film speaks nature and if the ontology of film shows nature, what is the difference between this "showing" and this "speaking"? How can we speak of the contemporaneity of nature from something that *was* to something that *is* or *still is* and, perhaps, still "*speaks*"—as it did before the death of God, in the form of the mythological and pagan gods of the earth, those ancient forces of enchantment linking the physical and metaphysical realms by way of an inscrutable swathe of metaphorical resonances widening endlessly towards the unity of all things? How might we then distinguish the cryptic voices of the gods from our own projecting voices, or are both voices required to reveal and revel in nature in all its glory?

I am brought to the question "how to speak?" for two reasons. First, there is a sense in which what we call "nature" lies *beyond* language such that reaching it entails giving voice to the inexpressible. The following batch of readymade phrases with nature as their focus acknowledge something fundamentally out of reach in this regard: "home of the animal," "the primordial soup," "source of wonder," "enemy and victim of culture," "paradise lost," "mother nature," and so on. Second, there is equally a sense, and it is also sometimes said, that works of art—their nature, as it were—are irreducible to our language, blocking or intimidating reciprocal responses rather than inviting our need to speak, to give voice to powerful aesthetic experiences. A few testimonials from philosophy and criticism might run like this: "Art is the sensible presentation of the idea," "This work makes little sense … but I like it all the same," "The work of art works in mysterious ways," "Look *before* thinking, for open eyes are the key to an open mind," "I am satisfied with my speechlessness," "I am forever changed," and so on. Art and nature are united in their conflict with language, which is to say they put up resistance within the realm of humanistic understanding and partly position themselves outside such understanding, at least as demonstrated by our language. In this picture, art and nature are separate processes or vehicles that trigger the transcendence of conceptual categories and the authority of the word ("In the beginning was the word …"), with the former doing so aesthetically and the latter empirically, each managing in its own way to turn language on its head and back into *silence*. So the question, again, is *how to speak*, for we are in need of a certain language or bravery of language to speak art's "spoken speechlessness of nature" and, in particular, film's disclosure of the revelation that is nature—a speaking at the crossroads between how nature appears in representation and its presence as an appearance in excess of representation. Speechlessness in the face of nature and art constitutes romantic frameworks of human finitude that, taken together, may appear to have little to do with each other as they sulk over words too small or weak for some of the more heightened occasions of aesthetic experience. Nevertheless, the alterity of the natural and artistic worlds is brought face to face in film, as they illuminate each other and speak through each other's sealed mouth. The ontology of film shows/speaks nature's primordial silence as a *meeting place* in which art retains a vital dimension of artlessness, where nature is reconciled with the artificial or mechanical, and the unswayable muteness of the world's independence from us resonates within all discourse. The task, as I see it, involves walking the line between the coarse materiality and metaphysical ineffability of nature on film as a force which faces us and faces away, standing both near and far from the human world, by turns beautiful and terrifying. A sublime source of both lucidity and mystery, nature comes to light as a great power that was, is, or still is, yet whose future has become uncertain.

II. Dramaturgy of Nature

As we all know by now, cinema as an art does not exactly imitate nature even if a part of its own nature is to draw on it directly. Cinema and nature have, if you will, a *natural affinity*: the core principle of the cinematic apparatus accepts what it "sees and hears," allowing the sights and sounds of nature to take root and grow within the aesthetic without being subject to use or other biases and blindnesses which limit ecological awareness. The ontology of film, in calling out to the nature of things, is heeded by nature as the unifying force of all things; and the things which heed the call most readily, becoming the most luminous onscreen, are often those which belong to the grand luminosity of nature itself. By contrast, only during periods of aesthetic contemplation, defined by a sense of calm and care, can human beings fully attend to nature's poetry and experience it for what it is rather than for some other purpose, be it mining nature for riches (exploitation) or reading nature for signs (astrology). Now the manifestations of this affinity between cinema and nature in the *art* as opposed to the ontology of film are far from straightforward, for insofar as the natural world, like our own human nature, is simultaneously in the background and at the center of consciousness, at once deeply fundamental and yet somehow totally incomprehensible or alto-gether excised from modern life, it is similarly with respect to the medium of film both mimetically mirrored by the moving image and more or less eclipsed by the anthropocentric demands of audiovisual mise-en-scène and storytelling conventions. These demands are neither native to the moving image nor completely alien to it. Rather, the cinematic narrativization of nature embodies an idea of *culture* that measures its strides in consultation with nature—an art of film dynamized by the *friction* between the ontology of the moving image (facticity) and the epistemology of cinematic discourse and montage (fiction).

To return to the overshadowed piece of apocrypha from the early history of film that I briefly discussed in Chapter One, we may recall that spectators of the turn-of-the-century Lumière short, *A Baby's Dinner* (France, 1895), are believed to have responded with a passive or contemplative astonishment towards the accidental, inconspicuous, and virtually meaningless presence of nature: trees blowing in the wind, branches swaying, leaves rustling, nothing more.[1] Deep in the distant background and off to the side of an ordinary domestic scene featuring a family enjoying afternoon tea out on the terrace, this small glimpse of nature allegedly stood out and shone like the sun—and we can still imagine it having such an effect, with nebulous contingency over-powering the straightforwardness of ostensible subject matter—in marked contrast to the notorious black train speeding towards the camera in *Arrival of a Train at La Ciotat* (France, 1895), a film believed by many to set a rigid course for the haptic pleasures of affect and escapism in mainstream cinema (see **Figs 1.4, 1.5**). The brand new and spectacular appearance of the much-anticipated moving image, which had declared itself so dramatically, even violently, with the Lumière train, was in all likelihood experienced with a thin-skin intimacy and perhaps more deeply on its own terms as a kind of natural phenomenon in itself—the natural as rendered by the technological—such that those soft focus trees as captured, intentionally or not, by the Lumières were thrown into sharp relief by the very simple portrait of a young family of three unaccustomed to the absolute democracy of the moving image, one in which the world is nothing like the stage and where there are other things of interest besides them. An aesthetic moral, so to speak, to be derived in retrospect is that *nature trumps narrative* in the perception of these viewers of early cinema, and it does so despite the fact that the subject of the staged slice of life is practically all-encompassing here. What is it, then, about this equally mundane piece of nature, stripped of all colors and sounds, that made it stand out from the background so strikingly, eclipsing the carefully positioned figures, the subtle family dynamics, the still-life spread of objects, and even the film itself on display for the first time? The beauty, contingency, and automatic poetry of wind-in-the-trees tip the scale of emphasis in its favor and make us question what counts as "subject matter," for to experience nature through its mechanical reproduction in both time and space is to read the world's palm and to rediscover a beauty which is *not* in the eye of the beholder.

No matter how quietly and daily the blatant disregard or destruction of nature is carried out, cinematic technology is uniquely sensitive and self-monitoring—encouraging its users to question the instinct of appropriation in the name of art—revealing and preserving nature in a place where it can be touched without leaving a trace: the moving image as a greenhouse sanctuary, not for nature *per se* so much as the consciousness of nature for its own sake. The encounter with nature onscreen through an *image* as opposed to a direct experience depends to a certain extent on a complex interplay of aesthetics and accident, factoring in whatever skepticism one holds over the rhetorical claims and seductions of images in general. This wind-in-the-trees appears despite the fact that it has no significant bearing on the filmed event and, in all likelihood, was not even noticed by the filmmakers themselves. It is the sort of detail that brushes by our more calculated intentions and priorities; the sort of phenomenon that becomes easily drowned out by thoughts, higher aims, ambitions. Nevertheless, the camera records it as though its value were beyond question. By appearing in the background, poking through like sunlight and waving its hand, it marks not only the world beyond the frame but the world *behind* it—nature as a character without face, name, or agenda. This figure teases or tickles the static frame and, in a sense, moves it, sending shivers through it, indicating that the world as a whole is moving and changing and aging. One gets the feeling that if a single leaf were to suddenly fall (too early for this time of year), the Lumières might catch the necessary inspiration to awaken to nature more fully and rewrite the history of the actuality by filming just the tree, inventing the closeup right then and there, perhaps a solitary and contemplative closeup that patiently awaits the decisive moment in which nature's clock starts to tick. While human affairs are always of interest and justifiably the main focus in most films, it is the metaphysical affairs, regardless of how small, that are surprisingly powerful in overwhelming perception, rerouting signification, and catching our consciousness off guard.

That film, like photography, can be said to have a more direct access to the natural world than other artforms is an argument that hinges on the capacity for the camera to record and thus *respect* what stands naked and true before it. Despite this privilege, most photographs (still or moving) of nature—where nature is the obvious subject or theme—participate in the landscape genre of painting, a genre with a long and complex history of changing modes of representation and exhibition, succinctly encapsulated by Martin Lefebvre in pictorial *and* spectatorial terms as "[t]he birth of a gaze (that of the painter, the collector, or the critic) by which what was once in the margin has now come to take its place at the centre."[2] Excluding anomalous cases from the avant-garde (often driven by the *abstraction* of landscape), the landscape genre as we know it does not seem to have clearly transferred over to the cinema nor continued its development under new time-based conditions, notwithstanding those aspects of films which harbor some resemblance to the landscape genre.[3] Films for which the name "landscape" would be an appropriate sounding description are few and far between; even a film like *La Région centrale* (Michael Snow, Canada, 1971), which attempts to map the spatial and temporal conditions of a landscape through the purely mechanical dance of perspective, subtracts the human element entirely in what is a self-contained experiment for which no further variations seem possible. The so-called "nature film" is also a poor fit for landscape and even nature as I understand it, for it appears to hold primarily for the scientific documentation or exploratory investigation of the lives of other living creatures—insects and animals and the microcosms of ecosystems—all living *implicitly beneath* the species with the will and means to capture them on film in their natural habitats, as if these filmmakers were nostalgically recalling a more peaceful and primitive mode of existence so as to make us appreciate just "how far" we have come as the "master species."

There is a finer distinction to be made between landscape and nature: the former refers to an entirely human aestheticization and mastery of the latter, which is often described as inherently wild and perhaps untamable. Nature which prevails as idea, context, or even character in a small group of narrative fiction films ultimately resists the landscape category because there is a sense in which nature on film is out of control or can bring about a loss of control. The filmmaker of today can choose to set the story in nature, or bring some aspect of nature from the background to the foreground of human affairs, or proceed to involve nature in the events of the narrative by expanding the range of the diegesis beyond its specifically and sometimes exclusively human horizon—but as long as the story still centers around flesh and blood characters, as it often does, then nature will serve to *reinforce* their tie to flesh and blood. Even if nature appears to remain hidden on the periphery of an anthropocentric aesthetic without managing to assert itself back on its own terms, into the grandeur of its totality, human beings will always constitute but a single part of nature—perhaps an insignificant part, for all we know.[4]

At least three modes or *senses* of nature are possible in film where the goal is to bind human and natural space and signification:

1. The representation of the presence of nature—the range of life between earth and sky, light and dark, life and death—projected before us, just as it was when captured by the audiovisual camera, existing in space and transpiring through time, "nature" as that which exists for itself or *just is*.
2. The idea of nature as an immemorial and potentially infinite process of rhythmic persistence or flow—eclipsing the brief span of an individual life and even the epic span of human history as a whole. Such persistence typically assumes the form and feel of a neutral or faceless *indifference* towards the hermetic motives, collective machinations, and exaggerated seriousness of human affairs. This indifference will be magnified within cultures conducted in separation from nature or in contempt of nature.
3. The hermeneutic processing or "digestion" of nature via the expressive vehicles of language, metaphor, and myth—refinements of a mode of aesthetic consciousness that can also be seen to historicize nature and, if pushed far enough, to speak through it anthropomorphically.[5]

The World War II film *The Thin Red Line* draws upon all three of the modes described above and sometimes all at once. The film investigates the metaphysical conditions of nature through the lens of war by asking (repeatedly) whether the logic of nature, be it as sanctuary or battlefield, supports or rejects the human appetite for domination and destruction. The soldiers in the film question nature's "morality" in the full awareness that an answer is not forthcoming, only silence; and even if some sort of answer were possible, it would not be decisive enough to clot the incessant outpour of questions. Such elliptical questioning stems from the characters *and* the film itself, leading Malick to emphasize a branch of the third mode described above: a poetic, confessional, and obsessively speculative series of voiceover monologues from the main characters, all of whom are members of the American allied forces fighting against the Japanese during the Battle of Guadalcanal (1942–3). From start to finish, these voices rise and fall in an unguarded and deeply probing philosophical manner, which becomes essential for an understanding of the film's commitment to and convictions about nature *as* war, even more so than the film's sublime imagery. Voices with tenuous and often interchangeable ties to the soldiers in combat resemble the cacophony of nature sounds emitted by the restless jungle in the South Pacific, voices adrift like the wind or pattering like rain, with no clear point of origin or final destination, echoing within the great divide between solitude (what one voice calls "the coal drawn from the fire") and salvation (what another voice—or is it the same one?—calls "the one big self"). What may sound like rhetorical questions seeking certainty or consensus are best described as prayers seeking solace, for in a world without God, especially that of world war, there can be no absolute or definitive voice from "the above and beyond" to answer them with the reassurance of divine benevolence.

Instead of constructing an ambivalently enchanted or merely nostalgic vision of nature, the film, aided by this chorus of questioning reverie, summons nature into a position where various perspectives on it can emerge. In this sense the film does more than establish nature as a setting, opting instead to rig the snare of nature as a *provocation*, a snare which I will tentatively call "thought." As the source of the fountain of eternal soul-searching, as kindling for the spark of inspiration and spontaneous song, nature seems to put human beings in the mood to question, contemplate, and create, remarkably in the midst of humanity's darkest and most desperate hours. This complex and competing series of relationships between the various perspectives on nature in the film and the photographic or profilmic presence of nature itself weaves an elaborate and often entangled tapestry of philosophical conversations, a perpetual strife between the figures of language and those of nature, between how nature is conceptualized by thought and what remains unthinkable about it, and even between what is thought in private and what is said in public. In thinking nature, the soldiers inevitably "draw a line," but since it is the fate of these soldiers to stand on the brink of death and face the unthinkability of the termination of thought, they are the only ones in a position to cross it. More on this later.

The Thin Red Line is exemplary of what I have been calling a new metaphysics because throughout the film nature is perceived as sentient and alive on the condition that "God is dead." The soldiers' default mode of voiceover address, or prayer, to a higher unifying power is not "God" but "You." And this secular "you" is often in reference to the "many," as in the question "Who are *you* who lives in all these *many* forms?" The slippery syntax suggests that if there is a God, it is not to be found idling *behind* things so much as broken up *in* things both beautiful and terrible, juggled about in an endless sea of variation and repetition. The thick rays of sunlight in the jungle may initially evoke a quality of the divine, but eventually their frequency becomes so ubiquitous, if not banal, that whatever symbolic power they once possessed is all but drained away. This is partly due to the irony that these "enchanting" rays of light can reach us only when diffused through the trees, specifically through holes in the leaves eaten away by voracious worms (the same worms which decompose the dead and represent "hell" in the minds of the soldiers). Furthermore, there is no image in the film which attempts to follow the divine ray of light all the way up to its source in the sun, either through camera movement or cutting: beyond the light Malick finds only birds flying in circles, eyeing potential prey or juicy remains. And in general, there is no image that is not filmed from the position *of the earth*, even the most skyward. The higher one gazes "into the heavens," the deeper one's body and soul are tied to the earth. Thus Malick eschews the classic bird's-eye view of the war genre's notorious battle scenes, where the camera ascends only to look down in a spirit of entrapment or judgment. If there is a god-witness in our midst, or if conscience is personified as god-like, why envision it as *looking down* upon us? The temptation to view the horrors of war from this old metaphysical vantage point betrays the earth in our eyes and seals off the sky in our minds.

––––––

The questioning of/through/with nature implies that nature itself is a fundamentally "open question."[6] When films turn their attention from humans to nature, we may ask what exactly they are asking of it, what these cinematic gazes are looking for? What is being done to nature when its aestheticization prompts a shift from mere beauty to a deeper profundity? And then there is the matter of our gaze, what we as spectators are looking for when given the chance to look and listen to nature in this way. Before turning over to an analysis of *The Thin Red Line*, it is necessary to employ one of the main methodologies of this book and rethink metaphysical concepts which have returned anew in the moving image, in this case the transformation of the concept of "God" (or, in less religious terms, the "numinous") into "nature."

In the wake of the death of God, is nature's primary mode of appearance that of an *extreme indifference* to us, as some philosophers are inclined to believe? Simon Critchley, in his essay on the film, observes that "[N]ature's indifference to human purposes follows from a broadly naturalistic conception of nature. Things are not enchanted in Malick's universe, they simply *are*, and we are things too. They are remote from us and continue on regardless of our strivings."[7] This rather simple idea that nature in the film "merely is," that the impression we have of its persistent being-for-itself is a sign of its remoteness, making us feel withdrawn from a larger, higher, possibly enchanted purpose through the relative insignificance of our daily strivings, resonates with Stanley Cavell's more general conception of the ontology of film, particularly as exemplified in his response to Malick's purely cinematographic efforts in *Days of Heaven* discussed in Chapter Two. In fact, Critchley's idea that in Malick's cinema "things merely are" aligns quite strongly with Cavell, for, as we saw earlier, Cavell put forth the idea that Malick discovered how to acknowledge a fundamental fact of film's photographic basis: that objects participate in the photographic presence of themselves onscreen such that the drama of human affairs is reduced in significance the less it participates in affairs external to the world of the human.[8] Cinema facilitates this fundamental participation in a way that human beings may be tempted to withdraw from it, or exchange their own being-in-the-world for various illusions of how things might be or ought to be for them—and this is a criterion for nature appearing indifferent *to us* without being indifferent to itself. In other words, if we can say that the things of nature are such that they are turned towards themselves like nothing else, participating uninhibited and alive in their own aesthetic recreation on film, then the human being that turns toward itself succeeds only in isolating itself, cutting all ties with the fold of nature. What is self-manifestation for nature is self-isolation for human nature.

Another key influence which Critchley neglects to mention is the very one which Cavell mentions only once in *The World Viewed* and in passing: André Bazin. There is a particular moment from Bazin that is worth drawing attention to in this conversation on cinema and nature. When theorizing cinema as a medium which represents and communicates by way of what is real, Bazin collapses fact and fiction, essence and appearance, in the stunning phrase "dramaturgy of Nature."[9] I am still quite amazed by the capitalization of the word "Nature" in this context, as it draws attention to a similar distinction between the mimetic and metaphysical "directives" of the moving image which I have been thinking through. The bold capitalization invites us to ask what cinema's ontological relationship to nature is, even though it is not exactly clear what Bazin wants to mean (or what his English translator, Hugh Gray, thinks he means) by emphasizing Nature in this manner. Is the Nature of nature analogous to the Being of beings? The ambiguity is enhanced by the metaphysical aspiration of the concept as it reaches for something more fundamental than nature itself, or perhaps fundamental *to* nature itself. Given Bazin's silence on the matter, we are invited or forced to imagine what a *dramaturgy* of Nature might be. Nature both capitalized and dramatized does not immediately refer to the natural world or to the nature within our midst, residing within us; neither does it merely carry the connotation of human nature. Specifying the concept as dramaturgical in form suggests that we are not dealing with nature *as such*—human or otherwise, the oneness or separateness of things—but rather with a technical and aesthetic dramatization of that which remains, or is believed to remain, indifferent to or beyond the reaches of history, culture, and human consciousness itself. If cinema dramatizes nature (whatever that will turn out to be), it begins by extracting it unawares like a precious resource for the film to feed on in its own unique way of being. Such an extraction maintains that it is possible for a dramaturgy to be based not just *on* but *in* nature—fictionalization of fact, textualization of truth—such that what is most dramatic is also what is most philosophic: the *becoming* of beings on film. More specifically, the question before us is whether Bazin's dramaturgy of Nature entails (aesthetically, perhaps even logically) a filmic discourse not only set in nature but *beset by* nature and its unquenchable "system" of moral ambiguities, unleashed in the realm of conscience by the obstinancy of nature's indifference to morality. If you want to examine the complexities and contradictions of human nature, you can start by placing humans in the neutral laboratory of nature itself, whose hierarchy is a unity in which all beings prey and perish. Survival of the fittest belongs only to "the whole," and the whole is never complete, never settled in its ways. And so one must *choose* a way. In the laboratory of nature, the humans are at first out of place in surroundings indifferent to their strivings, but then, having been put in their proper place of insignificance in the grand scheme of power relations, they start growing into themselves, discovering themselves, performing themselves—dramaturgically. Those who seek to become bigger than they are are soon cut down, just as those who fear growth are soon stomped. This may be the only law/act of nature which they can ascertain.

Bazin's ontological leanings will imply that the turn towards nature in narrative film can be viewed overall as an attempt to turn towards the nature of film, or to *digress*. Deliberate acts of digression from a film's narrative obligations can function to honor, let's say, its original or primordial obligation to the roots of human dwelling, striving, and suffering—nature in all its beauty and ugliness, contingency and absurdity, banality and mystery. In that sense, such digressions from the human to the non-human deflect the subjectivity and self-centeredness that haunt both outward and inward reflections on nature. However, if a film digresses to the site of nature as a metaphor for its own nature, as return or retreat to the station of revelation and world-disclosure, there is no point at which it can be said with any certainty that it has found either nature or itself. Digressions by their very definition lack *telos*, which is why they inevitably circle back to the narrative from which they took leave, suggesting that narrative may be as fundamental as nature in this regard. Perhaps we can say that a digression from narrative (directedness) to images of nature (openness)—to images left in a more natural cinematic state, free of narrativity—will be ontologically present while epistemologically absent, like the meaningful pauses in between stanzas or chapters. Then a dramaturgy of Nature will not interrupt the drama so much as direct it back to the elements of drama, which may be, in fact, the "four fundamental elements" for films set in nature. As immanent as these elements are, this directing back to nature in a narrative structure as complex as *The Thin Red Line* can come across not as finding a place of rest or truth within the structure but as stirring an event or force that penetrates *from outside the structure*, even though it is the manmade structure which has been imposed upon nature in the first place and without which there is nothing to show or speak of. Such revelatory, if not dramatic, fresh air from the outside is impossible to generate without a taut matrix of narrative operations, and more often than not it is generally quite insignificant unless it strikes the camera's or a character's receptive consciousness to nature, as if receiving a call from beyond that resonates deep within.

That the dramatic presence of nature in films elevating this figure to the level of heightened and intrusive expressiveness is sufficient unto itself, that there is nothing at all to be said about the contents and qualities of nature woven throughout the fabric of a narrative because nature is that which *says nothing* to the narrative, is without a doubt a legitimate hermeneutic obstacle or fear in dealing with films whose commitment to nature equals or even exceeds that of humans.[10] Nature being the most central and arguably most powerful element in a film as rich in significance as *The Thin Red Line*, coming to know the film involves following it from the house of narrative (the comfort zone of meaning) to the house of nature, the latter subscribing to rules of narrative and meaning-making which are very different. What makes matters even more complex, the film's significance, upon reflection, seems somehow tied to the remarkable degree to which its depiction of nature renders *insignificant* the very war it labors to accurately reconstruct and, by extension, the storytelling conventions of the war genre of which the film—despite breaking with many of these conventions—is nonetheless a member. Filmmakers like Malick and his Russian elder Andrei Tarkovsky obsessively draw on nature almost as a rule and out of love; and they tend to downplay the thematic, symbolic, and mythical possibilities of nature by assuming that these associations are so abundant and clichéd that viewers can be counted on to project what is most meaningful to them if provided with sufficient ambiguity in the "nature text." I can also imagine that audiences who respond to this type of approach may have as little interest in forming straightforward interpretations of nature as the filmmakers do in offering explanations for the way they use or emphasize or privilege nature above everything else.

Later in his career, Tarkovsky did address his audiences more frequently and found that many wished to know more about the meaning behind the singular and recurrent motifs of nature woven throughout his œuvre. In his book *Sculpting in Time*, he offers the following explanation for his *inability* to answer such questions in a way that will be satisfying or useful to viewers and himself:

> Rain, fire, water, snow, dew, the driving ground wind—all are part of the material setting in which we dwell; I would even say of the truth of our lives. I

am therefore puzzled when I am told that people cannot simply enjoy watching nature, when it is lovingly reproduced on the screen, but have to look for some hidden meaning they feel it must contain. Of course rain can just be seen as bad weather, whereas I use it to create a particular aesthetic setting in which to steep the action of the film. But that is not at all the same thing as bringing nature into my films as a symbol of something else—Heaven forbid! In commercial cinema nature often does not exist at all; all one has is the most advantageous lighting and interiors for the purpose of quick shooting— everybody follows the plot and no one is bothered by the artificiality of a setting that is more or less right, nor by the disregard for detail and atmosphere. When the screen brings the real world to the audience, the world as it actually is, so that it can be seen in depth and from all sides, evoking its very "smell", allowing audiences to feel on their skin its moisture or its dryness—it seems that the cinema-goer has so lost the capacity simply to surrender to an immediate, emotional aesthetic impression, that he instantly has to check himself, and ask: "Why? What for? What's the point?"[11]

Tarkovsky resists the idea that the persistent presence of nature in his work must mean *something else* by dispelling the idea that meaning is what lies beneath the surface, a meaning concealed by the author as in a game of hide-and-seek. He goes on to accede, with remarkable conviction and to my mind quite convincingly, that nature in film does, in fact, have meaning, albeit one of a different kind that puts us in touch with "the truth of our lives," even if nothing can or ought to be said about what this truth amounts to. For him, nature can be seen to function in four interconnected registers that must become immanent to the individual experience of each viewer.

1. Narrative invitations to nature constitute a direct acknowledgment of the fundamental conditions of our dwelling on earth.
2. Natural surroundings infuse the narrative events with a palpable and unified atmosphere.
3. Attention to the unique, complex, and sublime details of nature resists a utilitarian approach to filmmaking and consequently a utilitarian or largely consumptive approach to spectatorship.
4. Poetic attempts to evoke the *feel* of the world as the original house of humanity, the house in which we acquired the language necessary to share our experience of being-here, boldly summon the aesthetic sensibility of the viewer to become immersed in the atmosphere in which the film world has been *steeped*, to use Tarkovsky's fine turn of phrase, thus enabling him or her to exercise the muscles and tendons of a pre-linguistic awareness.

Tarkovsky's exasperation at the clear symbolic use of nature in film is due in large part to the perceived misguidedness of the questions—Why?

What for? What's the point?—which can have no definitive answer if the filmmaker, as far as Tarkovsky is concerned, has done his or her job correctly so that the viewers may take over and answer such questions for themselves. What I take from a filmmaker's signature silence over symbolism is that such questions are not questions at all but rather hasty, flabbergasted, and ultimately defensive *reactions* against a film aesthetic designed to expose us to a rich sense of atmosphere and the sublime mystery of *this* world. Getting over this skepticism of the world in its own image requires not a mastery of film language or history, but, first and foremost, a "surrendering to an immediate, emotional aesthetic impression." In the grip of the sort of wild abandon that is triggered by aesthetic experience in general, the right questions regarding the meaning of nature realized for its own sake—and no less for the benefit of the viewer estranged from nature—are *unknown* until those emotional–aesthetic impressions have been realized in the same way, as active thoughts rather than passive reactions.[12] "Rain, fire, water, snow, dew, the driving ground wind …"—the elements of life combine into the familiarity of an otherness, a river of truth that flows through the discrete registers of narrative, character, theme, and context, irrigating the film world so that it may yield *living* meaning, both necessary and contingent, in the process expanding the viewer's consciousness while providing access to the unconscious.

Before nature can be cast and characterized in some sort of atmospheric way, it must be presented such that it can *present itself,* which requires that it be provided with a tangible space in which *to appear*—a compositional clearing, as it were, fit to be occupied with an exteriority whose power exposes (and perhaps overexposes) the film with life. And with such clearings forged and engaged, nature can indeed make an appearance, a grand appearance, in the narrative structure alongside more conventional or generic elements which can then appear, depending on their weight, as contrived or even counterfeit by comparison. What I call an appearance on the stage of a clearing is the condition for an act of emergence or interruption from beyond the limits of both character psychology and cultural worldview; and it is something, I believe, that narrative structures in general do not quite know what to do with and hence cannot contain or can *almost* contain. Elements of nature, as I have already suggested, tend to stand in opposition to narrative elements insofar as their appearance, admitted on its own terms as a singular event, will show no sign of concern or support for the events of the narrative—what I spoke of earlier as nature's indifference. While the elements of nature are, in theory, brought to the narrative from somewhere "outside" the narrative, as grass grows between slabs of concrete, in reality there can be nothing that stands outside the text proper that is not a property, however inscrutable, of the text itself. So these appearances appear not *from* the outside but rather *as* the outside—as an "outsideness" of radical exteriority.

Now it has always been a possibility of cinema, arguably its original possibility from which it has strayed, to let the world happen or let nature take its course. But, as a rule, *nothing* seems to happen, or nothing of significance, we might say, unless such happenings are in some way staged. A filmmaker can cultivate a setting into a stage for a dramaturgy of nature to unfold by expanding the stage of life in all directions, using montage, for example, to cut away from the world of the human to the world of the non-human.[13] In films featuring the metaphysical figure of nature, the shift from a human being to a bird or leaf, like the move from the human face to hands or feet, requires a cut from one to the other that carries the force, it seems to me, of a *call*. When called, nature is brought out of the narrative at the expense of narrative and linear time swerves into circular time or the void of timelessness; and if called clearly and frequently enough, the persistence of nature can become a substitute for narrative persistence, and the happening of the world is established as the very location and life of narrative, a metaphysical location whose coordinates are always in motion. In calling out to the whirl of nature, Malick is aided by his willingness, after Tarkovsky, to orchestrate many of these calls using the human voice itself, drawing from the art of poetry by having the characters speak in a voiceover whose privacy is typically restricted to reading or thinking in silence. By bringing the inner voice of the soul out into the open (into the place conventionally occupied by third-person literary narration), the film's calls to nature are reinforced, if not fully realized, by the soldiers' various appeals to it—to everything from nature as savior to seal of sinfulness; and through these disparate voices, which shine unbeknownst to their outer identities (spared the inhibitions of military masculinity), the soldiers can call out and sing to nature as *one*—"the one big self"—in search of a backdoor to paradise lost. The film conducts this song with zeal and ushers the way to the misshapen door, above which it reads not the "machine" but the *war* at the heart of nature.

III. A Cinematic Sublime

Film expands our conception of nature into something for which linear human time is senseless: recurrence as change. Our lives repeat or evolve, but both at once? The cinematic representation of nature is better attuned to nature as "recurrent change" than any human bias towards unquestionable progress, yielding images which "take after nature" by coming to presence while passing away, passing us by, growing and perishing untragically, entering and exiting life in the same gesture of being—*becoming*.[14] Such statements are meant to address the intuition that what we are likely to have in mind when considering the animated appearance or live eventfulness of nature in narrative film goes beyond a *mere picture* of it, for nature, in perpetually coming to presence and passing away, can also be said *to transform*. That which defines the appearance of nature in art, that which affords it artistic rather than merely contingent significance (indiscernible, perhaps, from insignificance—signification's *reprieve*), is equally irreducible, if not hostile, to affirmative words such as "beautiful," "ineffable," "true," even the very word "nature." It is as if these word-pictures have grown silent in the face of what they are meant to refer to, insofar as their reference disguises a complex valuation of the recurrence and constancy of "changeableness" that pushes language and common sense to its limits. So when nature appears as the *process* (metamorphosis) that it is, appears suddenly, intensely, and ephemerally within a film, it steps out of its static picture to wash over the characters (not to mention the spectators), steeping them in an atmosphere of change that renders the uncertainties of life more bearable, if not the very force which bears them up. Nature's "appearance" in this sense not only represents nature to the characters and viewers but also, and more importantly, *exposes them* to nature as something more powerful and unknowable than what they were prepared for (what mere pictures of nature could prepare them for). Because the elements of nature can be seen as turned towards their own existence, hiding within themselves and at one with the whole, nature is also, in a way, *exposed to itself*, and when this self-exposure or metaphysical exposure becomes the object of cinematic representation, with the aid of the camera's openness and sensitivity to time, space, and above all light, nature may come to presence poetically, as Heidegger might say, and appear more pure and alive than representation typically permits, more attuned to itself and complete in its parts. Cinema can show instead of know nature, or show its knowledge of "that which is" as an exposure to nature, to that which sustains us and whose power compels us to empower ourselves or give thanks to the gods. In movies, nature is unable to tell us how to look at it or interpret it, rather only that we see into it and *be seen*, and I find this to be the case even if filmmakers are looking for something more than what meets the eye—their look will be one of many.[15]

The way nature comes out of its hiding in film as an "exposure" compels us to pursue a finer distinction between two overlapping terms: *objectivity* and *exteriority*. To return to our discussion of landscape, this genre may appear to fall into the category of objective picture of nature; however, Lefebvre offers the following definition of landscape as a coming together of outside and inside conditions that I see as essential to the concept of exteriority as the basis for what I am calling *exposure*: "Landscape is a *form of being* of external space in our minds."[16] In my analysis it should be obvious by now that this form of being cannot bring external space into our minds without *breaking through* the mind, resulting in an exposure to alterity—and, depending on the case, an *overexposure*—for which the primordial figure of nature provides the ideal mixture of nearness and farness, sublimity and precarity, life and death. Nature as that which is intrinsic to itself—facing itself and changing itself constantly—is perceived not as "outside us" but as "other to us"; our distance and alienation from what is, or ought to be, so near at hand transforms what we perceive into a cypher for what can no longer be touched. Read in this way, nature is that which remains ironically *untouched* by our own grasping nature, insofar as we find ourselves *out of touch* with what binds us to nature irrevocably to the end of our days. The distance from nature is also phenomenological in that it turns out to be essential for an appearance to become both foreign yet facing, to mingle with manmade structures of knowing and eventually break through the self-preserving structure of consciousness, or at least startle this authority of consciousness as an unnatural gap between beings, a filtering lens or diluting liquid against the forces of alterity. What the forceful and contingent presence of nature might *mean* in the various organizational structures of narrative film, and how nature can be seen to participate in film as a narrative element of its own, expanding or refracting the narrative as a whole, hinges on the possibility of there being (a sense of) not just a world outside the narrative which the latter cannot account for or is blind to, but a pervasive sense of otherness and unknownness in which the narrative world—the film world—is steeped to the point of intoxication. This is the lost enchantment and possible reenchantment of nature as primal poetry to be encountered and undergone face to face, as in Tarkovsky's *Stalker* (briefly discussed in Chapter One), where free-form reveries of nature grow out of the main character's mystical love for the Zone, a place where respect for nature is restored to the harmonious hitching of thought and action, human consciousness and world consciousness.

For aesthetics as much as for philosophy, such cinematic dawnings of the mysterious otherness of the world in which we live will not always fall squarely into the category of the natural world or any readymade conceptual category, for that matter. And if they are to be structurally anomalous or even destructively vertiginous to the whole, then nature's "presence character" in film requires *more* than a fleeting digression followed by a return to normalcy. *What* normalcy after *transgression*? A greater force is felt to be afoot, shaking the ground and awaiting acknowledgment from *everyone*. In awakening us from the autopilot stupor of habitual movie consciousness, this film phenomenology of nature radicalizes exteriority such that it may be interiorized, and enlivens the world in its own image by the possibility of the world existing in the image of a transcendent being. It is here that the experience of nature onscreen—orchestrated according to tensions between what is most familiar and unfamiliar about the world as a whole, tensions exacerbated by a world which is also *no longer whole*—may come into contact with what I will call a *cinematic sublime*.

We can begin to comprehend the mysterious affective quality of this type of encounter, which involves a reorientation of spectatorial posturing via *disorientation*, by grounding it more deeply within the aesthetic terrain of the sublime as theorized by Jean-François Lyotard in his essay "The Sublime and the Avant-Garde," a text which I briefly discussed in Chapter One. A theory is built around an inexplicable aesthetic event or epiphany that, for all its transformative power, is hidden deep within the cracks of our everyday experience, ironically concealed by its sheer transparency and interminability. Lyotard understands the essence of the sublime as an aesthetic event whose occurrence is strange and estranging—a stranger to consciousness—for drawing attention to the fact of its own happening in "the now," over and above "the new."[17] Ostensibly inspired by one of Ludwig Wittgenstein's razor remarks on the mystical from the *Tractatus Logico-Philosophicus*, Lyotard writes of this primordial temporality in such a way that everything hangs on the substitution of a single word, or breath between words:

> That it happens "precedes", so to speak, the question pertaining to what happens. Or rather, the question precedes itself, because "that it happens" is the question relevant as event, and it "then" pertains to the event that has just happened. The event happens as a question mark "before" happening as a question. *It happens* is rather "in the first place", *is it happening, is this it, is it possible*? Only "then" is any mark determined by the questioning: is this or that happening, is it this or something else, is it possible that this or that?[18]

Lyotard restricts his analysis here to the instant and the avant-garde, specifically the peak abstractions of high modernist painting which eschew all forms of representation and narrative for the sake of variations of pure form and color. His main reference point is an appropriately unfinished essay by the abstract expressionist/minimalist painter Barnett Newman entitled "The Sublime is Now." Informed by the idea that the sublime is always an experience *of* the sublime, an experience defined not by *what happens* but rather by *that it happens*, there is a further line of philosophical reasoning that I wish to develop in preparation for my reading of the narrative structure of *The Thin Red Line* as a movement to and away from this mystically momentous nowness. If it makes sense to ever ask such a question (perhaps it is more applicable to art than life): *what happens when "it happens"*? If it is the case that the "it happens" breaks down the image and breaks through our consciousness of it, as I argued in Chapter One, why is such a break, for all its danger and damage, registered as an inexplicable type of cathartic relief or cleansing (for the film characters experiencing them and for us experiencing their experience)—the taut entwinement of pleasure and pain, activity and passivity, exposure and withdrawal, that is given the name *sublime*? The great event (call it mystical for the sake of a name, as long as we remember that the "it happens" happens before anything at all can be named) still provokes the ancient and elusive question, ceaselessly resonating, of the phenomenon of being itself—the nature of nature—privy to those beings for whom Being is a pressing issue and not a learnable fact, the Being of beings as Heidegger calls "it": Did *that* just happen? It *happens*?

The "It happens" of the cinematic as opposed to the painterly sublime is so fleeting, like an honest greeting immediately upended by the pressures of ritualized conversation, that it is difficult to register as mattering or even belonging to the film as a whole. A good example of this is the scene from *The Thin Red Line* discussed in Chapter One of the American soldiers crossing paths with a local native man—the former going to war and the latter, by the casual looks of him, going home. The flabbergasted expression of a panicky soldier, Private Dale (Dash Mihok), cues us or perhaps permits us to undergo our own encounter with the sublime, here in response to a ripple running through the postcard picturing of natural beauty, in other words to nature assuming a human form: the holistic and uncorrupted purity of the jungle manifesting in a man who can mind his own business, think his own thoughts, whistle a tune if he likes, and walk freely and fearlessly against the grain of the military machine of armed men bound in single-file procession to be swallowed whole. This man taking a stroll during wartime—for him, *no war*. Such events, by virtue of a kind of aesthetic imperfection or dangling incompletion, resist easy identification and assimilation in the first place, and as a consequence of this resistance they initially fail to meet the requisite criteria of narrative or thematic specificity and coherence. In narrative as opposed to experimental film, the former by its very nature buffering spatial presentness and temporal nowness, the "It happens" harbors the power to potentially interrupt or shock linear time, diverting the flow of meaning back on itself for a moment that suspends. The *breakthrough* moment in *The Thin Red Line* is part of a narrative structure that turns on itself and cuts a hole in time; the entire jungle otherworldliness for the soldiers seems echoed in the native man who moves towards them and us, entering and exiting consciousness unconstituted—and this is particularly amplified within a cultural context, specifically that of popular film culture, determined in so many ways (aesthetically, cognitively, hermeneutically, even philosophically) by the "What is happening?" imperative of art. Of great importance for us as a measure for what matters or what *can* matter in the realm of the cinematic sublime—where what matters most is what is most often missed, *just this* and *right now*—is the capacity for film to suspend or altogether lift its own narrative and thematic projects (in this case, the American war effort and, I would say, the American war genre), creating characters who undergo the "What is happening?" while simultaneously faced with the "It happens" and the markless question—intensified when what is happening is beyond belief—"Is *is* happening?"

As we know, after their encounter with the warless Melanesian man, the soldiers and the film carry on as if nothing happened. The difficulty of the "It happens" is too easily assimilated by the "What does this mean?" and "What happens next?" questions of narration. Film narratives are like moving trains which struggle to slow down and rarely manage to come to a complete stop— to catch their breath, to console their characters, to reflect on the past, to truly think about what has happened (that *it* happens). But carrying on as if nothing happened is also a way of describing *shock*. While this encounter with the local man is a minor shock compared to the combat they will soon brave, the soldiers do not seem to deflect the shock entirely so much as carry it inside them as extra weight on their backs to the front (they carry on knowing that they *could* turn back). The shock of the "it happens" is an initial awakening to complex forces of nature—possibly divine, always in conflict—that include the war itself as the madness of reason and nature's twist on peace. Cavell, particularly in his work on American or post-Pollock abstract painting and Shakespearean tragedy, might describe such an awakening in ethical terms as a transformative leap from knowledge to acknowledgment—except I would add that such experiences may jolt one into *beginning* in a state of acknowledgment and *becoming* ethically open without making a conscious decision to do so.[19] Exposed by nature's knowledge, the plurality and simultaneity of which constitute nature's unknownness, the soldiers in the film will appear by turns elated, dumbfounded, abhorred, enlightened, and calmed by what they experience, ablaze in a single feeling or splayed prismatically across a shapeshifting mood; and within the harsh and sometimes blinding light of such an exposure, to a shard of beauty with sharp, terrorizing edges, they are as children facing what you might call "a first" rather than simply "a fear." (Death makes children of us all, and the fear of it can be consoled, it would seem, only by the elderhood of the dead. The dead—those who have *accomplished* death—are "metaphysical heroes.")[20]

In *The Thin Red Line*, the experience of exposure is specifically *to nature* as the vexing inseparableness of life and death. This constitutes a kind of double exposure that confounds the self, unhinges it, and in some cases completely annihilates it (the self no longer recognizing itself, new yet not necessarily improved). In the film the human tie to nature's vexed law is felt to be precarious (in need of reinforcement) or suspect (in need of permanent severing) or absolute (in need of practical realization), depending always on the personality and worldview of the man behind the uniform and the soul behind the man, so to speak. But all these various and competing ties to nature are, above all, direct exposures to *being in* nature and not being able to escape its light. In nature, the American soldiers are simultaneously at the heart of Home and very far away from the home they all wish to return to. To fight a war on behalf of one's country *in another country* entails being uprooted from one's culture and displaced into the uncanny zone *between* cultures. This too is nature—the unowned and contested field of battle where the soldiers, to quote one of many writers who wrestle with the film's complex sense of war, "encounter finitude in its rawest sense."[21] Nature appears where cultures clash, at the border where culture dissolves into young men fighting for their lives, seeing themselves reflected in their appointed enemies. To fall back into nature and awaken past its threshold, drenched in its humid heart and liquid interaction of life, is like arriving on another planet that belongs to no one and cannot be mastered. On the other planet that is Earth, life pours in. Those who dwell there (and die there) are shot through by rays of light, warmed by the blood of being cascading between bodies. Picture light streaming in, flooding the small aperture of a being qua being, and burning a hole or setting aflame rather than forming a perfectly recognizable impression of the world outside—as if every ray of light were drawn together by a magnet and entered us in a swift, solid blow, clicking into its rightful place, throwing our concepts, squaring us to the earth, bristling the oxygen in our veins, pulling the earth from under our feet like a rug, and scrambling our rote sense of what the everyday world is like; all to bypass or asphyxiate the screen-filter of consciousness—to rattle the cage of consciousness, or better yet to play the musical instrument that is consciousness, a string for every sense.[22]

———

The term "exposure" is equally applicable to the medium of film and the human mind.[23] For the former, the recording of images on film or by digital means depends on a technical process of exposure based on specific standards of optical visibility and perfected by the art of mechanical reproduction—an automatism of sight. An image can be overexposed or underexposed, made too bright or too dark to see by, but done correctly (which is its own artistry) the right amount of light in space and length in time will expose the materiality of the medium beyond recognition, albeit for the sake of a greater recognition—the world in its own image. If the medium itself, being intrinsically photo- or sensor-sensitive to the world through light, can be described as *ontologically impressionable*, then it is also, by definition, susceptible to under- and overexposure. Whereas underexposure blots out parts of the image or sometimes the whole image in swathes of darkness, overexposure overwhelms it—sometimes burns it—with excessive light too hot to handle. Now in what I would call the "psychology" of cinematic exposure, when the human figure appears on film it is doubly exposed beyond the criteria of the visible, for the mode of appearance of the human is already one of exposure: self-exposure. A cinematic exposure of a face exposes a face that is exposed to itself—naked and confessed before the camera "I"—a double exposure involving both mechanical and mental registers of consciousness. While an actor may temper or try to thwart his exposure through a timid or false performance, it is still always the actor—the real person—who stands there exposed by the camera eye-I, and this exposure as conditioned by the cinematic apparatus constitutes a brink of vulnerability that constantly risks *overexposure*. There is nowhere to *hide* in a film. It is then possible to say that film mechanically exposes people who are, in varying degrees, psychologi-cally overexposed; and if these people are professional actors, which is often the case, then the characters they portray—it does not matter who they are or what, if anything, motivates them—are born from this deep pool of light and these raw pangs of presence that mark a "double-exposure" far more pristine—too pristine, perhaps—than the murky superimposing of images typically associated with the term as a cinematographic technique.

The Thin Red Line is exponentially built out of such overlapping overexpo-sures insofar as the film exposes itself to war, exposes its actors/characters to war, exposes the environment to war, and exposes *us* to war. Any film about war must in some way be *at war with itself*—a cinematic battlefield of beauty, truth, and terror. And when this battlefield belongs inextricably to nature as the territory which belongs to no one (indifferent to all claims of ownership except its own *claim to be*), then war is both mirrored by and at the mercy of the greatest battle of them all: *life*. As a film about/of/at war, it is replete with such transformative exposures that engrave the skin of mind and body: men destroying men; men witnessing the destruction of men by men; men and women in synchronized longing from distant corners of the world; survivors who look the world in the eye as if for the first time, finding everything and nothing to live for; and last but not least, dread over the two deaths—the unimaginable death to come (gently rapping) and the all-too-real death itself (barging through the door). The unlucky soldiers on both sides of the struggle are indiscriminately blinded by the sight of death and unhinged, one by one, by the imminence of their own mortality (mere gasps away from the promise or complete futility of immortality); and depending on the person behind the uniform, they are repulsed or perplexed or enlightened—and sometimes all at once—by the power of nature "whose death captures all," as one voiceover ruminates in hushed tones. A death that captures all *captures life*, a metaphysical alchemy that rejects the false view that death is a failure or flaw in the fabric of being. Instead, death is form, light, love, and life itself—the ultimate overexposure.

Long stretches of the film are composed almost entirely from intense successions of cinematographic and psychological exposures and overexposures. Peak overexposures to death (also known as trauma) stand side by side with revelatory overexposures to life. Pleasure and pain, ecstasy and agony, can have similar faces, each testifying to transformations in consciousness that rumble as deeply as the bedrock of human identity—transformations to the core, as it were, that shatters a character's self-image as if a grenade went off in their subconscious sleep, never to awaken the same **(Figs 4.1, 4.2, 4.3)**.

Some overexposures in the heat just before, during, or after battle reach such feverish boiling points that certain characters are no longer recognizable by the actors who play them, suggesting that these actors have managed to expose themselves too, above all to the sufferings of their characters through a complex mixture of technique and intuition, acting and non-acting. And sometimes, given the uncontrollable chaos of war and the levelling effect it has on human agency (not to mention how the various hierarchies and complex bureaucracy of military operations reduce all individuals to faceless pieces in a game), as soon as a character is introduced we are hard pressed to distinguish him amidst the mangled pack of fear and trembling known as Charlie Company. We simply cannot with any ease find the key markers of difference among the anxious and fearful, the common ground of the soldiers being so precarious that it envelops them all in the raging pulse fueling both courage and cowardice. Identifying with these characters is not only difficult but impossible at times, at least in any conventional way, for what we want to call their "identity" is either in transit or physically coming apart at the seams. One soldier in particular, Sergeant McCron (John Savage), in a handful of short yet powerful scenes, descends into madness after witnessing the deaths of all twelve soldiers under his command. The most vivid of these scenes shows him agonizingly scrutinizing the name inscribed on his dog tag in a desperate attempt to recover a self that for all practical purposes no longer exists **(Figs 4.4, 4.5)**. It is as if we come to know these characters at their most *unknowable*, for as infantry or "frontline" soldiers they stand at a critical existential juncture in which their sense of self dangles on the precipice of one of the most wretched experiences of mortality imaginable.[24]

Together these exposures/overexposures as I have been describing them *expose the film's own gaze*, dislodging its unidirectional fixations and disorienting its hawk-eyed view of the story world, causing it to lose track of its narrative itinerary, which is only ever legible from "the ledge" of a stable sense of omniscience that the film forsakes right from the opening shot of a crocodile descending into a swamp, as if luring the film to join the murky waters and

Figures 4.1–4.3 *Faces exposed like sensitive celluloid:* The Thin Red Line *(Terrence Malick, USA, 1998).*

hold its breath alongside a dormant beast. Forgetting the names of characters, masking the profiles of star actors, wandering about the jungle in a contemplative and sometimes nervously pacing manner; summoned into reverie by inconsequential details like marching to the front, swimming in the ocean, or

Figures 4.4 and 4.5   *Total overexposures:* The Thin Red Line *(Terrence Malick, USA, 1998).*

just an abandoned fishing boat rocking in the waves; branching off into the great distances, measurable and immeasurable, between the human, animal, vegetal, and transcendent spheres of existence with a single cut; and going so far as to reach out to us, the audience, with strangely accusatory words ("Is this darkness in you too?"; "You're in a box—a moving box."), which expose us in turn … —the film's gaze is as perceptive and insightful as it is blind and dumbfounded and disoriented. Taking in, and taking to heart, the brute entropic chaos of war, the terrors and traumas endured by the film become over time *steeped* (again, in Tarkovsky's sense of the word) in the primordial brew of a higher redemptive truth—a possible order or secret to the chaos of war. But the substance of this truth (if that is what it is) is not lying in wait as explanation, justification, or even redemption. Rather "the truth of war," if it is not to become mere compensation for unanswered suffering and unspeakable injustice to human solidarity, is one which the film finds, albeit gradually, at the threshold of its falsity. Let me be clear: war is hell. Susan Sontag was right about that (and most things).[25] But the hell that is war is set, here at least, in heaven. What is more: the hell that is war *makes* heaven on earth: camara-derie, empathy, heroism, sacrifice, nature as our lost paradise where the soul is made flesh. Heaven on earth (nature) contains within it flashes of hell, and hell on earth (war) contains flashes of heaven. Man is at war, nature is at war, but together, somehow, they are at peace.

I have proposed that nature be thought of in relation to this film (and also film itself, though I realize this may be untenable) as dangerously sublime rather than innocuously beautiful, a mysterious force *to be faced* rather than a textual figure to be read. To describe streaming light or pouring rain or the wild stares of animals as "forces" is to say that they have the power to rend reason, to cause breaches in the *culture* of human consciousness. What the film refers to in its metaphysical preface as "the war at the heart of nature" suggests that nature is not neutral, not non-confrontational, and thus speaks to a situation where politics plays out within nature as if the latter were a sports arena of sorts, a space in which all the participants, large and small, are entangled in jarring collisions of beauty and terror, peaceful unity and adver-sarial competition, and, of course, life and death. In this widest of arenas, survival is best described as a necessity rather than a victory, unpunctuated by celebration or complaints. (Things merely are.) How, then, does Malick's emphasis on the beautiful natural environment of Guadalcanal, where all the film's battle scenes take place, square with the equal emphasis on the relentless and often ugly exposure of the soldiers of Charlie Company to the harsh reality of death at every turn? A preliminary answer arrives through the character of Private Witt (Jim Caviezel), a demoted and undisciplined soldier who appears to behold everything around him—life and death, order and chaos, good and evil, individual and group—with open and adoring eyes. He declares his worldview early on, practically introducing himself with his pseudo-philosophical beliefs, by insisting to his superior officer, a cold-blooded nihilist with a secret spark of humanity, that there is "another world," as he puts it, to be reckoned with—another way of looking at the sur-rounding death, destruction, and dehumanization of war non-cynically and perhaps even with a redemptive humility. Witt takes inspiration from both his mother and mother nature here: a well-kept memory/reverie of his mother perfectly calm on her deathbed, with the sky for a roof and an angel holding vigil, is unlocked by his time/timelessness spent with the indigenous peoples of the Melanesian islands, a life in the lap of nature which he admires and par-ticipates in while AWOL from Charlie Company. This Westerner's romantic notion that people who live off the land must be "of" the land or one with it, with nature, is checked by a brief yet significant conversation across the language barrier between Witt and a woman, also a mother, who contradicts his observation that her children never fight by replying, "Sometimes when you see them playing, they always fight." Conflict underlies Witt's vision of "indigenous paradise" and, more importantly, conflict is the key to the supreme calm he values, for without it the children are restless and the exhaustion of night eludes all living beings. With insights derived from both past and present experience, Witt sees, or thinks he sees, a calm in death and, if you will, a death in calm—a harmonious strife in the natural order of things where life and death are posited as one and the same process. Through the gaze of Witt, with which Malick identifies more than any other gaze, the war at the heart of nature—if it can be called a war at all, perhaps the word "war" can be differently intoned—appears as an organic and self-sustaining war that is vital to the persistence of life as a thriving, striving, dancing ordeal of death. Nature "naturalizes" whatever paradox prevents us from participating in this process ourselves, as equal parts of nature which power the whole beyond insight and comprehension. The big picture, as General Quintard (John Travolta) puts it, is something we will never get a complete grasp of. (And this impasse may also extend to the big picture of the film itself.)

The other war fought in nature (World War II) is historical and political, at least on the surface, and relatively manmade, though Malick would ask us to consider whether manmade in this case necessarily means unnatural. Obviously, the reasons behind this or any war are manifold and complex, and perhaps, as the military commanders in the film suggest (though they can hardly be objective about it), there is something natural or inevitable about the war instinct as a metaphysical condition for the renewal of peace. However, peace as the spoil of war is not world peace, far from it, but rather peace for the victor's vision of how the world ought to be (theirs). The film invites us to bear in mind that the victors who authorize wars do not fight them on the ground; for them survival is equated with posterity, with a utopian picture of plenitude and power beyond the reach of present-day sacrifice. Nothing less than the securing of property will guarantee the livelihood of this hypothetical tomorrow based on the preservation rather than the diversification of a particular strand of the species eager to sow more seeds. If nature's diversity never sleeps, humans, on the other hand, sleep all too soundly in their respective camps. Incredible, often reprehensible, and sometimes utterly insane measures are taken, by individuals and nations alike, for the sake of tomorrow and tomorrow's flood towards a vision of the distant future to ensure a sound sleep, for it seems nothing can soothe such a restless state of mind save for the ideological lullaby of domination, regardless of how "inclusive" such an ideology pretends to be. Human nature and metaphysical nature part ways, at least on the issue of war, given the former's tendency to dominate its own kind and the latter's acquiescence when subject to domination (the secret behind nature's projectless diversification). Nature is not weak in this regard but indifferent and anarchic, especially when it comes to systematic *negations* of difference.

One must be exposed to the cinematic sublime in order to read its wilderness of contradictions. In the case of *The Thin Red Line*, we are exposing ourselves to a film that is equally concerned with the life/death of metaphysical nature and the unnatural/natural death of human nature/culture at the hands of war. The film's exposure to its own subject releases questions, and the viewer's exposure to this flood of questions prompts interpretations, which can also flood the mind with equal force. Is the nature perceived via exteriority and exposure perceived *as* natural by the soldiers, filmmakers, and us, the viewers? Can nature be called "natural" as a surround for the *unnaturalness* of a species self-destructing? Is nature on some level responsible for such chaos? How much responsibility can *one person* take? ...[26] In a film where the fighting soldiers encounter nature as frequently and fervently as the film itself seems to do, there is an important distinction to be made (whether or not the film explicitly or even implicitly makes it, and whether or not such distinctions are conceivably clear-cut when it comes to movies) between nature as perceived by men shadowed by their own unfathomable and untimely mortality, and nature as it is sought *from behind* the mechanical (that is, immortal) camera, whose disembodied gaze can undergo extreme overexposure—bearing the full brunt of witnessing—without losing consciousness, as it were. Committed to being inside the fiery midst of hell-on-earth battle, the film also summons the necessary composure to attend to the plight of all the soldiers (a seemingly impossible task), taking the full measure of responsibility—an automatism of responsibility—by including the parallel predicaments and pain of *both sides* of the conflict. While the war may be narrated and exposed from the point of view of the Americans, once the Japanese are revealed behind their weapons and camouflage, the film loses all sense of a victor, as though each item in the rising death-toll bore a concentration of soul strong enough to tip the scale of justice off its delicate moorings. In this way the film embodies the constant threat of mortal interruption in a gaze that can be described as not only overexposed but *overwhelmed*. Here I am drawn to two complementary first-person point-of-view shots during the film's second major battle scene featuring a merciless raid by the Americans on the Japanese camp: the first shot advances upon a Japanese soldier in a state of surrender, and the second, stationed behind a Japanese firing position half-buried in the ground, jerks in response to a fatal gunshot delivered by an American soldier, as if the camera-eye/mind/body were also struck down. In both shots, the gaze of the film does more than identify with the winning and losing sides. Each point-of-view is internally split, enacting both victory and defeat, power and powerlessness, life and death, simultaneously. While each shot appears to embody a distinct perspective, both, in representing the victor, seem to empathize with the loser. Both "shots" let us feel the wrath of the Americans from their perspective and that of the Japanese whose perspective is being obliterated. In showing what it is like to be on the winning *and* losing sides of a battle, the film ends up recording a *double loss*—losing its dignity in the first shot and its very life in the second shot. The film, of course, is acting here, using the immortality of its camera character to vicariously experience the full cost of war: loss of life for those who lose and loss of soul for those who win.

This overwhelmed gaze (overwhelmed by a responsibility to death, regardless of who, even of what) often bears the mark of being lost, panicked, and stricken, and sometimes it just does not know where to turn when confronted by excessive pain, monotone shock, inflicted suffering, hot artillery, and the abrupt descent into death's unknown (what Sergeant Welsh (Sean Penn) refers to simply as "madness"). Lost and at a loss, the film's gaze can appear to cope with these horrors by *turning away* from them in reciprocal horror but also hope for redemption. And what it finds in its turning-away towards earth, horizon, and sky is the *site of nature*, which is presented as being what it is, spoken of as dying in order to live, and mythologized as the ineffable irreconcilable saving-power, perhaps to the point of ecstatic glorification **(Fig. 4.6)**. While there appear to be two distinct angles of nature at work, one connected to the soldiers and the other to the perspective of the film itself, cutting many of its images in half, as it were, nature and its presence as a non-human character are always in close proximity to the soldiers for whom death is an always lurking and likely possibility. It is *through them*—their shock and longing, peace and distress, love and hate, clarity and compunction amidst the tragic fist of war—that the film is able to experience nature up close and as a sight for sorest, saddest eyes, begging for signs that this

Figure 4.6   The camera's skyward supplication: The Thin Red Line *(Terrence Malick, USA, 1998).*

war—and possibly war itself—is somehow "natural" and "justified," even if the principle which governs it is not for them to know and smacks of lawlessness—at least then the casualties of war are "for a reason" (however cruel) and not "for the madness of powerful men" (whose cruelty is in vain). On top of that, the uncanny nearness of nature is amplified by the soliloquy-like voiceovers of the soldiers, which, taken together, filter it through a collective consciousness or unconsciousness and into a cacophony of unanswerable questions and questionable answers, both of which are inescapably stifled or foiled by the limits of human language when faced with (the metaphysics of) war. All this leads me to believe that the metaphysical gaze of the film and its automatisms of nature are unequivocally linked with the frontline soldiers in mutual solidarity—shooting images instead of bullets.

IV. Metaphysics of the Front

I have been describing the film's signature stream of voiceovers as a choir-like camp whose members strike different tones yet are nonetheless interchangeable with one another. This couldn't be further from the truth. There is a *lead* voice that leads us to and across the front. Most of the voiceovers in the film are spoken by a soldier whom we cannot readily identify once all the main characters have been introduced. He is given surprisingly little screen time and is altogether omitted from the film's pivotal battle scenes, though as a standing survivor at the end of the film it is implied that he fought along with the rest of the company (how *well* he fought we don't know, nor are we apt to care at this point). Malick's decision to appoint a peripheral character to the position of lead voice has thrown many commentators astray, resulting in lines of voiceover from this relative unknown being misattributed to the characters they are visually juxtaposed with onscreen. But these are honest mistakes, for the character chosen to deliver a significant portion of the film's metaphysics via voiceover is introduced only briefly near the beginning and does not return until after the battle at Guadalcanal. So, who is he and why is his character so deliberately minimized? Who speaks this gentle voice which speaks on behalf of the frontline soldiers, representing what Witt calls the "one big soul"?

In the first scene in the ship before the American soldiers land on the beach, we are introduced to a young soldier confessing to Welsh his extreme fear of death as simply unimaginable for someone who has the whole of his life to look forward to. Welsh and a group of soldiers are washing up in front of a row of mirrors, composing themselves, deflecting their fear with a familiar routine, choosing cleanliness prior to their encounter with death (the possibility of both killing and being killed). Welsh, looking unimpressed and quite frustrated with the young soldier's open display of cowardice, asks him for his name. He replies with his *full* name: Edward B. Train. Private Train (John Dee Smith) is compelled to state all three parts of his name as it might be etched on a gravestone. When Corporal Fife (Adrien Brody) overhears Train exclaim to Welsh, "We're all probably going to die before we even land," he immediately drops what he is doing (brushing his teeth) and flits his eyes back and forth in a rush of trepidation, instantly catching the cold of Train's fear confession. They are all full of fear, naturally. In fact, the entire scene in the ship revolves around how the soldiers cope with their fear: some use fear as fuel for hate, others manage only to don the mask of hate; some sit quietly with a calming activity like whittling or reading (probably rereading) letters; some try to sleep it off while others turn their bodies to the wall, walling themselves off from the world of war; a reckless soldier plots to steal a weapon for added protection and does so, but the weapon, ironically, is never brought out in combat and is never referred to again (he got by without it). Train, then, is the only one—and perhaps one of the youngest—who is brave enough, foolish enough, in his fully justified fearfulness to speak aloud what the entire company, including Welsh, is thinking and feeling in private. His is a loose tongue, tied more to his heart than to his mind, wise only in its spontaneity and transparency, in the way in which his "train of thought" speeds through his words and even outruns his words. As viewers we may also share this widespread fear and find relief in Train's child-like honesty. At the risk of giving Malick too much credit here, perhaps during these brief moments Train earns the right to speak on behalf of everyone who cannot or who refuses to acknowledge his vulnerability and fear. And it is as though the film nominates him to do just that. Through voiceover, his fear is transformed into a fascination with a world on the cusp of slipping away, into a sense of faith, too, that there is salvation at stake for everyone, a "new world" pressing through the pores of fear. But if death becomes us, only for the fear of death to unhinge us, then, as Wittgenstein reports from his post on the front, that is the fault of a false view of life. The false view, as I understand it, is the projection of a self with everything to lose, whereas the truth is that there is nothing at all to lose, hence nothing whatsoever to fear, if the only thing deemed to be worth losing is the self and all it might gain—the self as a clockwork morality of self-preservation via acquisition. At the end of the film, having spoken on behalf of the one big soul, Train addresses, as if for the first time, his own soul, now filled with courage and light. The whole film could be read as the journey taken by the sick soul of fear to the one big soul of peace, though such a reading would have too little to work with as far as Train's character arc is concerned. We must work with what the film works with and gives us and that is *nature*, albeit refracted through a prismatic hierarchy known as the military, or the dark side of human nature.

Sunlight through the trees, a hill covered in tall grass, a crocodile in a swamp, rosy-fingered dawn, a wounded bird, a face in the earth …, nature is *everywhere* in the film, side by side with war, like a river flowing through sheets of metal. The combat world of the film is cupped by nature or, as Tarkovsky prefers to say, steeped in nature. Malick begins and ends with images and sounds of nature and such images are woven seamlessly, ceaselessly throughout the near three-hour running time. To a certain extent this is to be expected since the entire film is not only *set* in nature, but unlike the earlier *Days of Heaven*, it is forcefully *beset* by nature at every turn—nature's question, as it were. The philosophical reveries of various soldiers, especially Train's, also directly concern nature. The opening line of voiceover from Train asks: "What's this war at the heart of nature?", and the closing line, also from Train, declares: "All things shining." (This final line, while not an answer to the film's opening question, is significantly *not* yet another question. The film gets somewhere: from metaphysical questioning to a three-word declaration inseparable from the metaphysics of the moving image. What shines other than the sun and moon?—All things which *pass through* this thing called "the mind.") As the film's metaphysical nature-narrative unfolds in tandem with the military project of the American soldiers—who land on the island of Guadalcanal, advance through the jungle, reach the hill, and win the battle against the Japanese—it gradually becomes apparent to everyone that nature, hovering in the background of linear and calculated warfare, is, in fact, deeply imbricated within the collective horizon of the soldiers rather than romantically or nostalgically cast away to the remote regions of such a horizon as a crude symbol of salvation or grace. This horizon, however, is equally fraught with a fear of death devoid of the abstractions and anxieties of objectless fears: it is a confrontation *with* death because it is a *real* fear. Now, just when absolute fear is primed to deal its own death-blow of blindness, it is at this point of extreme encounter, of complete physical and psychological disarmament, what I have been calling overexposure, that *nature appears*. In making its appearance from setting to situation and from background to foreground, nature collapses the distance from life that comes with the absence of any meaningful awareness or acknowledgment of death. The place where soldiers kill and are killed is not referred to as *the frontlines* for nothing, for it is here— literally and figuratively as befits imaginary lines, call them borders—that the soldiers, on their own or in groups, are exposed to the core of their being, their consciousness emptied of everything non-essential. Experiences associated with the words fear, pain, terror, hope, hate, anxiety, compassion, love, truth are undergone in a flash. And the nature they see amidst these flashes of insight (can insight be intrusive?) is not the nature we see, for "we see" while they *are seen*—the site of nature is also nature's "sight." They are not in the position, basically our position, to experience nature safely (aesthetically) from behind the barrier of a camera or screen or body or consciousness—a position fundamental to most conceptions of nature, perhaps even the very idea of nature itself which the film rethinks.

The opening section of *The Thin Red Line* features two AWOL American soldiers, one of whom is Witt, living in fairytale harmony with native Melanesians who are represented for the most part as naturally attuned to nature.[27] Witt sees them as a part of nature and sees himself as a part that has broken off. He is actually a part of Charlie Company, "my people," as he calls them, yet from whom he has fled seemingly in search of paradise. He is accused of running away from his duties to the war effort, but we can say in his defense (for he does not defend himself on this point) that he is desperate to dive into the war at the heart of nature. After this extended opening sequence, Malick jarringly shifts over to an American warship, where we first learn of the "false harmony" from which Witt attempted escape and perhaps, deep down, all the soldiers experience in different ways as soul-destroying: a rigid chain of command/hierarchy of power that seems to recede endlessly in all directions like one of Kafka's infinite regresses. On the deck of the ship, Colonel Tall (Nick Nolte) is preparing to carry out the obliteration of the Japanese position atop an intricate series of hills, and he is instructed by his commanding officer, General Quintard, to do so "without mercy." After expressing his admiration for Tall, who has chosen late in his career to lead a battalion in the war rather than land a cozy and "clean" office chair, Quintard reminds him that the Admiral (played by nobody—a hopelessly high-up and therefore utterly offscreen figure) will be watching the entire battle from afar, intimidating him further with the political and perhaps religious maxim, "There's always someone watching, like a hawk." With this threat Tall visibly loses his tree-like uprightness, wobbling into a skeptical self-consciousness at the thought of being watched and evaluated every step of the way by an authority eager to replace him if he fails to act in the best interest of the war. A strategic and unhesitating sacrifice of the soldiers who will carry out all the fighting is deemed the only viable path or acceptable "method" to victory. The analogy of the hawk resonates with the notion that those who have power over others are in the "privileged" position where they can *see without being seen*, remaining all but invisible and even invincible in comparison with those whose lives are actually on the line.[28] This is one of the many rungs of power operant within bureaucratic hierarchies, and the radical asymmetry it creates belongs to the very essence of power—what it means to *have* power (often at the expense of others). But if the Admiral is a hawk, then Colonel Tall is certainly no rabbit or mouse, for he holds his fair—or perhaps unfair—share of authority and control over those directly beneath him. When the fight for the hill ensues, Tall will station himself significantly behind the frontline battalion where the canons are, and from there gains a clear view (a wide shot) of the entire battlefield through a pair of binoculars. Of particular interest to him is the next link in the chain of command, a Captain Staros (Elias Koteas), to whom he ferociously (ambitiously) delivers his strict military orders by phone once the fighting commences. Admirals observe the progress of colonels and colonels observe the progress of captains and captains observe the progress of privates, with whom the command chain comes to an abrupt end, breaking off like a precipice and opening onto a frontline frontier where the power relations and perceptual logistics of the military machine dissolve into a violent storm of confrontations beyond the reaches and reason of even the highest hawk, perched too far back to see anything at all **(Figs 4.7, 4.8, 4.9, 4.10)**.

Amidst its sprawling coverage of the "two wars" (among humans and within nature), the film's gaze is aligned from the beginning with the American troops, hence with the frontline, even before the fighting begins. The film itself seems to *hesitate* on the threshold of the bloodshed and death-toll demanded by the war genre, delaying the inevitable horror the soldiers and viewers will face. When Colonel Tall orders Captain Staros to attack the Japanese position atop a series of hills by full frontal assault, the platoons begin their slithering advance through the tall grass in broad daylight, stopping at the base of the hill to receive the Captain's orders, which are, of course, a relay from the Colonel who also acts on behalf of a higher authority, that of the General, and so on. As we will see, the chain of command moves further and further away from the frontlines with every rank, leaving the soldiers to fend for themselves. The appointed leader of one of the platoons has received his assignment (for which he will be responsible yet by which he will be given a possibly life-saving degree of separation from the front), to locate and eliminate all hidden strongpoints of the enemy, and with this all members seem to be ready (as ready as can be) for the attack. But the daring frontal assault is not launched just yet. Without an official order or instruction from above, there is consensus that the attack will not commence until the next morning. While this may be standard military procedure, or just the common sense/decency to begin a difficult and decisive task first thing in the morning, Malick makes a conscious decision to unfold these idle, calm-before-the-storm moments in vivid detail. For the rest of the day and a full night, the film "waits," passing the time and holding onto these death-free moments slipping through the waist of the hourglass, with the knowledge that these precious hours are pressing to a point in time after which nothing

Figures 4.7–4.10 *Stops along the military chain of command on the way to nature:* The Thin Red Line *(Terrence Malick, USA, 1998).*

will be the same—a turning point, as we say, but not so much in the plot of the film as in the lives of its characters, who represent, after all, real people, many of whom perished in the historical Battle of Guadalcanal. This deliberate act of narrative hesitation at the threshold of war opens the film up to an embrace of fading light, rising silence, and cool air—ideal conditions for the solitary contemplation (here without voiceover accompaniment) of various members of the military machine who, regardless of their position, are free to let down their guard and face themselves for what may be the last time. The interlude sequence is constructed as follows (and in such a way that it can be easily overlooked if viewers are too anxious for the war/action to start):

1.   A slow panning shot from behind Staros, who stands alone in a field, surrounded by tall grass and a perimeter of trees.
2.   A telephoto shot of a small island in the distance that seems majestically reachable by canoe, awash in a soft blue twilight glow.
3.   A not-too-tall mountain gently backlit by the setting sun, with gray–pink clouds dusting the peak.
4.   Back to Staros, now shown head-on as he scans the horizon, perhaps trying to envision tomorrow's battle or, given his orthodox background, looking for some sort of "sign" (he moves his head at about the pace of the camera in shot #1).
5.   High-angle closeup of Staros praying intensely by candlelight in a space too dark to register clearly onscreen (it could be inside a tent, but it may as well be the space of prayer itself—a single fragile light surrounded by a void). Staring intently into the flame, he asks "Are you here?", then pleads "Let me not betray you; let me not betray my men. In you I place my trust." This prayer is intercut with closeups of the candle's thin flame flickering in the wind or from the whispery breath of prayer or—who knows?—from a response to the prayer.
6.   A calm river stretching towards a set of hills in the distance.
7.   A swirl of gray–pink clouds (looking like a river of clouds after the previous shot) juxtaposed with Tall's voiceover (the only voice we hear in the sequence) describing them in the Greek words of Homer, which he then translates into English as "rosy-fingered dawn" for the sake of Staros, to whom, it turns out, he is speaking (he knows Staros is Greek but assumes, probably correctly, that he might not comprehend *ancient* Greek). Rosy-fingered dawn is a very fine English phrase, and Tall delivers it with a grandeur befitting the occasion.

As a whole, this nature interlude opens the film widely enough to discover a connection between the passion/desperation of in-the-dark faith in an unnamed or forgotten deity and the luminous beauty of the Guadalcanal environs during the cinematically sacred periods of twilight and dawn. It is interesting that during the overnight waiting sequence we are given the distinct perspectives of Staros and Tall in their respective contemplations of nature, be it through poetry or prayer, since they each hold relatively fortified positions of power that will protect them from the real dawn of nature forthcoming on the frontlines of battle. Given their positions, both characters can perceive nature in a somewhat sentimental manner as something innocent, beautiful, mysterious, inviting, and completely non-threatening. And, of course, that is perfectly "natural" because, on top of their lack of anxiety over their own deaths, they have yet to be threatened in any way; the military plans are still freshly laid, uncontaminated by contingency; the commanders above them have yet to err (Quintard proudly remarks that the Marines have done their job, so now it is time for the infantry to follow suit); and no lives have been lost under their command (not a single drop of blood spilled). Furthermore, the film's own gaze, which up to this point has preferred the poetry and philosophy of the natural world, has yet to face the war at the heart of nature *as conducted by man*.

In the conclusion of his essay on landscape in film, Lefebvre turns to the concept of nature as territory, stating that "The definition [...] has the advantage of illustrating the 'possessive' character of territory which contrasts with the experience that one can make of space in terms of aesthetic contemplation."[29] I would like to apply Lefebvre's useful distinction to the nature interlude described above by suggesting that, at this moment in the film, nature is *not yet* territorialized. On a map it is, but in the consciousness of the soldiers, it is not. We can say this because nature is aesthetically perceived and contemplated with the poignant knowledge that, once fought over as property and bloodied with sacrifice, it will no longer be present, not to mention beautiful, *in and of itself*. But at the same time such an "unpossessed" experience of nature appears to result in little more than images *of* nature (rather than, say, nature in its own image)—static compositions and postcard beautifications which conceal as much as they reveal. For instance, the point of view of the infantry soldiers is conspicuously missing from the tense pre-war wait, as opposed to the scenes on the warship in which an anxiety utterly alien to the likes of Tall and Staros prevents the soldiers from enjoying the view of the rolling sea through the portholes beside their beds. What are they doing on the last night before battle? Are any of them admiring the beauty of their surroundings or gazing up into the heavens for support? Perhaps some of them do, but we have no way of knowing what the soldiers are thinking or doing in what may be their final night on earth, and this is significant. The higher authorities who direct rather than fight the war can look at nature and derive from it military or religious inspiration, whereas the soldiers, whether they view it this way or not, when it comes time to fight in the morning will be (and they know it) *forced into nature*, so deeply that the very distance required to perceive and interpret it collapses. The static picturesque image of grassy hills (one of the film's few establishing shots) is destroyed, formally speaking, once the soldiers are unleashed upon it in ant-like droves. Now the traditional picture of nature is seen in a new light of close shots, quick cuts, and rapid camera movement, dispersed across a hill which has been transformed into a deadly obstacle course. The resistance imposed by the steep incline of the hills becomes menacing, yet the tall grass provides excellent, almost angelic, camouflage. The once lovely invisibility of the pinnacle from which the Japanese forces rain down bullets has revealed itself to be akin to a volcanic eruption, yet the ridge layers are so pervasive that one is left unguarded, allowing the American soldiers to take refuge and rest—and think. The safety of the ridge allows an untouched Colonel Tall to come join them, and as bombs continue to drop just behind the ridge, close enough to obliterate them all, he is the only one not to flinch—because for him the hill is still just a hill.

How else does the film understand what it means to experience nature *from inside of nature*, framed by one's powerlessness and the sudden urgency of one's mortality? Consider a soldier during a brief stoppage in the battle for the hill, a soldier whom we have not seen before and, as far as I can tell, do not see again. (Overexposure can befall anyone at any time.) As he takes cover beneath the tall grass, watch him reach out to touch a single leaf that, to his surprise, folds up like a pair of butterfly wings pinned together by a drop of glue **(Fig. 4.11)**. It is tempting to read the human touch as poisonous here, or the worlds of nature and man as magnetically irreconcilable. But regardless of how we read it (or how we read the soldier's vaguely dejected reaction),

Figure 4.11   *Nature recoils:* The Thin Red Line *(Terrence Malick, USA, 1998).*

the closure of the leaf seems to me a candid gesture or gasp from nature, expressed in its own terms and in a language all its own. The moment echoes a later scene after the battle where Witt pours some water over a large jungle leaf, only to find, to his astonishment as well as ours, that the water speedily slides down the leaf as if it rejected the water on which its survival depends and of which it is largely made. At first glance this is yet another instance of nature recoiling from the human touch, but it is unlikely that the soldiers who experience nature up-close and from-within would describe it this way, or describe it *at all*. Witt is fascinated and delighted by this plant whose leaves let the water "roll off its back," leaves no thicker than skin but just as protective. Of course, everything in nature is protected, wears a shield of sorts, but this is a side of nature we have not seen before, in the film or anywhere in Malick's previous work. Nature reduced to beauty and tranquility fails to factor in nature's *armor*, which is apparent all the more to those who wish their skin were as thick and sharp as some trees. Contra Freud, the only thing in nature that appears to live physically unprotected is what we call "mind." The mind's lack of a barrier in its mechanisms of defense against the world and, above all, itself is unnatural and precarious, setting up the human condition's proximity to madness and possible descent if the mind becomes misshapen by the hands of trauma. When struck by trauma, the mind is drilled so deeply that the window of the face can become permanently sealed—a fate which befalls many of the soldiers on both sides of the front. And a face tragically shut down in this way is not a shield but a sign that whatever protection the mind could provide was betrayed, ironically, by its impressionability, by its susceptibility to exposure, by its capacity to absorb new experience and learn by it, changing in the process. Sadly, sometimes the only lesson to be taken from the *worst* experience is how to best avoid its recurrence.

Overprotection is also a problem in *The Thin Red Line*, and in its own way equally perilous. Let our grammar show us how: those who possess power are often described, without judgment, as being *in* power. Being in power is a privilege and a protection, yet it is also an *isolation*, a hermetic ensconcing within a position, a role, a fate really. In the film such figures can be identified through the statuesque gait of standing, observing, and commanding. (Everyone in the army, in fact, is capable of this action, or inaction, in certain moments, regardless of their status.) We see them looking on passively— and ironically, quite powerlessly—through binoculars and communicating indirectly through telephone. The price of power is a loss of *proximity*: Tall and Quintard and the phantom Admiral are all kept at a safe distance from the threats—but also the truths—of direct exposure and the possibility of overexposure as they direct the action of combat in a manner eerily reminiscent of a film director. To be distanced from the film's site of exposure is to be distanced from the reality of death—the most difficult and elusive of all realities—and into a position of relative ignorance, despite the wealth of military "intelligence" required to attain such elite positions behind the frontline. Such intelligence ought to know something about death; the truth is that it wants nothing to do with it, hence nothing to do with truth, just power.

Captain Staros represents an interesting case in that he genuinely carries the burden of responsibility for the welfare of his men, carries it deep within his soul as the previous praying scene suggests, rendering his position in the chain of command more precarious—even torturous—than we might have thought possible, especially given his relatively elevated status. As captain, it is Staros's job to witness head-on, in what he plainly describes as "suicide," the very deaths he orders on behalf of Tall (but also of his own volition since he is free, though not without penalty, to defy Tall and eventually does)—to *bear witness* to death from just outside the clutches of death, just far enough back from the frontline, where he is adequately (of course, not fully) protected from the brunt of enemy fire. In this way Staros is overexposed by the sight of death without having to face it in the flesh. This strategically measured arm's-length position exposes him less to the possibility of his own death than to the *responsibility* for the lives of his men (as in, grammatically speaking, "his children"), who, upon his command (albeit reluctant command), find themselves "cast by an external force into the mouth of a death machine."[30] Now he wouldn't want that fate either—who would?—but what he *has* instead is the basis for moral–spiritual death. In other words, his experience of death is reduced to the guilt in *bringing about* death, including that of a teenager, while deprived of the very possibility of his own death—the Heideggerian being-towards-death exemplified by Witt's existential aspiration, inspired by his mother's graceful deathbed demeanor, to be able to meet his fate when the time comes with a deep sense of calm, like a lake on a windless day whose reflection makes a world. If Staros discovers he is unable to emerge from the fog of guilt, he will become someone for whom the irredeemable terminus of death itself is fair punishment, as opposed to (though such a comparison is anything but fair) life everlasting.

In the world of this film, which is, above all, the world of war (no matter how beautiful the background), the more powerful someone is, the less visible they are (visible only to themselves), hence the more isolated they become and estranged from nature—from both the natural world and their own human nature. Those with power exceeding their measure "play roles they never conceived" (confessed by Tall via interior monologue). In directing the war rather than fighting it, upper-rung figures like Tall and, to a lesser extent, Staros are cut off from the *real* war, the war at the heart of nature, and suffer for it, paying the price of spiritual desolation (Tall) and spiritual desperation (Staros) **(Figs 4.12, 4.13)**. The Admiral is *so* completely removed from the film's sense of reality that he is not even represented as a human being at all. Mentioned only by title and described as someone who rises with the dawn, he emerges in our imagination as a sort of god-like overseer for the American troops, who must look like tiny chess-size pieces each with their own programmed assignment, or toy figurines that topple over with ease and are gathered up for the purpose of keeping score. Is such a man so effaced by his own aura of power even eligible for admittance into Witt's "one big soul that *everyone* is a part of"? Soulless in this sense, the Admiral stands perched on a tier of iron with an ideal view of the "theater of war." Cue on the soundtrack a high-pitched voiceover monologue that might begin with the obscene and laughable exclaim, "What a beautiful day for a battle!" It would be delivered with either a noxious pride or a counterfeit romanticism to convey the irony of an act of showmanship coming from a mere spectator who knows not what he says.

Figures 4.12 and 4.13   *Tortured souls cut off from the war at the heart of nature:* The Thin Red Line *(Terrence Malick, USA, 1998).*

Power is not only a condition of those too powerful even to be seen. It is a fundamental feature of hierarchies that each rung on the chain of command, regardless of how low, constitutes a separate microcosm with its own internal law and chain—and the closer it is to the front, the more lawless and loosely it dangles, the more fragile and altogether arbitrary such power relations become. Particularly in the midst of the chaotic enterprise that is war, links snap and are reinforced in the blink of an eye and laws are rewritten in pure action and blood. Soldiers rise and fall in spontaneous bursts of bravery ignited by conscience or madness, or some intoxicating combination of the two. According to Paul Virilio, in his bold cross-examination of war and cinema, "[*T*]*he history of battle is primarily the history of radically changing fields of perception.* In other words, war consists not so much in scoring territorial, economic or other material victories as in appropriating the 'immateriality' of perceptual fields."[31] To this I would add that films about and of war (a distinction I believe to be worth stressing) are capable of dramatizing such appropriations while simultaneously undergoing the perceptual *transformations* that can only be described as immaterial with some hesitation. The Admiral, Tall, and Staros remain, like us, *viewers* of war: we all may be shocked or moved to tears by what we see, yet only those stationed on the frontlines— that is, only those who attempt to push the line forward (as in a game of North American football)—find themselves in a position and a place where the fields of perception and power are in constant flux.

After a maelstrom of consternation and strenuous soul-searching over Colonel Tall's decision to launch what will be, for the Americans, a deadly frontal assault on the hill occupied by the opposing Japanese, Charlie Company faces the long-awaited and undoubtedly dreaded moment of first blood (dreadful even for those who long to draw blood)—the living proof that the war, World War II as it is written in the headlines and history books, is *their* war, their *lived experience*. As the troops hesitantly ascend the first hill, lurching through the tall, parched grass, Lieutenant Whyte (Jared Leto) abruptly signals to the platoon in his command to lie low, transforming like magic a hill swarmed with soldiers into a vacant and untrodden landscape. Crouched beneath the grass in seamless camouflage, an intensely focused yet overzealous Whyte impulsively orders two soldiers lying on the ground about ten yards ahead—on the very edge of the frontline—to blow their cover and venture up the hill into the unknown. After exchanging vibrating glances of excruciating alarm, this unlucky pair heed the command and begin their doomed ascent. They journey up there like two space probes sent to explore a foreign and dangerous land, fated never to return, sacrificed for the sake of knowledge; or like two feet gradually dipped into freezing cold water so the body-brain may gauge the threat of exposure and shirk back if need be. (Are feet expendable?—Of course not.) Whyte, a soldier with relatively little or minor power in the grand scheme of the American side (not sufficiently powerful to be *under*exposed), now finds himself tucked behind the frontline, observing the outcome of his decision—*his*, it would seem, and not Tall's or Staros's—with unspeakable intensity and trepidation. Staros, who finds himself stationed behind the entire battalion directing the attack on behalf of Tall (who is another full position behind, like a full stop in cinematographic terms), observes the suspenseful scene through binoculars, a camera-like device that foregrounds his inability, from *this* position, to see it with his own two eyes. (Filmmakers, too, can use cameras to see what would otherwise be blinding.) In this sense, Staros sees the action precisely as "a scene," the one we too are watching as nothing more than a scene, or an action scene in genre terms; and for both him and us, to be able to monitor, adjust focus, and perhaps painfully relish the dynamics of this unfolding horror from behind glass or screen has the consequence of limiting any significant transgression of distance (physical and psychological), a distance maintained by the abstraction of sight from the body that bears it. In this context, to see unseen is akin, as Witt remarks in voiceover, to a piece of coal drawn from the fire. The self is born as an island cools, deprived of yet also spared the fires of universality. Of course, such distances and schemes of surveillance are, like our very own systems of belief, never as full proof as they seem: the two soldiers dispatched by Whyte are suddenly shot and killed without warning by enemy fire so well hidden that it is as if the hill has its own safeguarded set of eyes from which deadly laser beams are launched. The victims are seen perishing from the point of view of Staros looking through these glasses, a view which becomes ours as well; and almost in that very same moment, as a reflex of his agitated and cumbersome humanity, he quickly removes the device from his face in a gesture of disbelief that "the show" is really happening and isn't just a movie or nightmare or practice drill—and we too may undergo a similar reality check. Malick then returns to the closeup of Whyte, who witnesses the whole incident—the first blow to bodies and morale—with his two *naked* eyes. First, he blinks, rather his eyes blink, and then he shakes his head, rather his head shakes—he is like a turtle without its shell, a child suddenly gripped by the feeling of being lost in the woods. He can barely sustain the triple impact of the sight of death, the closeness of his own death, and the responsibility he now bears for the two soldiers who died on a whim—his whim. Embarrassed in the most debilitating, guilt-ridden sense of the word, he drops his head, absorbs the undeniable event like a fresh sponge, and quickly tries to recompose himself, to wring himself dry for the war which is about to rear its ugly head.

With the stable, somewhat scripted viewing positions of Staros and Whyte instantly uprooted, shot through and shattered by the all-too-real sight of death, nature makes its first major appearance at the front and in tandem with death, bringing the action to a halt and dramatically influencing the course of events. A gust of wind (an evolved and exaggerated version of the background breeze from the Lumière film *A Baby's Dinner*) stirs the tall grass beneath which the two bodies lie dead, as if they found their final resting place and are one with nature now. Above, the clouds part and release a wave of light over not just the dead bodies but the entire area where the American soldiers have attempted to conceal themselves. Revealed indiscriminately by the high-noon light, this seemingly sinister interjection of nature affects all the soldiers equally and in one fell swoop, allowing the Japanese forces the full advantage of seeing their enemies like sitting ducks, whom they now strike without mercy in a storm of annihilation. The Japanese are fortuitously aided by this raid of sunlight, this massive bomb of exposure which rips the links in the chain of command, overexposing all members of the Company as dwelling on the same level of extreme vulnerability and mutual flame-fragile mortality. What begins as a sublime event or even a mysterious sign of grace or guardianship from above—light breaking through clouds in the wake of first blood and illuminating a hill destined for the sky—ends up turning the American soldiers in, rendering them asymmetrically visible to the enemy **(Figs 4.14, 4.15, 4.16)**. They are thrown out into the open, where there is no longer any place to hide from death: a *thrownness* that repeats the agony and ecstasy of being born, an *openness* where human beings are exposed as the mortal creatures they are (dangerous to each other despite their capacity for friendship and love), a *radiance* which measures the individual flame within the bonfire of an unfathomable whole and deems it pale. The dark lining of this golden light from above exudes both heavenly pathos *and* hellish malevolence. One may be tempted to say, metaphysically, that good and evil are at war in this death-dealing light, and that this war is the very heart of nature whose blood courses through all living beings—but it is not clear who is who or which is which because, well, these great forces appear to be working together and for the same inexplicably paradoxical "purpose." The continuum of light and dark may be the only "thing" for which manmade divisions (even the thinnest of lines) are useless; even the smallest of increments can be divided *ad infinitum*. No concept will help us to settle the paradox that light and dark are betrothed, each inhering in the other's bosom. If we want to press on and say "light is grace," then we are bound by the familiar picture of humans as the beings who have fallen from grace yet for whom absolute light is deadly, as it is to the dark underworld of the vampire. Whichever way we look at it, the sun and the cloud which covers it redeem and condemn *simultaneously*, such that any god—even godlessness, call it the devil—lurking behind this metaphysical

Figures 4.14–4.16   *Nature's metaphysical interjection in the war:* The Thin Red Line *(Terrence Malick, USA, 1998).*

battle between light and dark would have to flash both a tear and a laugh to save face.

After Staros bears witness to the numerous casualties caused by both military and metaphysical powers, Tall orders yet another dangerous frontal

attack, orders it from far behind the frontlines, of course, so far behind
that he is forced to stare through a long pair of binoculars and rely on radio
updates just to keep up with what is going on, not to mention who is dying
and how (such details are beyond his *professional* comprehension). Over the
phone Staros maintains that his men cannot take such a suicidal position,
and he ends the heated dispute by bravely, if not heroically, refusing to obey
Tall's order. We saw Staros witness many soldiers perish in the first attack,
including one of the youngest (whose final words, "Oh, Captain," could be
taken as an expression of bewildered condemnation directed at Staros). He is
not about to betray his men a second time. Refusing to rescind the order, Tall
ferociously and contemptuously declares that he will make his way to where
Staros is hiding, behind a ridge with what is left of the company, including
his intention to take into account any "extenuating circumstances" which
he might have overlooked from his insular perch of power behind the line.
What interests me here is Tall's solitary walk through a smoldering battlefield
towards the frontline and how Malick depicts this movement as a stream of
consciousness which flows against the grain of willful conquest. Tall climbs
down from his seat of power, only to carry it with him as he rides the open
path cleared by his troops. Accompanied by Captain Gaff (John Cusack) who
trails behind, they march through clouds of smoke issuing from the aftermath
of the horrendous battle we have just witnessed. The fresh aftermath, which
ought to supply plenty of vivid evidence of the bloody consequences of Tall's
merciless military strategy, is almost completely obscured by the smoke,
which also obscures his vision as he wades through the wreckage. Before, the
sun picked out every blade of grass, whereas now it is impossible to imagine
grass ever growing again. In vain, Tall glances about the smokey white abyss,
spinning around twice as he walks and looking back, however briefly, for the
first time in the film. The veiled battlefield with its black blood and guts is a
kind of psychological aftermath, a personal hell if you will. On the deck of
the ship, when General Quintard asked Tall how much he desired to win this
battle and claim the prize of valuable territory, Tall responded with a hint of
cynicism and humility: "As much as I have to." But it now appears that he
underestimated his own ambition and pursuit of glory for its own sake, which
led him in his most reckless decision to press on without sufficient water
for his men. Success without *any* compromises can leave a bitter aftertaste
of ash—vanity. Tall's somber voiceover begins: "Shut up in a tomb. Can't
lift the lid." Should I be criticizing Tall for causing so much death when he
himself is already dead? Sauntering quite casually now through the smoke,
knowing that nothing will touch him and, as the price for this alien sense of
invincibility, not being able to touch anything around him—this metaphor of
being shut in a tomb is quite apt. Witt's coal drawn from the fire has started

to decompose. Welsh's dismissal of the entire military as "a moving box" has besieged Tall, and perhaps Welsh too: power buries you alive and promotions add another nail in the coffin. Tall's passage through the smoke is vividly echoed later on, in a terrifying scene leading up to the film's second battle sequence where Charlie Company moves through a thick cloud of fog in the jungle towards the Japanese camp. Here, their inability to see transforms the fog-eclipsed jungle into a monstrous personification of the enemy as bullets from beyond flash by like rabid teeth. One gets the feeling that if Tall were by their side in the fog, he would gladly take (on) a bullet to prove a point, rather than watch them whip by in utter disbelief. Tall's problem is not just that he can't lift the lid off his own tomb—he can't despite the fact that it has been shut from within.

Upon arriving at the frontline to reprimand Staros, Tall embodies a metallic skin-thickness befitting his underexposure to the chaotic climate of war and its random showering of death from above. As I mentioned before, a shell explodes mere yards from the position of the remaining soldiers, causing everyone, including Staros, to cower in fear, all except Tall who does not so much as flinch. I could accept his refusal to react to such a threat as an old-school tactic to further secure or polish his authority, demonstrating his immaculate courage and sending a message to the soldiers that fear is a counterproductive and debilitating *decision*. Nevertheless, I find it quite striking, even frightening, that he is so completely unfazed by this brush with death, as if his being were incapable of responding to danger—lacks this all-too-human instinct—because, at least on the surface of his character, he is the image of single-minded purpose oblivious to everything else, or because, beneath that surface, he has not been exposed to serious danger and will not be (this being his "first war" as someone who has studied and trained his way to the top). His tomb and its firmly shut lid deny him access to the vulnerability of his own body, which is, after all, whether he likes it or not, the foundation of his mortality, the roots of his "tallness." Tall's fearlessness may also have its source in the weakness of an ignorance pointed out by Staros: not knowing what it feels like to have someone die in your arms. (Tall looks long and hard at Staros at this point, digesting this gap in experience and saying in his silence, "True, I don't, and wouldn't want to. If I were the kind of person to do that, I wouldn't be here. Which brings me to my question: Why are you here, Staros?") So, without any battle scars or traumatic wounds to his credit, Tall may stand as tall and unflappable as his name suggests. When, at rest after the second battle, he finally does open his eyes to the war, appearing to awaken to the consequences of his actions in the war—the existential poison that is war—it is almost too late, seeing nothing but the tagged bodies of American soldiers and the few remaining undestroyed objects in the Japanese camp before a wave of emotion *almost* overtakes him. Holding it back at the last second springs only a small leak of feeling yet seals his fate as his own gravedigger, the one who holds down the lid from inside his spirit tomb. For Tall, power is all but blinding, the extent of human ambition is falling in line, coveted distances blight the death which captures all, and the path to clarity cuts through intimacy—a faith in others which he squandered long ago: "All I might have given for love's sake. Too late." Should he ever change his mind, or his life, a change of heart may not be forthcoming.

　　In conversation with Staros, lecturing him on the folly of military soft-heartedness, Tall carries himself to the conviction that nature is at bottom "cruel," rationalizing war as an extension of this metaphysical cruelty. But nature is cruel because he *wants it to be*; it is his calling; it is his *nature*. When we first encounter him on the ship prior to the battle, he reveals through voice-over this truth about himself, something deep *within* himself to be concealed from all his professional interactions and perhaps from himself as well once he steps into the commanding role of a colonel: that this cruelty of nature which belongs to him has leached into the marrow of his soul, resulting in a man "dying slow as a tree." A tree may stand tall and still be dying, its roots underground shriveling into a closed fist. He is suffocating in the open air. Tall might say, "My soul has been crushed by the *politics* of war, the real death-machine." The brain as opposed to the mouth of war never stops justifying its own madness, never stops obsessing over what Quintard keeps calling "the big picture." And when Quintard offers his diagnosis of the hierarchy of power in which a figure like the Admiral does his "fighting," complaining how difficult it is to remain "upright," Tall, who agrees, knows that there is no such thing as an upright dead tree. It merely appears that way.

————

In war, the frontline is where the opposing sides meet for the first time and for the last time. The soldiers on the ground who constitute and negotiate this "line" are face to face with each other, facing what philosophy calls (too conveniently, if you ask me) "the other." The bitter irony of hands outstretched unto strangers is that here they go for the throat when they are not holding guns and grenades. There is no better dramatization of the horrors of same-species otherness than the figure of "the enemy." The enemy is the figure whose otherness is held against him and used to identify him *as* the enemy, serving as not only the motivation but the very principle used to destroy him. Perhaps this tragic experience of alterity is more characteristic of face-to-face warfare, whereas with developments in artillery and especially the advent of guns, the otherness of the enemy retains a degree of inscrutable mystery, the long-range weapon throwing the face out of focus, creating comfort zones of annihilation that sidestep the complexities and contingencies of the face-to-face encounter. Lacking a face to see or speak to, the enemy-other can assume an almost mythical monstrousness or uncanny ghostliness. That a soldier may be killed even if he surrenders unconditionally, waving his humanity like a flag for all to see, suggests that the flag of the face is illegible from the great distances of the gun, or altogether invisible from the bomb's remote or top-secret space of detonation.

Fighting to the death, both the Americans and the Japanese are past the point of no return. Borders are in motion. There is no time or space left for negotiations; "kill or be killed," the law of the jungle peers through the human law once again. In addition to acting as the site from which the call of the other can best be heard, the frontline, as I have suggested, is where nature makes metaphysical as opposed to romantic appearances. If the overly powerful are blind to these appearances, if only because they are nowhere near them and so cannot be blinded by death, then logically the criterion for their emergence as presences is *powerlessness*, specifically over one's fate. Most of the shots of nature in *The Thin Red Line* are quite fittingly taken near, from, or slightly past this decisive, contested, and mobile line (the very line, perhaps, from which the film takes its title). And I believe this explains why the great majority of these images are not wide-angle landscapes but closeups (of trees, leaves, grass, birds, insects, light, and so on)—fleeting, jagged, out of place or placeless.[32] In the wake of battle—where survivors discover that they have become both victims and murderers, where the moving lines of combat come to a standstill to act as a shroud for the newly dead—the human other on the other side and the otherness of nature spanning both sides crystallize into what Robert Silberman calls the film's "moral climax."[33] I am not sure such a moment should be labeled at all, perhaps only described, and I am not sure it can be effectively described either without slipping into an analysis in which labels abound. Nevertheless, he is not wrong.

At the top of the battle hill lies an extreme closeup of the face of the enemy and the face of the earth, fused together. A young Japanese soldier, dead and half-covered in the dark, dry, bombed-out ground, buried by the cold–hot chaos hands of artillery, his face perfectly flush with the surface of the earth, staring back at us with the peacefulness of a plant, putting a face on nature itself as that which binds all living beings. Witt—the romantic soldier seeking reentry into paradise, whether among the indigenous or Charlie Company, whether in a culture rooted in nature or, like his own, a culture rooted in warfare—stands above the face as if paying his respect to the deceased in an open casket, gazes down stiffly and intently, calmly and with extreme concentration. For such a contemplative sensibility as Witt's,

susceptible to poignant bouts of wonder and reverie, this "earth-face of the
enemy-other" is the longest he looks at anything (except the Japanese soldier
holding him at gunpoint and pleading with him to surrender near the end
of the film, though perhaps the length of Witt's stare here turns completely
inward by virtue of the dawning of his own imminent death: he *must* remain
calm). This complex image, which Witt sees only after it has been firmly
established for our consideration/contemplation, possibly as a moral climax,
feels like the longest shot of "nature" in the film, without a doubt the heaviest
and most vexing **(Figs 4.17, 4.18)**. The smoke from battle and trees ablaze
(the same smoke that before obscured Tall's perception of the battlefield)
wafts in and out in spurts, concealing and revealing the earth-face by turns—a
moving expression of the Japanese soldier's half-shut or vaguely open eyes.
Not solely an image of the natural world or a closeup of a dead person's face,
this sublime and dream-like aberration combines both in a deeply haunting
and profound, puzzling way. It is as if the figures of human-nature and non-
human-nature have become two rivers of time flowing in opposite directions

Figures 4.17 and 4.18   *Witt studies the earth-face of the enemy-other:* The Thin Red Line *(Terrence
Malick, USA, 1998).*

on a collision course—caught in the last instant by the film image into which both empty and become one. I am inclined to say that this image enacts the "discordia concors" of metaphysical poetry in its wild welding of opposites, scrambling philosophy's Great Chain of Being into the circle or perhaps the spiral that it is. When Malick follows this image with a stark low-angle closeup of Witt's probing gaze, looking as if he is trying to peer beneath the stony lids of the soldier's infinitely inward eyes, we can comprehend, if not share, his paralyzing obsession with the face and the futility of turning away satisfied with having properly seen and understood it. I think many viewers (and Witt, too, is a viewer with aesthetic consciousness) can find themselves staring just as hard—restlessly and inconclusively. The Japanese soldier's earth-face is hard to see, as in "hard to accept," let alone to decipher a viable meaning from. And yet, as difficult as it is to see/accept, it is almost impossible to look away/deny.

This is what we and Witt see and can't see, but since seeing is such that it can point to the world without describing anything beyond its surface, stabilizing subject–object relations while casting shadows over the other senses, let's shift sensorial registers in this scene and ask what is to be *heard*. Of equal importance and the more challenging in significance is the emergence of voiceover at this profuse juncture, adding more layers to an already overburdened (overexposed) image. This voice without body, like Witt's body without voice and the Japanese soldier's "face without face," injects another gaze—not so much from offscreen as, let's say, from "inscreen"—a soul-gaze with provisional ties to the metaphysical interiors of the two present figures: the dead yet spirited soldier from beyond the world, and Witt himself, who is still alive in *this* world yet seems to be openly awaiting his own death, holding a secret sense of calm that gives him an almost reckless form of courage. Now, if we listen carefully to the voice without attaching it solely to what we see, we will "see" that it does not belong to either face involved—Witt or the nameless soldier—but rather to *Staros* and his questioning mode of prayer: Staros, the softhearted captain who arguably has the hardest time coping with the war, crumbling under the weight of lives lost for "the greater good," so much so that he accepts his irrational dismissal from Tall as the only safe road back to civilized justice. As a spiritual surrogate for the dead soldier, his voice pours out Judgment Day-type questions, seemingly on behalf of the stoic earth-face image: "Are you righteous? Kind? Does your confidence lie in this?" Malick has singled Staros out, calling upon him at the threshold, summoning him from a literal army of inspired voice poets scattered throughout the film, whose medium is the excruciating silence of the living intertwined with the dead. The absolute silence of the dead and the living's failed comprehension of the dead—the dead's silencing of the clamor of the living—come together in the gentle voice and weighted words of Staros for reasons which are not very clear, or are about as clear as Malick's decision to appoint Private Train as the collective voice of Charlie Company. But Staros is here and speaks for a reason even if Malick is not fully in the know. Perhaps being banished from the war on the grounds that "nature is cruel" (in other words, "too cruel for you"), allows Staros to pronounce judgment on human nature's share in that cruelty. This doesn't mean he isn't capable of any cruelty and has no stake in power and its price (he is a lawyer, after all); rather it can only mean that he derives no unwavering sense of purpose or pleasure from their whipcracking effectiveness in reducing the various courts of human life to miniature battlefields.

Staros's voiceover as an inflection of the earth-face—filling the gap or diffusing the tension between Witt's reflective face and the dead soldier's recalcitrant facelessness and unbridled return to nature—concludes with the following poignant and reluctantly rhetorical question: "Do you imagine your sufferings will be less because you loved goodness? Truth?" The object of his address or self-address here is fraught with much ambiguity, for this "you" and its unrequited love of goodness and truth fit the film's tragic search for beauty in terror, order in chaos, peace in war. But even if we were to restrict our focus to this scene alone, both Staros and Witt, in their unconditional, self-sacrificing love of the Good, are strong candidates for *receiving* rather than posing such a question. An even stranger candidate for posing this question to them is the skeptical on-the-fence nihilism of Sergeant Welsh, who asks Witt during one of their philosophical feuds, "What difference do you think you can make, one single man in all this madness?" Welsh's voice is also echoed in Staros' resounding question, and if he were the one to pose it he would surely take square aim at the moral belief systems of these two men as nothing more than exercises in wish-fulfillment, particularly on the point that the good life entitles one to compensation or, at the very least, absence of pain. Welsh's questioning via the earth-face manifests the skeptical side or undercurrent of Witt's fervent romanticism, the *counter-voice* that Witt might hear as his own quiet yet irrepressible self-questioning (perhaps a process-ing of the secret magnetizing the animosity of their intellectual friendship). But, since Welsh has his own distinct voice, and since Staros uses his voice to speak for those who lack one, I want to consider the possibility that the dead soldier may be the only one in a position to *truly question* them on their capacity (and the human capacity in general) for justice when the just ought to expect, in return, *injustice*—a question that the Staros–Witt amalgam knows yet cannot state without the help of a victim, a ghost, a haunting. In representing their human fate that only fortune can keep death at bay and that goodness will always be an uphill battle against a world of shifting, hence uneven, terrain, the dead soldier—*not of this world*—becomes in this respect a representative of transcendental justice granted to the victims of injustice: for to kill another human being, as everybody knows, even when on the defense, is to break the social contract at every joint, even if the motivation or ultimate goal, in the case of war, are to protect one's country and vision of humanity. While engrossed in the bottomless, vertiginous, inscrutable depths of nature, the other, and death—the three faces of the earth-face—Witt's face is blindingly overexposed into a blank page of consciousness that is capable, at last, of experiencing "Nature" uncolored by beliefs about its undividedness or gracefulness or deification—an experience in "full color" which returns his head from the smooth ivory clouds of ideas and back to the earth where, as expressed in the film's final line of voiceover, *all things shine.*

What does this mean for Witt's grand metaphysical hypothesis, by far the most ambitious and optimistic in the film: that humanity has "one big soul that everyone is a part of." As Staros and his rhetorical questions on behalf of the dead soldier fill him with skepticism, Witt must look even deeper and think without finalizing his thoughts (hence the absence of voiceover from him) to see whether the one big soul of humanity encompasses nature in addition to culture. Might the earth-face symbolize a return to the earth where man and nature are perceived as having a family resemblance? Or is it the case that being buried beneath the earth, sealed in a box, keeps man tied to the soul of *his* as opposed to *all* people? Normally, Witt is more than capable of reflecting on his poetic experience, expressing himself simply yet philosophically; and throughout the film his character is all too quick to find patterns of meaning within all manner of diversity and discord. But now, standing up and staring down, stiff as a statue, he appears too overwhelmed by the harsh realization that the Tower of Babel's only root is the graveyard of absolute silence. Like an upside-down "devil tree,"[34] the vision of a common unilingual humanity retreats into the depths of the earth where, as another voice puts it over an earlier image of a dying bird, "Death's got the final word, it's laughing at him." We shall all speak the same language, once again, only in death.

The whole film up to this point (about the halfway point, as it happens) has been pressing towards this moment where Witt (the human open to otherness) encounters the absolutely other (the dead enemy soldier) in the form of nature (the life of death), now visible, now invisible through the smoky wake of warfare wafting in and out of the frame—fading out and back in again as movies do when they wish to *move past something.* On top of the hill, under the sky and in the broad afternoon light, in the naked aftermath of war and on the other side of the frontline, Witt throws himself into his attentive gaze with the entirety of his consciousness, without blinking, completely exposed to—overexposed by—the paradox of the death of life (the soldier's muddy death mask) and the life of death (nature's stewing persistence, thanks to death). He stares as if into a deep, dark well, straight through his imaginary reflection, and if we venture along with him, we may be reminded of the film's staring opening image of a crocodile dropping down into a viscous swamp, shutting one of its eyes just before it touches the water. This memorable opening image is followed by the first of the film's many unanswered (and unanswerable) voiced out questions, *the* metaphysical question as far as Malick and I are concerned: "What's this war at the heart of nature?" My various ways of working on this question imply that the heart of nature beats at the crossroads of human nature and the natural world, and since it is human nature to take dominion over nature (the crocodile, possibly the very same one, is later captured by the American soldiers), the war is at the heart of what it is to be human—and our blood is part poison. Nature lives along the line separating self from other, life from death, humanity from animality, ... where it blurs the line. Such lines dissolve as soon as they are crossed, inevitably, in the honest fight for truth. And what, to conclude, is a line in this sense?—Fundamentally *thin*. Lines are the work of willful hands, the index finger of the mind, better known as the tongue: drawn in the sand and erased by the waves.

— — — — —

Is nature without meaning on film? It is oversaturated with meaning. It is the very possibility of meaning. That is how it overexposes us who look to it *for* meaning. But it remains ambiguous and mysterious as well. A landscape is something we gaze upon and admire, whereas the life force is an inexplicable power that is received or denied, or receives or denies *us*. The wake of the death of God has nature growing more deeply into itself as "alive"—indeed, this is what makes nature come out of its hiding and appear wild and free, or as Nietzsche might say, beyond good and evil. In the innermost thoughts of the soldiers in the film, there is no certainty or consensus, be it in terms of knowledge or faith, as to whether the "book of nature" could ever have (or ever have had) a single divine author, not to mention one that will disclose itself to them in their time of desperation and despair. (If nature is written in this sense at all, it must be read that way, first *as* written, and second as written *for you and you alone*.) When the world in its own image takes the form of the unity of nature, and when the world in our image takes the form of the chaos of war, and if ours is a world where the old metaphysical questions go unanswered and cinema's world shows that this absence of an answer is the best possible answer—then it is true enough what Witt, the "Yang" of

Malick's spirituality, says as a retort to Welsh, the "Yin" of Malick's skepticism and tendencies towards nihilism: "I've seen *another* world." We may not see another world the way Witt does (finding order in chaos, calmness in fear, family among friends, life in death, even the "spark" in poor Welsh), but to see another world that is also *this world* is what cinema itself does, how it helps us to see and perhaps to live with seeing too much.

"Mother, I am Dumb ...": The Reevaluation of Friedrich Nietzsche in The Turin Horse

> — We are conducting an experiment with truth! Perhaps mankind will perish
> because of it! Fine!
> > — Friedrich Nietzsche, *The Will to Power*

> Unequivocal rejection of all philosophy is an attitude that always deserves
> respect, for it contains more of philosophy than it itself knows.
> > — Martin Heidegger, *Nietzsche*

Béla Tarr's most recent and, by his own admission, final film *The Turin Horse* (Hungary, 2011) returns us to the beginning of this book in Nietzsche's concept of the death of God, the end of metaphysics, and cinema's new metaphysics. The film declares itself to be following the trajectory of the horse whose abuse at the hands of a raging cabman made Nietzsche weep— these tears being a metaphor for an epic recantation not only of an entire philosophy but the way of life such a philosophy demands of its author: Nietzsche's way. Or so the story goes. It is one of the most famous stories in the history of Western philosophy, a seductive piece of apocrypha that few readers of Nietzsche can resist indulging. Of the handful of fictional films about Nietzsche's life, as far as I know, none of them, including Tarr's, dares to dramatize the incident with the horse. But *The Turin Horse* stands as the only "Nietzsche film" committed to following the cabman, his horse, and the afterlife of this legendary turn of events in which Nietzsche's philosophy, particularly of the overman and will to power, came crashing down upon him. In taking this perspective Tarr seems to be asking why Nietzsche wept with pity when he believed, at least at the end, only in the honoring of power. Given that the film is set during what appears to be an apocalypse of total erasure, a preliminary answer in the form of an allegory is that a metaphysical force beyond human understanding is weeping, too, perhaps over life itself, life as power, or over a new and greater power, call it powerlessness ... The film, however, is not conventionally philosophical enough to concretely ask or answer such questions. Its philosophy comes in taking the road less trave- led, rejecting the rules of historical biography and cinema's biopic genre by portraying the horse instead of Nietzsche, animal as opposed to man, silence over speech. On its own path and amidst this silence which recalls the first films ever made, the horse can be seen as the missing link between the end of metaphysics in philosophy and the return of metaphysics in film, which is not unlike seeing the horse for what it is—in its own image.

Before proceeding, it is important for me to say that the film, while resonating with a metaphysical conception of film-as-such (in many ways it is the very film I had been waiting for in crystalizing the view of cinema—and perhaps philosophy, too—in this book), is not necessarily exemplary of this or any view one might bring to bear. Not to say that a model form of exemplification is possible or even desirable, for what I am aiming for—what I presume all film-philosophers want—is a *conversation* between the film and the philosophical heritage of which it is conscious and to which it contributes in its own unique (that is, traditionally *non*-philosophical) way. In fact, there may even be aspects of the film which seem to fly under the radar, or directly in the face, of the view I have expounded regarding the significance of the return of metaphysics in a post-metaphysical (i.e., analytical, scientific, political, postmodern, post-truth, post-Nietzschean, above all image-obsessed) age. I am not bothered by this in the least because for a film to be able to do philosophy in its own way, it cannot be known ahead of time what in it might count as philosophy. Perhaps its most ostensibly philosophical aspects would end up garnering the least attention—wouldn't that be cinematic! Furthermore, any effort at *mere* exemplification (teaching a film what you know, or think you know, rather than being taught by it as part of a conversation that can go anywhere) will show that neither film nor philosophy is likely to benefit much from transaction under duress. In resisting the temptation to exemplify, I remind myself of other equally perilous pitfalls I have sought to avoid in reaching this point: there is no one symptom of the death of God and no end of metaphysics that is not also a beginning, just as there is no absolute figure for the world in its own image or absolute film which commemorates the birth of film.

Beginning after the end of Nietzsche's philosophical life, in the wake of his mental breakdown in 1889 and before his death in 1900, hence beginning before the birth of cinema (1896) and after the death of God (1882), *The Turin Horse* imagines the birth of film *before* film-as-such and *after* philosophy's dismantling of metaphysics and reevaluation of all values. It imagines the world as it was *before* "the world in its own image" and *after* "the world in the image of God." It therefore imagines the world "*as it is.*" The film imagines itself to be not only the first film ever made, but, with its apocalyptic vision devoid of redemption, also the *last* film ever made (its apocalypse is not just thematic but *formal*). In this sense, the film is the moving image of eternal recurrence. At bottom, it imagines the horse over which Nietzsche wept and withdrew into a speechless and motionless madness, the horse which Nietzsche understood better than Zarathustra, as it happens, for the horse is a product of taming by a creature that successfully tamed itself long ago, or never needed taming in the first place: Man. Man is a *tamer* of what he fears most—the wild and unknown—and what is tamed in this way becomes "knowledge." The tamed horse then becomes a symbol of knowledge *concealing the unknowable.* We may have sought to free it, or to free ourselves, for that's what we want, or think we want, but in the end knowledge makes specimens. In place of being wild, of being truly alive, the tamer becomes a trapper of *power without will.* The horse's power, as it happens, is *not* will to power. The specimen is still alive somewhere; it abides without participating in the plans of its captor, dying only in terms of *our notion of how it lives.* But I am running ahead of myself.

Let's back up to the idea that *The Turin Horse* imagines itself to be the last film ever made and the first film ever made, harking back to the early beginnings of the medium as a silent and gray aftermath of the death of God, the world in all its bareness and barrenness. Even though the film was made over 100 years after the birth of film, it is closer to the spirit of early silent cinema than to any of its twenty-first-century counterparts and even, ironically, the majority of the silent film canon. With scant dialogue, a soundtrack dominated by repetitions of music and wind, extreme spatial confinement, and the most minimal of narratives, the primal silence of cinema at work in Tarr's film is not specifically defined by the absence of sound. Rather, the silence which sound actually helps to discover more deeply is expressed in the muteness of animal life, the physiognomy of faces, the mechanical gestures of domestic routine, the supernatural constancy of nature, the inevitability of time's passage or exhaustion, and the fundamental wordlessness of the world in its own image. In general, the film uses sound to amplify the silence of a world folding in on itself, the word caving in on itself, the animal (a horse) bearing witness to the end of an old way of life and the start, perhaps, of a new one.

As far as the history of film is concerned, the beginning is not the word but the image, or *the word of the image,* for the word on its own could never speak silence and so could never sound the arrival of this new world and its new metaphysics—to be disclosed only by the infancy of cinema in a flash of light, being, and truth, for all to see and hear, and to speak of only after the fact, if at all, as the world wails inconsolably.

In *The Turin Horse*, a father (János Derzsi), his daughter (Erika Bók), and their horse (?) are isolated on a farm amidst a valley surrounded by endlessly receding plains and incessant winds. Their daily labor, which makes up the substance of their daily life, is tracked through six days of menial repetition, broken only by shifts in light and markers of the passing days—their actions and movements and gestures verging upon a sense of eternal recurrence that blurs the line between freedom and necessity.[1] As time's river dries up and the winds continue to howl as if from the bowels of the earth, there is a palpable premonition from the very first scene that life is coming to an end, that an apocalypse is at work to sap the will of being and spread impenetrable darkness throughout the world. But of course, the apocalypse has already taken place: it is the death of God, the end of all endings, and what is more, as Nietzsche goes on to report, a God killed by us prematurely and without complete understanding of the consequences of such a hubristic deed.[2] On the razor threshold of this decisive historical and existential moment, the film asks its characters and viewers to exfoliate a will to live based on notions of salvation in various forms of afterworld (be it metaphysical or pragmatic), and find solace in a will to power that is tied to what Nietzsche never hesitates to call, simply and with confident naïveté, "a love for and faith in the meaning of the earth."[3] Here such a love is put to the test by an earth that has lost its color (the film is in black and white), forever awaiting the coming of the overman and a new palette of being in the world. But the open door that is the earth is open only to itself. While the temptation may be to wait for a dramatic sign of redemption or perhaps revolution in the nature of things, the film remains remarkably attentive and vigilant in the endurance by which it abides by the ordinary details of life for their own sake, completely avoiding anything we might associate with narrative fabrication or even progression, unless we come to see *destruction* as a form of creation and catharsis.

The periods of rest in between chores, when the father and daughter take turns watching, perhaps studying the windstorm through their front window, hint that they may have alternative plans for such a world that seems to be slowly closing its fist on them—however, we are not privy to their thoughts and their contemplations are as routine as anything else they do. The horse, too, is sometimes shown just standing and staring into the void of space, perhaps contemplating its own bleak fate. The film gives us no reason to think that *humans alone* can think and compose themselves through thought, with animals left to drift in a wild domain of the moment lacking rhyme or reason; nor are we reassured that what may simply be the *appearance* of thinking in the human face is necessarily a search for ultimate meanings or a practical interpretation of contingent and chaotic events. The film's magnification and ballet-like orchestration of daily life make no appeal for an external meaning or outcome to justify the epic ardors of persistence in the face of apocalypse; and in this sense the moral of this refusal to moralize is that as agents we must relinquish our hold on everything except *that which holds us*, which is the will to live or love *for nothing*, an incredibly strong but by no means automatic and immortal flame, exemplified less by the freedom of the subject than by the gravity of the object—gravity as an unyielding "yes" to this earth, this life, drained of the values which history has bestowed to give gravity a false levity in the form of illusions, entire cities stationed in the clouds. In Tarr's vision the end of metaphysics gives way to the cinematic dawning and redistribution of life in the luminous materiality of things, in everyday activities such as cooking, eating, cleaning, getting dressed in the morning, fetching water from the well, chopping wood, and sleeping, so as to start the process all over again. Yet as humans build, nature destroys—that is what it means to be overpowered and exhausted, despite one's greatest efforts. After the death of God, what humans do to create meaning has lost all meaning, and no new meaning will fill the void; rather it is the letting go of meaning that will give us the strength to face the void. And so this human earthbound ballet of misplaced striving is refracted through the gaze of a horse who endures the burden of being not with dignity, not without dignity, but *abidingly*. For the horse, the world itself is fate, a fate to be neither accepted nor denied but *loved*, not in the deepest sense but the *only* sense of surrender.

The film opens with a voiceover prologue on a black screen, the content of which immediately piqued my interest for reasons both obvious to me and beckoning deeper reflection. Here is the text in full:

> In Turin, on January 3rd, 1889, Friedrich Nietzsche steps out of the door of number six Via Carlo Alberto, perhaps to take a stroll, perhaps to go by the post office to collect his mail. Not far from him, or indeed very far removed from him, a cabman is having trouble with his stubborn horse. Despite all his urging, the horse refuses to move, whereupon the cabman ... Giuseppe? Carlo? Ettore? ... loses his patience and takes his whip to it. Nietzsche comes up to the throng and puts an end to the brutal scene of the cabman, who by this time is foaming with rage. The solidly built and full-mustached Nietzsche suddenly jumps up to the cab and throws his arms around the horse's neck, sobbing. His neighbor takes him home, where he lies still and silent for two days on a divan, until he mutters the obligatory last words, 'Mutter, ich bin dumm' *(Mother, I am dumb)*, and lives for another ten years, gentle and demented, in the care of his mother and sisters. Of the horse, we know nothing.

If we follow the logic of this well-known tale of philosophy—and there is no reason to regard it as anything but that, a story, if not a legend that is impossible to verify—the film's implied historical setting becomes pertinent in its precision to my way of thinking about the film and even film as such. Beginning on the cusp of two interrelated paradigm shifts, one philosophical and the other technological or techno-poetic, the prologue suggests that the diegetic events be seen as taking place *after* the end of Nietzsche's philosophical life (in the ruinous wake of the death of God or the end of metaphysics as an ecstatic yet precarious emancipation from the absolute) and immediately *before* the birth of cinema (the return or resurrection of metaphysics in material life freed from abstraction, in a new absolute which spreads out into a luminous sea of singularities that is the world on film). So we could say that the film is set more clearly in *time* than space, on a "double hinge" where metaphysics swings in both directions, flapping in the winds of monumental change: like a door which closes what Siegfried Kracauer calls "the ruins of ancient beliefs,"[4] opens what Nietzsche calls the reevaluation of all values, closes the transcendent realm of the absolute, opening onto an immanent realm of the absolute image—a film set in the midst of that disorienting yet peaceful pause of time where the cultural itinerary of everyday life is no longer given, where the deep ruts of our various routines and habits appear like strange traces of an alien civilization. Not unlike those rare occasions where we mislabel a familiar face or thing, stunned by its truth, or when, just before dawn, we take our first frail steps without a pair of glasses and reach about for support in a liquid haze of colors and sounds, none brighter than darkness and none louder than silence.

Whether the apocryphal incident in Turin has any historical veracity to it, I regard Nietzsche's presence in the film as conveyed by the prologue to be primarily a fictional if not a fantastical one.[5] When the film's main action commences, Nietzsche becomes like a ghostly specter for whom haunting is hiding, a presence whose madness and ensuing silence hover over the film world without further reflection or judgment. The backdrop of his philosophy falls to the floor and is trampled upon by the rigorous activities of father, daughter, and horse within a world systematically erased by an apocalyptic wind. While Nietzsche did not live to witness or at least contemplate the cinema as we know it today (and this is significant), I think it is worth mentioning that a short, silent, black-and-white film reconstruction/reenactment of the philosopher's last days was produced by two German artists, Sabine Schirdewahn and Sven Hain. The film, entitled *Elisabeths Wille* (2000), is based on the controversial series of photographs taken by Hans Olde in 1899 of Nietzsche's post-philosophical period of convalescence (the very period that the prologue makes reference to). The film appears to weave together these photographic documents with fictional reenactments in an effort to bring Nietzsche himself (or what was left of him) and this pre-cinematic moment to life. Here Nietzsche's debilitating illness is dramatized so that the great philosopher looks hopelessly lost in the woods of his own mind, utterly oblivious to the camera zeroing in on his face and hands in search of the lost spark. In a similar vein as *The Turin Horse*, this fiction poses not only as a very early film recording but perhaps as *the first* conceivable moving image recording in the history of film, pre-dating both the Lumière brothers' and Thomas Edison's first filmic forays (1895 and 1893, respectively) if we imagine that Nietzsche had been filmed shortly after his initial collapse in Turin. As a fake and somewhat fetishistic film based on real photographs, it should in no way be taken as holding any historical value with respect to philosophy (the life of Nietzsche) or film (the origins of film). That being said, even though Nietzsche and cinema never crossed paths in such a manner, the film does manage to envision the encounter (convincingly or not will depend on the viewer) and in so doing pushes us to reflect on the implications of its uncanny timing: the death of God and the birth of film. For its first glimpse of the world, a "truth machine" captures the man who philosophized with a hammer and destroyed all claims to truth for a living, diagnosing truth as error, illusion, and absurdity.[6] The first manifestation of the world in its own image features the thinker who destroyed the world as we know it (God, morality, truth—everything great!), the thinker for whom the great lie of the image is the only remaining truth. Except now such irony turns into tragedy, for he is destroyed too, and the cinema dawns to affirm this devastation, this collapse of the overman back into the mere man that he is. And in affirming such devastation and impending death, it finds, intact, the world—life.

Interestingly, the father character in *The Turin Horse* bears a faint physical resemblance to the convalescent Nietzsche, and Tarr films him with the same gentle yet unromantic concentration as the photographs by Olde, allowing the camera to see nothing more or less than a man. Most likely Tarr had seen Olde's photographs and possibly their transformation into *Elisabeths Wille*. From within the lie of the latter he might have strived to create a deeper truth out of Nietzsche's tragic and bewildering demise. If so, he knew better than to take the last ten years of Nietzsche's life as his subject, for no philosopher (even a dying one) can ever hope to completely outwit philosophy's default mastery over the world and the times, which are always infinitely more complex than any philosophy. It is for this reason that Tarr's cinematic imagination leads him down the path of the horse, the horse that Nietzsche witnessed being beaten publicly on the street (the street as the site of the unexpected, of resistance to philosophy's hammer), whose pain and suffering trigger a wave of pity that contradicts his entire philosophy, hence his entire

Figure 5.1   *The apocryphal horse of Turin:* The Turin Horse *(Béla Tarr, Hungary, 2011).*

life, resulting in a psychotic break and decade-long silence from which he would never emerge until his inevitable death. The scene of the cabman and his horse interrupts Nietzsche, overexposing and questioning him in a disturbingly non-philosophical way (hence, for him, the shock of it), hitting the nerve of his final philosophical testament known as "will to power." If God is dead and might makes right, who will take care of the weak? Apparently, Nietzsche of all people—and that marks his end **(Fig. 5.1)**.

After the voiceover prologue, the first of the film's lengthy and seemingly unbroken sequence shots depicts what we are led to assume is the same cabman and horse making their way back home through a heavy wind storm sweeping the countryside.[7] Without documenting their arrival, the next sequence shot shows an isolated country house surrounded by barren hills with nothing but a lonely tree in the distance, a landscape reminiscent of the set from Beckett's *Waiting for Godot* **(Fig. 5.2)**. The domestic lives of the cabman-father and his daughter are tracked over six days, during which routine chores to be equated with "daily living" are repeated like clockwork against the background of the raging storm. These ritual-like tasks are performed with such heightened attention to detail on the part of the actors and filmmakers that the main source of drama or eventfulness in these routines becomes the gradual yet utterly mysterious collapse of the business—the busyness—of everyday life. As the days unfold to the hauntingly musical sound of the incessant unidirectional

Figure 5.2 *The desolate surroundings of the country house:* The Turin Horse *(Béla Tarr, Hungary, 2011).*

wind, it dawns on father and daughter, without them ever overtly discussing the matter, that this is no mere storm: the mechanical routines of life begin to break down, one by one, starting with the horse, who is like a barometer of apocalypse. First the horse refuses to move when harnessed, and shortly after will not eat or drink. A distant neighbor comes in search of brandy, and while waiting for the preparation of the bottle, delivers a dense philosophical interpretation of the storm, asserting that what lies at the root of the phenomenon is nothing elemental or even eschatological but a catastrophic accumulation of human greed, political misdeeds, and sanctioned corruption for reckless personal gain—an irreversible debasement of life at the hands of what sounds like capitalism (the loaded term is never explicitly mentioned; fittingly, no facile "isms" are deployed here). Before long, the well water inexplicably dries up, causing the father to panic and prepare for immediate departure. As the solitary pair venture out into the storm, the wind proves too strong and a thick dust cloud makes navigation all but impossible, thus forcing them back home. Faced with their bleak fate, the light of the sun suddenly dies out, lamps extinguish and cannot be rekindled, hot embers go cold. Throughout it all we may have noticed that the wind harbors subtle supernatural qualities: it is always blowing from the same direction (we never learn *from which* direction) and the droning howling sound slips into a rhythm that is eerily reminiscent of a choir of high-pitched screams. Nature has lost its sense of proportion, balance, and flowering randomness; it has become a crooked mouthpiece for something dreadful and dire lurking behind it. These are shaping up to be the six days of *decreation*, and on the seventh day, which is not shown, there will be no rest, no sense of accomplishment, anticipation, memorialization, or catharsis. The restoration of absolute nothingness and an ending to mark all endings constitute a return to the beginning before there was any such thing as intended light; before a sense of history, purpose, and hope for the future conspired to give shape to the epic horizon of our strange human existence, conditioned as it is to always seek out and will into being a light at the end of the tunnel.

In the biblical story of Noah, the apocalypse flood is meant for humans alone, the innate sinners. A sovereign exception is made for Noah and his family because they practice supreme virtue and devotion, are "good" in the eyes of God. Terrestrial animals are spared unconditionally—though not *all* animals, of course, only a representative sample—because as the embodiment of paradisiacal innocence they have remained a part of nature and have not (or not yet) drifted out of the divine orbit. In *The Turin Horse*, however, the apocalypse is, on the contrary, completely indiscriminate: if you believe, like Noah, that there will be a flood of global magnitude, then you can spend your summer building an ark; but if you look out the window, day after day, and see nothing but wind and debris, a wind element which goes on to obliterate the vital elements of earth, water, fire, and breathable air, then this apocalypse is not underwritten by the possibility of human or animal redemption, which is to say it is presented as final, absolute, without appeal.[8] Despite this, we might expect or want the horse, devoid as it is of the human capacity to debase, to bear witness to the last judgment or personify the force of judgment itself. Just think of all those animals in the history of cinema (take my analysis of the deer scene from *In the Bedroom* or Bresson's *Balthazar*) whose blank, wild, and inscrutable stares prompt the human characters to feel as if they are being watched and perhaps judged by a higher power, when it is really just the tingle of their own overactive conscience. But animals are no more innocent than children, and what are humans if not animals too? The idea of a pure aura of innocence surrounding the animal, signifying salvation or judgment or both, could be a symptom of what I will call a "metaphysical nostalgia" for a time before the human animal stood up into its signature stature as "most powerful." In the end, the horse is a horse (!), and while it is indeed graceful, grace will not save it. It will not be spared for anything, as this apocalypse is without a vision of redemption in paradise. The horse bears physical rather than spiritual burdens and so cannot bear witness in the only way it makes sense to do so: through the mirror of consciousness and the law. Not only does Tarr refuse to thematize the horse as a judge/witness of human debasement, he goes so far as to deprive the animal of a perspective by which to do so, for this is often a false perspective generated by anthropomorphist projection onto the white screen of the animal's open yet impenetrable face, resulting in a sentimental and displaced experience of conscience with no sincere plans for ethical action.

And yet, I maintain that there is still some core of strength in the horse's powerlessness and ensuing paralysis—strength in the dirt-encrusted texture of its coat, in its capacity to shed voluminous tears when being urged on by the whip, and most of all in its dependency, like all living things, on the *spirit of care*—a softening of will and invitation to love whose "power" Nietzsche must have overlooked, that is, until the horse met his gaze. After the death of a certain god and the failure of human morality to fill the gaping void of skepticism, the flickering instinct to provide care to dependent life (and all life is dependent on life, affirms the animal) endures in what one might call the unbidden yet binding affect of ethics, an ethics without content, without speech **(Fig. 5.3)**. Such a feeling is tied to the horse's almost immediate antenna-like registration of the apocalyptic extinguishing of will to power in the very flesh and pulse of beings. Perhaps Being itself has lost its will to be and become. The horse senses—knows—that life is coming to an end, for it and for all. It does not resist this fate. It does not ask why. Most importantly, *it does not pretend otherwise*. It has nothing in common with its owners who persist, persist, persist, while the world vanishes before them in a sea of dust. As life itself loses the will to live in the hold of humanity's destructive will to power, one thing in this world is left clearly intact: the strength of the horse's weakness in submitting

Figure 5.3 *Spirit of care:* The Turin Horse *(Béla Tarr, Hungary, 2011).*

to a destruction in which it plays no part. Father and daughter do not seem to have a hand in it either. How could they? They simply live. But how do they live, exactly? By grasping, grasping, grasping. Persisting, persisting, persisting. Nothing can put a stop to their rigorous itinerary of chopping, cooking, cleaning, eating and drinking, and back to working—so much expenditure for nothing nobler than their own pleasureless survival. Why work to live? How has it come to this, where work is the only *way* to live? I do not know, but the price of such a life is the world in the palm of the hand. We have been holding the world like this for so long that we fail to realize just how tightly and desperately we squeeze the life out of it. As the neighbor in search of brandy makes clear, there is nothing we cannot grab hold of and exploit—nothing sacred.[9] Nothing can put a stop to this poisonous will except an apocalypse of *pure will*—wind—that effaces everything man has sought for personal gain and which only serves to exacerbate his hunger. And as this self-destructive will is being drained away to the last drop, it is noteworthy that of the living creatures in the film the horse is the first to be sapped. Father and daughter show no signs of weakening until the bitter end. Persistent as ever—carry on, carry on—chop, pour, scrape, saddle, stare … But in carrying on like this so blindly, without truly realizing it, they find themselves *carrying the horse* like a sack of potatoes or wheelbarrow full of wood—except they carry it because they love it. This brings us to what is, for me, the most thought-provoking, important, and moving scene in the film (though I confess to having completely missed it on my preliminary viewings, a fact which I also regard as part of its power).

When the father decides to abandon the house because the water well has mysteriously run dry, he gives his daughter orders that only essentials be packed on a two-wheel pull cart, a smaller version of the wagon used to hitch the horse. When the horse is brought out of the stable, our assumption might be that it is being labeled not as an essential but rather as the engine for this new vehicle, that the plan is to assign the horse its primary duty and have it pull the cart through the wind storm. If this is the implied plan (it is never discussed), we might find ourselves cringing with dread, for on the previous occasion when the horse was ordered to work it wouldn't budge at all and received a goading beating from the father, resulting in an unforgettable document of an animal crying (these tears are *real*, I'm afraid, not apocryphal). Instead, I am astonished to see that the two of them, perhaps recalling the horse's fearful stubbornness or feeling guilty for having punished it unduly, attach its muzzle to the back of the cart, where it will be carried along mainly by the daughter who, unlike father, has the use of both of her arms. Maybe I make too much of this reversal and the horse is really no different from the other meager possessions packed for the trip—but if the horse cannot pull the cart and is of no use to them as a working horse (no longer denotes "work" in their eyes), why would they bring it with them in what is bound to be a precarious and possibly fatal journey into the unknown? What could they *want* with a horse that cannot work, will not eat or drink, and what is more, a horse which neither one, as far as I can tell, has managed to embrace wholeheartedly as a companion? Here as elsewhere, there is no discussion or debate between the characters about how to proceed and to what end. They know what they must do and act together without any planning, weighing of options, justification of reasons, or conflict of values. The father, no longer seated above the horse as its forceful master, is dethroned and decentered; his good hand, which no longer holds the whip, has softened like a father's hand in gently guiding the horse by its muzzle. The horse, no longer harnessed to lead the way, walks protected at the rear, plodding along at a comfortable pace. And when the daughter starts to pull the cart with the horse attached behind it, pulling with all her body across mean terrain and vicious winds, I don't believe I exaggerate when I say that she has *become the horse*. All three beings—human and animal, animal and human—*walk in unison*, magnetized by the old rickety cart which will soon become the unexpected focus of Tarr's concern **(Fig. 5.4)**.

That man, woman, and animal are now equal is also an understatement, for the animal is not just spared the ordeal but served like a prince; the ancient master–servant dyad is not only reversed but altogether cancelled, because here a human being respects the animal by *becoming* the animal that he/she is. There is nothing degrading about this, nor grandiose. The struggling yet resilient gait of the daughter–horse is remarkably devoid of anything resembling a proud rhetoric of humility, sacrifice, or self-overcoming. No facial closeups, no music, no suspense, not even a hint of irony—the cinematic event is unembellished, again remarkably, allowing the viewer to experience the redistribution of emphasis and reevaluation of power where he or she sees and feels it most deeply. I therefore do not immediately notice what is actually going on here between the humans and the horse; I have to *go back*. And the only thing that the filmmaker emphasizes for our consideration, in a rare closeup at the tail end of a monumental sequence shot, is a seemingly trivial tangent: one of the wooden wheel's of the cart spinning round and round, on the verge of collapse yet holding on, cutting through the parched earth ridden with debris **(Fig. 5.5)**.

If we go back and look more closely at this scene through this detail, new questions come to the fore, the "wheel of thought" is in motion. Is circular repetition the secret to forward progress? Is it the cost? The brake? Is Tarr's piqued interest in the epochal advent of the spinning wheel triggered by the renewed propulsion of man-becoming-animal, a propulsion indifferent to

Figure 5.4   *Role reversal between human and horse:* The Turin Horse *(Béla Tarr, Hungary, 2011).*

Figure 5.5   *The camera lingers on the rickety wheel of the pull cart:* The Turin Horse *(Béla Tarr, Hungary, 2011).*

distant horizons, goal-oriented gazes, and potential frontiers of conquest? It strikes me that *this* wheel in *these* circumstances is an important piece of a new metaphysics in which rational human progress is made irrationally yet responsibly; the legacy of linear thinking is put in check, spun around itself without altogether tying itself into a hopeless knot, almost but not fully abandoning the Western model of progress for, say, the aberration of eternal recurrence. The exposed wheel at the foundation of this quest seems to suggest, or dare I say *say*, that progress is not necessarily always straight and ascending. We don't know what counts as genuine progress. What looks like a step forward may be a step backward, or, which is more likely the case, a step in the same spot. Nothing is more frustrating or disappointing than unwanted, imprisoning repetition. Just because the old can be made new again does not mean that we progress *from* the old *to* the new. That old model led us nowhere and left us gasping. Perhaps there is a paradise life of repetition, each circle of which introduces a new dynamic variation, playful variations unbeholden to either a mythical source in the past or the sorcery of the myth that the future is ours and not time's. That may be the *extent* of what we call "progress"—turning back, turning round, dancing. All great journeys pass through an even greater sense of "home." In the wake of metaphysics, the dance of progress carries us home, which is precisely where father and daughter end up, *back home*, as if they passed through a circle and performed a tango led by the wind.

There is another reason why Tarr is so interested in the structural details of the pull cart. Despite appearances, this is no ordinary cart but a replica of the one featured in this group portrait of Nietzsche, Paul Rée, and Lou Salomé, the doomed love triangle that failed to resolve in anyone's favor **(Fig. 5.6)**. I could hardly believe my eyes (and my luck) when I happened upon this photograph and saw the same pull cart staring back at me, the same number of figures differently arranged, and a possible historical source of inspiration for Tarr. As you can see, Nietzsche stands in the place of the daughter (thus assuming the position of the horse, that is, a working horse), Rée stands in the place of the father, and Salomé crouches down on the cart where the horse of Turin finds itself in tow. Whether Tarr consciously adapted this photograph or not, the uncanny parallel gently summons Nietzsche's unbridled identification with the horse and self-deprecating masochism as the unrequited lover of Salomé who, allegedly upon Nietzsche's direction, proudly brandishes the whip. The whip object, however, is excluded from Tarr's reevaluation, which substitutes a radical form of selflessness for the dangerous game of love, a selflessness through which the remnants of power are pooled together as in a desert oasis. The static nature of the photograph itself is also invoked, as the cart's wheel, so exaggerated in Tarr's version, rotates/repeats like a moment forever trapped in time, perhaps envisioning a time when Nietzsche, Salomé, and Rée, performing their psycho-sexual escapades out in public, will become as anonymous as the father and daughter and every horse that ever lived.

Figure 5.6   *A possible historical source behind* The Turin Horse's *climactic pull cart scene: (Left to right) Lou Andreas-Salomé, Paul Rée, and Friedrich Nietzsche (Jules Bonnet Photo Studio, Lucerne, 1882). Credit: Archiv für Kunst und Geschichte, Berlin; and Joachim Köhler,* Who Was Friedrich Nietzsche?, *ed. Georg M. Blochmann, trans. Ronald Taylor (Bonn: Inter Nationes, 2000).*

After this reversal in the order of Nietzschean will to power, the apocalypse quickens and father and daughter begin to accept their fate. They do not say "yes" to fate and they do not say "no." (They continue to remain silent on all matters of philosophical or existential import.) They continue to live, to fight, until they too are drained of will. They had been willing themselves along splendidly, completing various tasks and securing their livelihood day in and day out. Was it all worth it? Was it all *progress*? Their subservience to the horse, and especially the daughter's embodiment of the horse (and Nietzsche), have cast a new light on their world. How small it is, how simple! Father and daughter, man and woman, do the same things every day, *the same new thing* regardless of the metaphysical state of things. Like the horse, they have no names. Like the horse, they are practically without speech. And like the horse, they are powerless over the world and the mess the human race has made of it. They thought they possessed great power and destiny over their lives, but that thought blinded them to the fact that the real outcome in taking care of business, as it were, has been that of taking care of each other so immaculately that they never had any need to *show* that they care. They live as one, thriving in this way only. *I live in this world, and while living here I act, or not, for others. If I act mostly for myself, then my world is small; if I act exclusively for myself, then I am my world. But if two people act together and as one then even a domestic routine performed mechanically and without speaking can constitute a world—and, indeed, such a world is what remains intact and in bloom when the world has ended.*

In the final scene of the film, on the sixth day of decreation, the terrible winds having ceased at last, leaving an infinite sea of primordial darkness and silence outside, an inexplicable "sourceless" light enters the frame like a new post-apocalyptic dawn, revealing the father and daughter still visible in the home, sitting across from each other at the table where they have their daily meal of one potato each. They do not look at each other since, in reality, there is nothing to see. We can all stop relying so much on our eyes for knowing each other and, yes, even for watching films. Instead, they sit in the presence of each other as they have always done during suppertime. They know what time it is, even though time has stopped. They adhere to the ritual, even though the potatoes are raw and they, like the horse, have permanently lost their appetite, hence the will to live but also the will to die. Will to power is on its deathbed. But this mysterious light on the last day of decreation—where could it be coming from, how can it be, when there is no light left in this world, indeed when there is no world at all to speak of? Has the camera acclimatized to the darkness like our eyes sometimes do at night? Or is the light of cinema itself shining through the darkness after decreation? I would like to believe that the camera (the body of cinema) and the world in its own image (the soul of cinema) are responding here to responsibility itself, and that the image registers it as if it were a glue-like substance glowing in the dark. The two of them together, nameless in this new worldless world, sitting face to face and self to self, are lit by the other's presence and their own persistence despite themselves, gazing deep within so as to better face the end as one being, or one becoming. With eyes averted, lips sealed, and hands (palms down) on the wooden table that separates them, the core of human connection in the absence of will, want, and work is an interminable light source visible only when the sun ceases to burn and darkness reigns. It is a light perhaps more ancient than the sun, a light by which the cinema seeks to light the *inner life*: love. Love is light, and this light from within is closer to the divine light than anything we might find outside us, in forms of nature that intimate "the beyond." May the death of God find new life as pure light—light before being, or the being of light   a light without source—cinematic sorcery **(Fig. 5.7)**.

Figure 5.7 *Father and daughter mysteriously illuminated in the darkness after decreation:* The Turin Horse *(Béla Tarr, Hungary, 2011).*

But what of the horse? Isn't it a part of this metaphysical spectrum of love and light? Isn't the love between human and animal based almost exclusively on wordless presence? Perhaps, but we would do well to recall again the film's opening narration regarding the horse and its availability to narrative comprehension: "Of the horse we know nothing." No one knows for sure if such a horse existed; no one knows for sure if Nietzsche wept over its pathetic plight. We do not know if it had owners resembling this father and daughter, if it dwelled in stables erected on windswept plains in the middle of nowhere. It is a *darkness*, a dark spot in history, a history which is still *all-too-human*. It is therefore fitting that the horse is excluded from the final scene of impossible light at the end of the world, for now both father and daughter appear horse-like in the way their heads droop with eyes downcast, warming each other with the certainty that they are not alone. If Nietzsche wept and went dumb over the horse, surely it is because it reminded him of the suffering of his fellow man, and perhaps his own inconsolable suffering as well (not to be overcome). The simple bond between human and animal is a reminder that the more complex love between human beings is, or can be, just as simple and sweet.

* * *

In art, truth depends on acts of trickery as much as on acts of trust. There are no rules. Fiction is the first trick or turn towards trickery, evident in the belief that fiction is not only the mandatory path to truth but the *preferred* one. The films explored throughout this book all go further than fiction, drawing upon forms reminiscent of the magician's set of tricks for the working of "miracles on film." Aesthetically speaking, the gentle light that dawns amidst complete and utter darkness at the end of *The Turin Horse* is as miraculously conjured as the cycling, cocooning ripples of river water in the wake of Mouchette's suicidal plunge at the end of Bresson's film. I also detect a similar quality of magic in the wildly unexpected telephone call to the Zone in *Stalker*, a call which disenchants the Zone (or reenchants what may already be a disenchanted space) and helps awaken the characters to the moral dilemma of supreme wish-fulfillment. Perhaps the most mesmerizing miracle-trick occurs in *The Thin Red Line*, when a wash of sunlight descends over the hills "in honor of" the two soldiers who perished at the edge of the frontline, a light made to bless the dead and curse the living in a double-exposure that confounds the dualistic tendencies of thought. Such filmic revelations are possible for the simple reason that their metaphysics are shaped according to the rules or, since there are no rules, through an artform half-ruled by life itself—by the elements of nature, the dimensions of space and time, the crossroads of human, animal, and mechanical consciousness. On top of everything else I have said about the audiovisual camera, I will end by suggesting that it is also a wand. It makes the world appear and disappear, leaving it to the filmmaker to remake it and decide: what kind of world? Rather than wish for a better or changed world, the filmmaker–magician begins by affirming a *living world*, even if what is ultimately unleashed from such a world turns out to be irrational or lethal. Just when life appears to be as dead as a rock, the rock moves, the rock *can* be moved, so watch out. In film, skepticism and spirituality are not as far apart as we thought. Looking up to "the heavens" of the world in its own image, these filmmakers are brave (self-effacing) enough to find and pull life's enchanted strings, channeling a more primal and powerful creative force through the medium of film. The moments in which time seems to come to a standstill are movie magic in the metaphysical sense. And, of course, they are only the heightened or punctuated moments—the totalities, soundings, and climaxes of metaphysical films—which, as we have seen, function meaningfully in the context of a larger narrative and aesthetic whole. But even if we restrict our experience to just these miracle tricks, we cease to be merely viewers and become *witnesses*. If we are not careful, such revelations will be passed over, or worse, mistaken for an accident, error, or lapse of reason, perhaps even a lapse of judgment. They will fail to make an impression on our consciousness if we do not believe that such things are actually possible where to believe is also to see. For the time being, at least for as long as we are invested in a film, we *do* believe, we perform the form of belief (the content of which may or may not be worthy of belief), for the so-called "willing suspension of disbelief" is the spectator's supreme reflex. Miracles are possible in the world of film— possible and probable—commonplace and universal—the caveat being that *anything* in a film can be experienced as miraculous and only in *that "world"* whose metaphysics we have just begun to discover.

Notes

INTRODUCTION

1. Nietzsche's point (though that is not exactly the right word) is clear (as clear as he would ever want it to be): it is not that we shouldn't believe in God, but rather that there is no God without the process of belief, or what he consistently calls *value*. The powers within belief might be better spent creating *new* gods. See Friedrich Nietzsche, *The Gay Science*, trans. Walter Kaufmann (New York: Vintage Books, 1974), pp. 181–2.
2. Film-philosophy regards film as capable of illustrating philosophical ideas, contributing to philosophical debates, and, in its most radical form, functioning in the mode of philosophy itself (sometimes with *anti-philosophical* results). Metametaphysics is an absurd "hall of mirrors" term, referring to a kind of post-metaphysical reassessment and renewal of the spirit of metaphysics, one which proceeds with heightened self-awareness by asking questions *about* metaphysics and about what metaphysics can (still) do. Its pertinence is epitomized in Allan Hazlett's perceptive remark when introducing a collection of essays on the subject: "It is an embarrassment to the critics of metaphysics that, having been declared dead a thousand times, it keeps showing up alive." Hazlett, "Introduction," in *New Waves in Metaphysics*, ed. Allan Hazlett (Basingstoke and New York: Palgrave Macmillan, 2010), p. 7.
3. Maxim Gorky, "Maxim Gorky on the Lumiére Program, 1896," trans. Leda Swan, in *Kino: A History of the Russian and Soviet film*, ed. Jay Leyda (New York, Macmillan, 1960), p. 407.
4. See Trevor Mowchun, "A Machine's First Glimpse in Time and Space," *Evental Aesthetics* (2015), 4 (2): pp. 77–102.
5. This phenomenology of cinematic dispossession is evoked by Stanley Cavell throughout *The World Viewed* as a dramatic seal of the world's mind-independence: in other words, cinema reinforces the world as "complete without me," in need of acknowledgment as opposed to knowledge. For Cavell this phenomenon is not exclusive to cinema, as he also finds it enacted in the "total thereness" and "candidness" of modern abstract painting. See Stanley Cavell, *The World Viewed: Reflections on the Ontology of Film*, Enlarged Edition (London and Cambridge, MA: Harvard University Press, 1979), p. 111 and pp. 159–60.

6. See, in particular, Noël Carroll, "Forget the Medium!," in *Engaging the Moving Image* (New Haven, CT, and London: Yale University Press, 2003), pp. 1–9; and D. N. Rodowick, *The Virtual Life of Film* (Cambridge, MA: Harvard University Press, 2007).

7. Nathan Andersen, in his philosophical study of film, specifically emphasizes the surface-depth paradox: "[A]ppearances themselves have depth." Andersen, *Film, Philosophy, and Reality: Ancient Greece to Godard* (London and New York: Routledge, 2019), p. 121.

8. See Daniel Yacavone, *Film Worlds: A Philosophical Aesthetics of Cinema* (New York: Columbia University Press, 2015).

9. Cavell, *The World Viewed*, p. 24.

10. This sense of film being "of" the world might even hold, albeit to a lesser degree, for animated films, where no photographic trace or digital capture of the world is in effect. What I find interesting about this is that films not beholden to the world, which are free to form themselves in accordance with their own aesthetic principles, in many cases adopt mimetic operations and conventions of representation no different than films whose mechanical recordings ontologically mandate a foundation of verisimilitude, be it to the world as we know it or the world as we can only dream of it.

11. This is the infectious pun-title of Rothman's book, *The "I" of the Camera: Essays in Film Criticism, History, and Aesthetics* (Cambridge, MA: Cambridge University Press, 2014).

12. André Bazin, "The Ontology of the Photographic Image," in *What is Cinema?*, Volume 1, trans. and ed. Hugh Gray (Berkeley, Los Angeles, and London: University of California Press, 1967), p. 14; Siegfried Kracauer, *Theory of Film: The Redemption of Physical Reality* (Princeton, NJ: Princeton University Press, 1997), p. 299; Jean Epstein, "The Senses I (b)," in *French Film Theory and Criticism: A History/Anthology 1907–1939*, Volume 1: 1907–1929, trans. Tom Milne, ed. Richard Abel (Princeton, NJ: Princeton University Press, 1988), p. 242; Christian Metz (unpublished manuscript); Cavell, *The World Viewed*, p. xvi.

13. In the field of art history, the concept of medium is traditionally conceived of in terms of "message," and so for Panofsky the medium of film overwhelms its own message, with physical reality as the very substance out of which art is to be made. His critique of films which "prestylize" reality implies that artistic expression will function best through a dialogue with cinema's ontological grammar of the real. For an art historian, the "canvas" of film is like the physical and historical space in which the painter works, a space and a time that most paintings reveal only indirectly and, even then, only with the help of art historical analysis. Erwin Panofsky, "Style and Medium in the Motion Pictures," in *Three Essays on Style*, ed. Irving Lavin (Cambridge, MA: MIT Press, 1995), pp. 122–3.

14. Martin Lefebvre, "The Art of Pointing: On Peirce, Indexicality, and Photographic Images," in *Photography Theory*, ed. James Elkins (New York and London: Routledge, 2007), pp. 220–44. See also, Philip Rosen, *Change Mummified: Cinema, Historicity, Theory* (Minneapolis: University of Minnesota Press, 2001) and Mary

Ann Doane, "Indexicality: Trace and Sign: Introduction," *Differences* (May 1, 2007), 18 (1): 1–6.

15. Malcolm Turvey, *Doubting Vision: Film and the Revelationist Tradition* (Oxford and New York: Oxford University Press, 2008).

16. Cavell, *The World Viewed*, p. 17.

17. Stanley Cavell, "The World as Things: Collecting Thoughts on Collecting," in *Cavell on Film*, ed. William Rothman (Albany: State University of New York Press, 2005), pp. 241–79; Ludwig Wittgenstein, *Tractatus Logico-Philosophicus*, trans. D. F. Pears and B. F. McGuinness (London and New York: Routledge, 2003).

CHAPTER ONE

1. Whether such a project can stand under its own weight is something that readers must determine for themselves. It depends on whether or not, in the context of philosophy, one can accept the logic of poetry. Heidegger's project is the invention of a way of thinking oriented or calibrated towards whatever it is that makes art art—the Being of art—which ultimately leads to the invention of a new philosophical discourse. The degree to which thinking the work of art alters the language of philosophy, expanding it into poetry, is precisely what makes this essay so provocative and imaginative, its infamous difficulties worth dealing with. See Martin Heidegger, "The Origin of the Work of Art," in *Poetry, Language, Thought*, trans. Albert Hofstadter (New York: Harper & Row, 1971), pp. 17–86.

2. Ibid., p. 38.

3. See Ludwig Wittgenstein, *On Certainty*, trans. Denis Paul and G. E. M. Anscombe, ed. G. E. M. Anscombe and G. H. von Wright (Oxford: Blackwell, 1977).

4. See Gianni Vattimo, *Art's Claim to Truth*, trans. Luca D'Isanto, ed. Santiago Zabala (New York: Columbia University Press, 2008).

5. Ibid., p. xvi.

6. See Norman Bryson, "The Natural Attitude," in *Visual Culture: The Reader*, ed. Jessica Evans and Stuart Hall (London, Thousand Oaks, CA, and New Delhi: Sage, 1999), pp. 23–32.

7. See T. J. Clark, *Picasso and Truth: From Cubism to Guernica* (Princeton, NJ: Princeton University Press, 2013).

8. Ibid., p. 282.

9. See Michael Fried, *Why Photography Matters as Art as Never Before* (New Haven, CT: Yale University Press, 2008), pp. 37–93.

10. Ibid., p. 50.

11. See Roland Barthes, *Camera Lucida: Reflections on Photography*, trans. Richard Howard (New York: The Noonday Press and Farrar, Straus and Giroux, 1981).

12. André Bazin, "The Ontology of the Photographic Image," in *What is Cinema?*, Volume 1, trans. and ed. Hugh Gray (Berkeley, Los Angeles, and London: University of California Press, 1967), p. 13.

13. Ibid.

14. Robert Ray, *The Structure of Complex Images* (Cham, Switzerland: Palgrave Macmillan, 2020), p. 62.

15. See Jean-Luc Comolli and Jean Narboni, "Cinema/Criticism/Ideology," in *Film Theory and Criticism*, ed. Leo Braudy and Marshall Cohen, 5th Edition (New York and Oxford: Oxford University Press, 1999), pp. 752–9.

16. Stanley Cavell, *The World Viewed: Reflections on the Ontology of Film*, Enlarged Edition (London and Cambridge, MA: Harvard University Press, 1979), p. xiv.

17. Though I do not wish to give undue weight to frivolous terminology, perhaps this situation can illuminate the difference between (our use of) the more casual term "movie" and the more formal/technical term "film." The word "film" implies that the filming process might peel away the very surfaces of the world, suggesting that a film image consists in a removable, reproducible, and verisimilar topsoil of being. Here, the material of the medium has a distinct origin which its projection summons, whereas the immateriality of the digital, which Cavell could not have foreseen, spiritualizes its own substance by hiding itself from view and wishing its ontological problems away.

18. Cavell, *The World Viewed*, p. xix.

19. Ibid., pp. xiv and 162.

20. Ibid., p. 72.

21. See Cavell, "More of *The World Viewed*," in *The World Viewed*, pp. 162–230.

22. Gilles Deleuze, *Cinema 2: The Time-Image*, trans. Hugh Tomlinson and Robert Galeta (London and New York: Bloomsbury Academic, 2013), pp. 171–3 and 201. In an earlier draft of my book, in a separate chapter which was eventually excised, I discussed at some length Deleuze's theory of the cinematic time-image, specifically his claim that post-WWII cinema records a direct image of time, and reached the conclusion that such a theory constitutes its own *metaphysics of time*. Of the many reasons for this chapter's exclusion, the fact that Deleuze's theory is all but incommensurable with my own undoubtedly played a significant part, for his position is that cinema reveals time itself not from its inception but rather upon its death, or paralysis, as a highly sensitive cultural barometer of post-war disorientation and trauma throughout Europe. The incommensurability likely stems from my regarding cinema as more tightly bound with the "death of God" as opposed to Deleuze's implied emphasis on the "death of man as a moral being."

23. Cavell, *The World Viewed*, p. 189. Even though Cavell was writing in the predigital era, the claim that cinema is a moving image of skepticism does not strike me as indebted, at least not in any obvious way, to the question of whether an image was produced photochemically or digitally, or through intricate combinations thereof. When approaching movies *philosophically*, whether one's ultimate motives are primarily phenomenological, like Cavell's, or metaphysical, like my own, it does not really matter how movies are made in a material sense as long as they open a world and represent it to us as paradoxically present, which is what most movies do and what we do with movies, I should think. It is, however, certainly worth considering how the opening of the world has changed in the

digital age (with cleaner shots, smoother cuts, smaller screens) and to what extent viewers guard themselves from trusting a representation of the world, the presence of which, in many cases, is known ahead of time to be forged rather than filmed.

24. Perhaps Cavell's semi-rhetorical question at the end of *The Claim of Reason* should, for our purposes, be slightly rephrased from "Can philosophy become literature and still know itself?" to "Can philosophy become art and still know the world?" The answer, which we all must work out for ourselves, might ultimately depend on *beginning* rather than ending with such a question, or by being prompted to begin a quest for knowledge in a new light—without questions. *The Claim of Reason: Wittgenstein, Skepticism, Morality and Tragedy* (New York and Oxford: Oxford University Press, 1999), p. 496.

25. Ibid., p. 189.

26. Ibid., p. 41.

27. Ibid., p. 17.

28. See Cora Diamond, "The Difficulty of Reality and the Difficulty of Philosophy," in *Philosophy and Animal Life* (New York: Columbia University Press, 2008), pp. 43–90.

29. It is interesting how a philosophical investigation like Cavell's can get underway not just with a declaration of ignorance but with a confession of intellectual limitations, without which there can be no philosophy but with which, ironically, there can also be no philosophy. Our explanations of the nature of photographs and films warrant constant repeating, a situation which only serves to add fuel to the fire of ontological restlessness. And this might explain the equal inclination to leave them be, to relinquish understanding that which defies understanding— one of a multitude of acts of intellectual self-preservation that we might call the bliss of *informed* ignorance.

30. Cavell, *The World Viewed*, p. 39.

31. See Walter Benjamin, "The Work of Art in the Age of Its Technological Reproducibility: Second Version," in *The Work of Art in the Age of Its Technological Reproducibility, and Other Writings on Media*, trans. Edmund Jephcott and Rodney Livingstone, ed. Michael W. Jennings, Brigid Doherty, and Thomas Levin (Cambridge, MA: Belknap Press of Harvard University Press, 2008), pp. 19–55.

32. See Jean-François Lyotard, "The Sublime and the Avant-Garde," trans. Lisa Liebmann, with Geoff Bennington and Marian Hobson, in *The Continental Aesthetics Reader*, ed. Clive Cazeaux (London and New York: Routledge, 2008), pp. 453–64.

33. Unfortunately, this night scene from *In the Bedroom* is too dark to effectively reproduce here. Instead, I offer you a similar, if less portentous, moment from the end of *La Dolce Vita* (Federico Fellini, Italy/France, 1960) when the decadent protagonist, Marcello, stares into the black eye of a large ray fish and finds nothingness itself reflected back at him.

34. For a succinct explanation of the index and its relevancy for the photographic arts, see Mary Ann Doane, "Indexicality: Trace and Sign: Introduction," *Differences*

(May 1, 2007), 18 (1): 1–6. For a more detailed account of the Peircean legacy of this complex, contested, and often misunderstood concept, see Martin Lefebvre, "The Art of Pointing: On Peirce, Indexicality, and Photographic Images," in *Photography Theory*, ed. James Elkins (New York and London: Routledge, 2007), pp. 220–44.

35. This view of human consciousness and subjectivity can be found almost anywhere in Levinas' writings, albeit in piecemeal and often convoluted forms of expression obsessed with undermining the hidden violence of Western metaphysics. I refer the reader to an early attempt made by Levinas in a series of lucid lectures to narrate "the story of consciousness" from nothingness to inception to encounters with alterity, an impressively "smooth" account of the paradoxes of ethics which the majority of his philosophy thereafter seems to deliberately entangle in an effort, perhaps all but futile, to do ethics metaphysically. See Emmanuel Levinas, *Time and the Other*, trans. Richard A. Cohen (Pittsburgh: Duquesne University Press, 1987).

Chapter Two

1. The title alone suggests that this age may coincide with what Heidegger elsewhere calls a "darkening of the world." Darkening as a symptom of picturing implies a world in which to see is already to speak and ideology is default. See Martin Heidegger, "The Age of the World Picture," in *The Question Concerning Technology and Other Essays*, trans. William Lovitt (New York: Harper & Row, 1977), pp. 115–54.

2. The word "arrogation" seems to be deployed by Cavell more as a description than a criticism of philosophical tonality and temperament. See Stanley Cavell, "Philosophy and the Arrogation of Voice," in *A Pitch of Philosophy: Autobiographical Exercises* (Cambridge, MA, and London: Harvard University Press, 1994), pp. 1–51.

3. See Thomas Kuhn, "Revolutions as Changes of Worldview," in *The Structure of Scientific Revolutions* (Chicago and London: University of Chicago Press, 2012), pp. 111–34. This radical account of worldview ontology is more pronounced and unabashed in the first edition. Kuhn tempered the sweeping nature and decisive dynamism of the paradigm shift thesis in later editions, a recanting which could not quite undo the major impact it had on American intellectual culture. Of course, history books naturally have their own histories as well, largely untold.

4. Ludwig Wittgenstein, *Philosophical Investigations*, trans. G. E. M. Anscombe (Oxford and Malden, MA: Blackwell, 2001), §118.

5. For Wittgenstein's metaphor, see ibid., §119.

6. What Rorty has in mind is a metaphor for the mind's perceptual orientation, tendency towards binary opposition, and pursuit of knowledge of that which is external to it—the external world posited as something fundamentally foreign or other which the mind can reflect through various picture-making practices.

These pictures "point" and so are often presented as accurate reflections of the real, but the reality, as it were, is that they are only acts of sense-making which rarely take their own procedures and proclivities into account. See Richard Rorty, *Philosophy and the Mirror of Nature* (Princeton, NJ: Princeton University Press, 1979).

7. Friedrich Nietzsche, *Thus Spoke Zarathustra*, in *The Portable Nietzsche*, trans. and ed. Walter Kaufmann (New York: Penguin Books, 1982), p. 307 (italics in original).

8. See Martin Heidegger, "The Word of Nietzsche: 'God Is Dead'," in *The Question Concerning Technology and Other Essays*, pp. 53–112.

9. Schopenhauer's conception of the will is also a part of this transformative moment, as is Peirce's objective idealism which posits matter in terms of effete mind.

10. Heidegger, "Language," in *Poetry, Language, Thought*, trans. Albert Hofstadter (New York: Harper & Row, 1971), p. 207.

11. Ludwig Wittgenstein, *Tractatus Logico-Philosophicus*, trans. D. F. Pears and B. F. McGuinness (London and New York: Routledge, 2003), p. 5.

12. A. J. Ayer, *Language, Truth and Logic* (London: Penguin, 2001), p. 27.

13. Rorty, *Philosophy and the Mirror of Nature*, p. 170.

14. Ibid., p. 179.

15. Wittgenstein, *Tractatus Logico-Philosophicus*, p. 89.

16. Stanley Cavell, *The World Viewed: Reflections on the Ontology of Film*, Enlarged Edition (London and Cambridge, MA: Harvard University Press, 1979), pp. 101–2.

17. André Bazin, "The Myth of Total Cinema," in *What is Cinema?*, Volume 1, trans. and ed. Hugh Gray (Berkeley, Los Angeles, and London: University of California Press, 1967), p. 21.

18. John Keats, *The Complete Poetical Works and Letters of John Keats* (Cambridge, UK: Houghton, Mifflin and Company, 1899), p. 277.

19. Bazin, "The Ontology of the Photographic Image," in *What is Cinema?*, p. 13. Bazin and V. I. Pudovkin before him also conceive of this phenomenon through the deceivingly simple word "transfer." Now, of course, the romanticism of the realist perspective can be seen to have a political corollary as well. Theorists of the latter persuasion, suspicious of cinema's—particularly Hollywood cinema's—persuasiveness as a transmitter of ideology, typically operate by emphasizing the *culture* as opposed to the nature of cinema as that which affects us like a natural phenomenon, digesting ideology into breathable air. The innocence and indeterminacy of cinematic nature make it exploitable into an effective vehicle for mass enculturation. While the ontology of film, being what it is, does not erect an impasse to ideology, what is often lacking in these ideological critiques are *alternatives* to critique: in other words, openness to a medium whose fundamental openness to the world renders its instances open to interpretation, despite what may appear to be nothing more than a worrisome ideology in need of questioning.

20. Bazin's theory can seem irreconcilable with his practice as a critic. (I, too, see the tension in my own work here and will do my best to dynamize it). In theory,

cinema is the world in its own image, but *in practice* it remains an image of the world, or a series of images, that must be articulated, and the articulations which circulate today become property of the medium tomorrow and thus an extension of the world's self-image and self-imaging capabilities.

21. Cavell, *The World Viewed*, pp. 72, 105, and 201.

22. More recently, Daniel Yacavone, in his exploration of "film worlds," makes a fundamental distinction between the fictional world *in* a cinematic work and the more than fictional and narrative world *of* it. The world *of* a particular film is a movement towards the Bazinian idea of the world in its own image and the Cavellian idea of world projection. The distinction between the "in" and the "of," analogous to the distinction between what cinema "is" and what it can "do," is contingent upon both the representational and presentational dimensions of film. And it is the presentational dimension in particular—undergirding the representational and making cinema's dimensionality possible—which functions as the gateway into the philosophical dimension of film, a dimension apparent to those who seek an essence, knowing that they shall not necessarily find it—for experience teaches that to seek is also to find. See Daniel Yacavone, *Film Worlds: A Philosophical Aesthetics of Cinema* (New York: Columbia University Press, 2015), p. xxii.

23. Heidegger, "The Question Concerning Technology," in *The Question Concerning Technology and Other Essays*, p. 27.

24. Ibid.

25. Heidegger, "The Age of the World Picture," in *The Question Concerning Technology and Other Essays*, p. 132.

26. Heidegger, "The Question Concerning Technology," in *The Question Concerning Technology and Other Essays*, p. 23.

27. Cavell, *The World Viewed*, p. 20.

28. The distinction becomes clear in the following case, if the veracity of photography is compared with the expressive capabilities of other artistic images. The photograph may offer a better likeness of my father, while the painted portrait offers a better (truer?) sense of who he is—his mannerisms, temperament, worldly disposition, way of life. Herein lies a difference between candid photography and photographic art: the ability to use the medium to make a great and revealing portrait equal in that regard to a painting, with the crucial difference being that only the photograph reveals at the same time as it creates.

29. Robert Bresson, *Notes on the Cinematograph*, trans. Jonathan Griffin (New York: New York Review of Books, 2016), p. 69.

30. Cavell, *The World Viewed*, p. xiv.

31. Ibid., p. xix.

32. Cavell was referring to Malick's early work (his current and only work at the time) and so am I, with *The Thin Red Line* marking the end of the early period (or as the sole member of a middle period) despite the twenty-year gap between it and *Days of Heaven*. The late period begins with *The Tree of Life* (USA, 2011), a film whose metaphysical scope stretches even wider than *2001: A Space Odyssey*

(Stanley Kubrick, UK/USA, 1968), and the first of his to be filmed digitally. To make sense of the highly impressionistic drift of Malick's recent work, could we say that he has retreated *back* to philosophy? My understanding of the controversial evolution of Malick's œuvre is as follows: Malick is a compelling, brooding, nearly flawless yet sporadic filmmaker in the pre-digital era of cinema. When he discovers the many efficacies of the digital medium and its corresponding digital consciousness, he is led in a sudden surge of films including *To the Wonder* (USA, 2012), *Knight of Cups* (USA, 2015), and *Song to Song* (2017, USA) to either overthink the world or dissolve it into a muddy stream of innocuous impressions, many of which eddy into monotonous loops that go nowhere. With storytelling, character development, and genre conventions at a bare minimum, the human lives onscreen seem detached from each other and the world by their own existential obsessions and interminable thoughts, devouring themselves like a solipsistic Ouroboros. The divine also shifts registers from an intimate force which characters question, covet, or ridicule in their brightest or darkest hour, to an impersonal and diaphanous resonance that seems to say (to us more than to them): "The chaos you perceive is a projection of your own troubled mind, for naturally all is one." Such metaphysical generalizations fall flat in movies unless they come from a particular place, like a character on the brink of madness or war as the naturalization of madness (re: *The Thin Red Line*). Ingmar Bergman was probably the best at writing out his philosophical ideas and beliefs *for* rather than *through* his characters, perhaps because for him the crises which characters face inevitably bring on a change in beliefs, sometimes a total loss of belief; and it is that discovery, sometimes a despair, over new ways of thinking which gives philosophical ideas their *dramatic* power.

33. Ibid., pp. xv–xvi. I find it interesting that Cavell, in one of his most ambitious expressions of the ontology of film, appears to inherit (without quoting) Bazin's commitment to the term "recreation" as a description of how objects appear on film: they do not merely appear, they come to life. In his work Bazin ensures that cinematic representation is not dismissed as a mere copy of the world, and Cavell's debt to Bazin is evident in his avoidance, when possible, of the static term "representation" when discussing film's "ontology," a term he also borrows from Bazin's inspired usage.

34. See Martin Heidegger, "Memorial Address," in *Discourse on Thinking*, trans. John M. Anderson and E. Hans Freund (New York: Harper & Row, 1966), pp. 43–57.

35. Cavell, *The World Viewed*, p. xiv.

36. See Cavell's excursus chapter "Some Modernist Painting," in *The World Viewed*, pp. 108–18. It turns out that what film does automatically is not unique to film but rather to modernism, though film may be unique insofar as it is *born modern*. The method of this excursus has a touch of madness in it, but if ever a digression from the primary path of one's thought, or "argument," were justified and, in retrospect, proved vital to a course reaching its end (for in philosophy the shortest distance between two points is often a shortcut), this is it.

37. Malick, for example, filmed only during the twilight "magic hour" moments, setting the film in this brief picturesque light interval. The entire production revolved around this special light, even though the script rarely indicates a time more specific than the conventional vagary of "day or night." See Terrence Malick, *Days of Heaven: An Original Screenplay* (Hollywood: Script City, 1976).

38. Heidegger, "The Origin of the Work of Art," in *Poetry, Language, Thought*, pp. 82–3. In Heidegger's discussions of the poetry of Rilke and Hölderlin, in order for the poet to heed the call of Being and in the process repair or redeem our estranged relationship with Being, he or she will find a way, every time anew, to bring out the being of language, language being the very house of Being.

39. This unique coinage from Heidegger can be found in "The Worldhood of the World" (Section 3, Division 1) in *Being and Time*, trans. John Macquarrie and Edward Robinson (San Francisco: Harper & Row, 1962), pp. 91–148.

40. I first heard of the term "camera consciousness" as an interpretive tool from a wonderful talk given by Adam Rosadiuk at the Society for Cinema and Media Studies annual conference. When I refer to the camera as "conscious" I am giving credence to its automatism, of course, but I am also projecting the camera's automatism *into* the images I experience onscreen. I know these images are the work of conscious beings, and yet my experience of the recreation of the world in its own image transforms human consciousness into mechanical consciousness. I explore this reversal more fully in the following chapter.

41. In any privileging of the auteur it seems to me necessary, where the art of formal radiance and world-disclosure is concerned, that in the very least both director and cinematographer be simultaneously acknowledged. *Days of Heaven* presents a complex case in that it was filmed by two cinematographers in succession, and in circumstances that cannot be described as part of the production plan. The older and more traditional Néstor Almendros was relieved by the younger *cinema vérité*-inspired Haskell Wexler due to scheduling as opposed to artistic conflicts. Despite his distinct visual sensibility, Wexler claims to have pursued aesthetic consistency at all costs by successfully mimicking Almendros's cinematography, heavily reliant as it is upon natural light and semi-artful if self-effacing camerawork. In my own experience as a filmmaker, directors are deeply involved in the cinematography and cinematographers can do some significant directing: together they are the mind's eye of the film. It is common knowledge kept secret that sometimes cinematographers can do *more* directing than the director himself, particularly when the realization of the image becomes a matter of executing a preconceived set of rote technicalities and conventions. Detailed and honest accounts of directing experiences—from directors *and* cinematographers—are all too scarce and therefore always welcome. Malick has remained stubbornly silent on such matters, as if he gave up his tongue when he gave up philosophy for art.

42. We may also want to ask to what extent the frame of a moving image of the world constitutes its *own* horizon where on- and offscreen sights and sounds are negotiated, where the specificity and selectivity of the frame itself expand

and retract. The cinematic frame, belonging exclusively to neither picture nor sound, contains within its coming and going, holding and hiding, seeing and hearing, an image's mode of allocation in apprehending the world. The pure decision and resolve of an image-horizon can lead us to consider what the image is doing in order *not* to be carried away by adjacent sights and sounds. Further illuminating the relationship between earth and sky, the image-horizon foregrounds (or meta-foregrounds) exchanges and compromises between the visible and invisible, the audible and inaudible, that belong to the very habitability of the world on film.

43. The idea that movies have minds and can "think" is pushed to the limit by Daniel Frampton in *Filmosophy* (London and New York: Wallflower Press, 2006).

44. In his classic work of phenomenology, *The Poetics of Space*, Gaston Bachelard writes, "Before he is 'cast out into the world,' as claimed by certain hasty metaphysicians, man is laid in the cradle of the house." Few philosophers are as refreshingly optimistic and down-to-earth as Bachelard, and to my knowledge he may be the only one to deliver so swift a critique, or reversal, of the methods of metaphysics with words like "house" and "haste." Of course, the claim that "house" precedes "world" excludes those who are born or become homeless. But for the most part our first world is an extension of the womb and some form of house, a nest to shelter us *from* the world. Bachelard, *The Poetics of Space*, trans. Maria Jolas (New York: The Orion Press, 1964), p. 7.

CHAPTER THREE

1. Stanley Cavell, *The World Viewed: Reflections on the Ontology of Film*, Enlarged Edition (London and Cambridge, MA: Harvard University Press, 1979), p. 39.

2. Two canonical works of classical film theory in this respect, arguably the first to make the case that for film to become art it must override or subvert its mimetic basis, are Rudolph Arnheim's *Film as Art* (Berkeley: University of California Press, 2007) and Hugo Münsterberg's "The Photoplay: A Psychological Study," in *Hugo Münsterberg on Film: The Photoplay—A Psychological Study and Other Writings*, ed. Allan Langdale (New York: Routledge, 2002), pp. 45–164.

3. For a fascinating study of the persistence in Western philosophy of the theme of human imperfection as a helpless fallenness in need of constant redemption, see Stephen Mulhall, *Philosophical Myths of the Fall* (Princeton, NJ, and Oxford: Princeton University Press, 2007).

4. Cavell, *The World Viewed*, pp. 72–3, 104–6, 146–7; see also Chapter 14 on "Automatism," pp. 101–8. According to Cavell, projecting the world in succession is the only thing film does automatically, which implies that it is not enough to make film into an art. Making a succession of automatic world projections artistically expressive requires what Cavell calls the discovery of automatisms, mediums within the medium, as it were, that upon activation call for a range of expressions that may become the basis for a new genre or tradition to emerge. Cavell's analysis of automatism is twofold, beginning as a technical description

of the ontology of film and evolving into an exploration of the tasks of modernism to create new automatisms at a time when the old ones no longer hold sway. Save for a perceived affinity between automatism and autonomy, between art as happening by itself and existing by itself, our analyses diverge.

5. I am borrowing my sense of redemption here directly from the subtitle of Siegfried Kracauer's *Theory of Film: The Redemption of Physical Reality*. The stakes of Kracauer's book are also deeply eschatological but where the approach to film is far more systematic, even taxonomical. His methodology and general way of thinking seem to deflect the spirited project of messianic redemption, at least until the book's provocative epilogue—a sweeping history of ideas starring the cinema as counter-history—disclosing what I believe are its most pressing inner motives. A personal point regarding this astonishing epilogue: one may end by concluding, as we are trained to do, or by *confessing*, which cannot be taught, unless it is possible to teach complete honesty with oneself and trust in one's readers.

6. Heinrich von Kleist, "On the Marionette Theater," in *German Romantic Criticism*, trans. Christian-Albrecht Gollub, ed. A. Leslie Willson (New York: Continuum, 1982), pp. 238–44; Robert Bresson, *Notes on the Cinematograph*, trans. Jonathan Griffin (New York: New York Review of Books, 2016). I discovered Bresson's little book under a slightly different name in the first English translation, also by Griffin, published in 1977: *Notes on Cinematography*. The two editions are identical except for the title and minor differences in the thematic organization of the material. I assume the word "cinematograph" is a more accurate translation of the French, hearkening back to cinema's inaugural name given by the Lumière brothers. It certainly suits Bresson's emphasis on the medium as a whole along with his auteurist leanings, deemphasizing the role of the cinematographer as we understand it today. However, the new term excludes the theoretical and perhaps uniquely French understanding of cinematography as a form of *image writing*.

7. I understand epiphany as an insight which human reason is potentially unfit to grasp without feeling threatened or obsolete, especially when such a truth is shown to come at the expense of reason itself. An epiphany is a festive occasion for the soul, a long-awaited yet ultimately unexpected reward for intellectual and general life labors that seemed to be going nowhere until one sees that hard work pays off in mysterious ways. We just do not know when we are able to change until change is upon us, and time and again the moral of the story is that patience brings roses. But there is another side to the story of the epiphany, a Romantic and much darker aspect in which the change of heart is undergone reluctantly because the pain of change is just as great. The philosophy that endures, I would say, is the result of such uncompromising, if not cruel, transformations of thought—sacrifices made to the new self who writes on the back of the old self. The new self sheds tears over the burial of the old self, or the new self is haunted by the ghost of the old self, because the epiphany imposes itself regardless of continuity and consent. For philosophy lacking signs of empathy, its epiphanies are most likely *learned*, not earned. Philosophy

textbooks, for example, are raised upon many little epiphanies, reaping them like a crop of tears.

8. Kleist, "On the Marionette Theater," p. 241.

9. Hell might be Franz Kafka's "The Metamorphosis": awakening to find oneself changed into a hideously oversized insect. By discovering one day that he is unable to speak or work or live with purpose, Gregor Samsa's new bug life is a scary reprieve from the paradoxes of modernity in which productivity masquerades as freedom. In protest, Gregor slips into a state of grace so radically foreign to himself and his family, to Kafka and his readers, that all must fail to comprehend it and, in failing so miserably, find its sublime beauty repulsive in the extreme. See Franz Kafka, "The Metamorphosis," in *The Complete Stories*, trans. Willa and Edwin Muir, ed. Nahum N. Glatzer (New York: Schocken Books, 1971), pp. 89–139.

10. Kleist, "On the Marionette Theater," p. 244.

11. Ibid.

12. Along with Chekhov and Kafka, who are undoubtedly influenced by him, Kleist is a master of writing short stories with the weight of novels, an act/art of refinement which I also associate with an aversion to vanity. When put into practice, whether in art or in life, the true measure of modesty is not self-effacement but self-criticism. The repeated distillations which reduce an artwork to its essence have systematically done away with the juicy bits of fat that artists sometimes use to pay themselves in absent praise, or simply to prove to themselves and others that they are in fact "good artists." My experience of Kleist—and Chekhov and Kafka—is that sentences tend to be realized on the condition that no personal validation is derived from them, and that, if I may be so bold, the prose is approved as if by a higher power. For examples—though, of course, readers will have to judge for themselves—see Kleist's short stories "The Marquise of O" and "The Earthquake in Chile." My favorite is the novella *Michael Kohlhaas*, which in heavier hands might have been a tome or been composed in the tone of a tome.

13. Kleist, "On the Marionette Theater," pp. 243–4.

14. Ibid., p. 244.

15. The hints of histrionics in Laydu's spiritualizing of the true believer's tortured flesh—as when he appears to look into himself to listen to the excruciating word of God and, armed/burdened with the truth, looks up to impart that word to others, a gesture which sometimes comes across as *looking down* upon uninspired souls—would be overcome by the time Bresson reached his own version of the Joan of Arc story, *The Trial of Joan of Arc* (France, 1962). While no film about Joan could ever hope to escape the monumentality of Dreyer's silent masterpiece, Bresson's humbling of the lead's performance (what is her name?) can be read as a critique of Dreyer's deferrence to dramatic acting, particularly the freedom given to the actors and obsessive use of closeups which magnify their every gesture. For the sake of argument, you could say that Dreyer puts his faith in Falconetti, whereas Bresson puts his faith demandingly in the audience.

16. Perhaps film actors discover, instinctively or through experience, that they do not have to project themselves all that much because they are already, in a sense, projected by the medium. Bresson might agree, if only actors had it within them not to project themselves *at all*.

17. An example of Bresson's criteria for rightness over expressiveness can be found in the *Notes*: "*Right* intonations when your model exercises no control over them." Bresson, *Notes on the Cinematograph*, p. 51 (italics in original).

18. Ibid., p. 74.

19. The ethical problems of the voyeur would take on an aesthetic complexion if Bresson were to actually film this scene using actors/models. The camera-eye, being unable to distinguish between authentic and inauthentic movements and expressions, would "assume" that the actions it records are revelatory of those who make them, and so any action which suffers a concealment of consciousness will still be treated as a candidate for grace. The filmmaker has to ensure, somehow, that the camera itself can follow through on its promise to faithfully record what may or may not be worthy of such faithfulness. It is as if Bresson strives to gain the trust of the camera instead of the actors, with the use of models over actors serving as a key part of that pact.

20. I have adapted this phrase from the subtitle of *Institute Benjamenta: This Dream People Call Human Life* (Quay Brothers, Germany–Japan–UK, 1996), although the sense of dream in this film is far more conventional than anything in Bresson. Of course, there are (can be) no dream scenes in Bresson's films, and the subject of dreams is of little concern in the *Notes*. I take this conspicuous absence of the dream to indicate Bresson's interest in the methods and not the tropes of surrealism.

21. Bresson, *Notes on the Cinematograph*, p. 5.

22. See Walter Benjamin, *The Writer of Modern Life: Essays on Charles Baudelaire* (Cambridge, MA, and London, UK: The Belknap Press of Harvard University Press, 2006).

23. Bresson, *Notes on the Cinematograph*, p. 40. The well-known line from the New Testament is "Seek, and ye shall find" (Matthew 7: 7–8, King James Version).

24. Ibid., p. 88. Capital letters in original.

25. This view of the camera's commensurability with (non-)human consciousness is not incompatible with the French philosopher Maurice Merleau-Ponty's lone essay on the cinema, defining it as a mode of perception and expression which is resolutely *exterior*, in contradistinction to literature's obsession with inhabiting the psychological interiors of characters and the theater's obsession with projecting the psychology of characters to an audience. See Merleau-Ponty, "The Film and the New Psychology," in *Sense and Non-Sense*, trans. Hubert L. Dreyfus and Patricia Allen Dreyfus (Chicago: Northwestern University Press, 1964), pp. 48–59.

26. Bresson seems to have found a way to completely bypass the gaze of the model, preventing it from meeting his gaze in a dream-shattering self-awareness, by

casting in a lead role an animal instead of a human being—a donkey in particular—in *Au hasard Balthazar* (France-Sweden, 1966).

27. Bresson, *Notes on the Cinematograph*, p. 66.
28. André Bazin, "The Ontology of the Photographic Image," in *What is Cinema?*, Volume 1, trans. and ed. Hugh Gray (Berkeley, Los Angeles, and London: University of California Press, 1967), p. 14.
29. Bresson, *Notes on the Cinematograph*, pp. 74 and 40 (italics in original).
30. In painting, the model also does not act; mostly he or she just stands there posing. And, in a sense, this is what Bresson also seeks from his models, perhaps informed by his prior experience as a painter: someone who just stands there, instead of acting. The challenge is in developing this sense of standing and thereness—this "presentness"—across narrative time. The model becomes more like a landscape or found object than an actor. If there is something Bazinian at stake here, it may be this "transfer," from model to character by way of automatism, bypassing the artifice and with it the art of acting as we know it.
31. Bresson, *Notes on the Cinematograph*, p. 13 (italics in original).
32. Ibid. (italics in original).
33. Ibid., p. 51.
34. Ibid., p. 33 (italics in original).
35. Ibid., p. 17. The note from which this technique is drawn is expressed with Bresson's signature combination of precision and restraint: "Models who have become automatic (everything weighed, measured, timed, repeated ten, twenty times) and are then dropped in the medium of the events of your film—their relations with the objects and persons around them will be *right*, because they will not be *thought*" (italics in original).
36. Ibid., p. 24.
37. Paul Schrader, *Transcendental Style in Film: Ozu, Bresson, Dreyer* (Berkeley: Da Capo Press, 1972), pp. 82–3. Schrader gives scant attention to *Mouchette*, claiming it lacks the "resolution" of the earlier films about physical and spiritual imprisonment while confessing that "it may be too early to tell" (p. 60). He does not catch Bresson's saving gesture (it took me many viewings), and one wonders what he might have made of it.
38. Bresson, *Notes on the Cinematograph*, p. 59.
39. By "silent" I mean pre- or non-linguistic expression. The sheep are not exactly silent: their bells chime with the same serene clamor heard in the beginning of the film when Balthazar, still a foal, is shown feeding on his mother's teat. We can then say that the herd of sheep at Balthazar's deathbed consoles him with the memory of his mother, a childhood memory rooted in sensations of touch, of closeness and its consequent smell and taste, hence of bondage with the higher power of that which gave him life. As Mother was Goddess to the infant, so She becomes God to any dying creature blessed to have had a mother, or mothering, if only for the brief period in which her abiding strength is converted into the fledgling's inspired first flight of independence.

40. Brief interviews with the main cast of *Mouchette* attest to this. Significantly, these are *not* insightful interviews into their creative process as "actors." The feeling, rather, is that they don't know why anyone would bother to interview them about acting or filmmaking. They just want to get back to their lives.

41. Bresson has a strong preference for the beauty, intensity, and troubled aloofness of youth. The young man at the baths in Kleist's essay would surely have been the main focus of a Bresson film version (if we care to imagine something so strange). But if Bresson's goal can be summarized as that of suppressing conscious intention, mechanizing the face, emptying out the mental interior and so on, why not restrict casting solely to children or even animals, those with less human experience or non-human experience? Mouchette may be the youngest character of about 13–14 years, though her problems in life exceed those of the average adult. As the primary caregiver of the household, she seems never to have known a real moment of child-like innocence and exuberance. Bresson made only one film about an animal and that is *Balthazar*, yet despite having the ideal material for a model—a donkey cannot act other than a donkey, I should think—Bresson devotes much of the film to the people who surround Balthazar, his owners (albeit he is never owned for very long). One of the few scenes in which Balthazar is not overshadowed by humans is at a circus, where he performs with human-like intelligence, answering math questions by tapping his hooves. In general, Bresson prefers not the mythical innocence of children or animals but the *twilight innocence of youth*: youths not being young or enjoying their youth. Actors whose faces exude the beauty and suffering of youth, like Greta Garbo, James Dean, Marlon Brando, or Montgomery Clift in their prime, would fit perfectly in a Bresson film if not for their transferable star power and thespian skill sets. Gaunt and lost-looking, solitary and soft-spoken, fragile yet fierce, fully grown yet still growing into themselves, the personalities of Bresson's youths are mapped across their face, body, and voice at that special in-bloom juncture just before a steady base of life experience solidifies into "knowledge." They are cast in such a way and at such a time as to be caught in the midst of their own quietly raging fire, surrounded by the cool cement of sidewalks and rough country roads—smack in between the dreaminess of childhood innocence and the dreamless adjustedness of adulthood, during that inimitable liminal interval when the serene archipelago of facial features and slightly awkward gait tread water in a storm-prone ocean of possibilities and chance occurrences.

42. Bresson, *Notes on the Cinematograph*, p. 83 (italics in original).

Chapter Four

1. It could be argued that contingencies of a poetic or even metaphysical nature radically distinguished the Lumière films from those Thomas Edison produced in his Black Maria studio. Edison's pitch-black, tar-coated backdrop systematically "walled off" the noise of the outside world, as if he sought the sterile and controllable conditions of the experimental laboratory, conditions more abstract

than the theater whose black walls function more like a painter's canvas. In Lumiére, the capacity for viewers to freely roam from the foregrounded world of humans to the backgrounded world of nature, or reverse the order of significance even for just a brief flash of consciousness, seems to have played an important role in the success of their films around the world and, more importantly, in the evolution of the cinema into an artform of heightened sensorial and panoramic proportions.

2. Martin Lefebvre, "Between Setting and Landscape in the Cinema," in *Landscape and Film*, ed. Martin Lefebvre (New York and London: Routledge, 2006), p. 27.

3. See the previously cited edited collection *Landscape and Film* and Lefebvre's companion piece, "On Landscape in Narrative Cinema," *Canadian Journal of Film Studies* (Spring 2011), 20 (1): pp. 61–78.

4. When films reduce nature to human nature, isolating human nature into a whole whose parts are in disarray, then natural forces such as sex, violence, love, and death can come across as "unnatural," as if the human tie to nature *gives in* to nature and risks unleashing a far from innocent animal.

5. Traditionally, animated or CGI films depicting nature as a living being with big eyes are acts of what I would call "animistic anthropomorphism," hence traces of the lost age of animism. These traces, however, are still disenchanted insofar as the very concept of animation breaks nature down into "frames" and makes it appear comprehensible *to us* rather than genuinely and mysteriously alive.

6. I borrow this phrase from D. N. Rodowick, who is fond of using it to describe the ideal state of philosophy as a discourse that must constantly question itself and possibly reinvent itself. The appeal to openness can also be somewhat misleading, for the perpetual demand to question makes sense only if there are provisional answers in place that no longer hold sway. See Rodowick, *Philosophy's Artful Conversation* (Cambridge, MA, and London: Harvard University Press, 2015).

7. Simon Critchley, "Calm—On Terrence Malick's *The Thin Red Line*," in *The Thin Red Line*, ed. David Davies (London and New York: Routledge, 2009), p. 26 (italics in original). Ben McCann evokes the concept of contingency in reference to the representation of nature's indifference in Malick's work prior to *The Thin Red Line*: "[N]ature as uncompromising, possessing an arbitrariness with no fixed scheme." See McCann, "'Enjoying the Scenery': Landscape and the Fetishization of Nature in *Badlands* and *Days of Heaven*," in *The Cinema of Terrence Malick: Poetic Visions of America*, ed. Hannah Patterson (London and New York: Wallflower Press, 2003), p. 80.

8. Stanley Cavell, *The World Viewed: Reflections on the Ontology of Film*, Enlarged Edition (London and Cambridge, MA: Harvard University Press, 1979), p. xvi.

9. André Bazin, "Theater and Cinema (part 2)," in *What is Cinema?* Volume 1, trans. and ed. Hugh Gray (Berkeley, Los Angeles, and London: University of California Press, 1967), p. 110.

10. Leo Bersani and Ulysse Dutoit conclude their study of *The Thin Red Line* not with the feeling of having reached a deeper understanding of its meaning and

methods, but rather with what strikes me as a resigned acceptance of the film's representations of presence, in other words the *(in)significance* of its various individual and interconnected presences which have not been forced into the symbolic register. They describe images of nature as resonating with each other, occasionally touching each other, and meaningful only insofar as they are present onscreen, to us, and to other presences within the film's metaphysical network of being. See Bersani and Dutoit, *Forms of Being: Cinema, Aesthetics, Subjectivity* (London: British Film Institute, 2004), p. 175.

11. Andrei Tarkovsky, *Sculpting in Time*, trans. Kitty Hunter-Blair (Austin: University of Texas Press Printing, 2000), pp. 212–13.

12. The activation of the "thought" of an emotional–aesthetic impression can occur through what David Davies describes in his essay on *The Thin Red Line* as an emphasis on the articulation of form, the painterly qualities of things, and texture over shape. I believe Davies is mistaken, however, in his binary distinction between "sensation" and "understanding," especially in the suggestion that the former must come at the expense of the latter. See David Davies, "Vision, Touch, and Embodiment in *The Thin Red Line*," in *The Thin Red Line*, ed. David Davies (London and New York: Routledge, 2009), p. 57.

13. Such cuts can also occur *internally* within the image, as when the frame is gradually or suddenly cleared of its human inhabitants. For example, in the films of Michelangelo Antonioni, characters will walk out of the frame while the view is held deliberately on the "empty" natural or urban environs.

14. Of all the philosophers who have been inspired to express nature in terms of constant change, going all the way back to Heraclitus, I offer Ralph Waldo Emerson's passage from "The Poet" for its syntactical struggle to keep up with its own (changing) conception of nature as the being which never sleeps, as the Being which answers to none: "What we call nature is a certain self-regulated motion or change; and nature does all things by her own hands, and does not leave another to baptize her but baptizes herself; and this through the metamorphosis again." Ralph Waldo Emerson, "The Poet," in *The Portable Emerson*, ed. Carl Bode and Malcolm Cowley (New York: Penguin Books, 1981), p. 253.

15. "Nature appearances" in cinema can be artificially rendered through various effects, from artificial lights that simulate the sun to sprinklers that simulate rain, or painted backdrops that simulate the sky, or wind machines that simulate windy conditions, or in our day and age a thousand digital creations imperceptible to the eye. But what are such artificial representations of nature ultimately for? What do they dramatize?—*Forces beyond human control*. Filmmakers can still value such forces by making rather than chasing storms, controlling rather than catching nature. Fabricated nature may have a more natural effect, exposing characters and viewers to forms of nature that are rare, unpredictable, or near impossible to get close to. It is revealing that our capacity through film to control these forces beyond our control has resulted in nature being imagined more often in terms of disaster or even apocalypse rather than the sublime and

its return to paradise. An optimistic interpretation of this phenomenon might state that "controlling the uncontrollable" is not necessarily an attempt to conquer our fears by way of gross indulgence as it is an act of communicating the finitude of the human condition, reminding us of the value of our small-ness and powerlessness when the temptation to control the world threatens to isolate us from the world and each other.

16. Lefebvre, "Between Setting and Landscape in the Cinema," p. 51 (italics in original).

17. Jean-François Lyotard, "The Sublime and the Avant-Garde," trans. Lisa Liebmann, with Geoff Bennington and Marian Hobson, in *The Continental Aesthetics Reader*, ed. Clive Cazeaux (London and New York: Routledge, 2008), p. 453.

18. Ibid., p. 454 (italics in original).

19. Cavell, *The World Viewed*, p. 110. See also Cavell, "Knowing and Acknowledging," in *Must We Mean What We Say?*, Updated Edition (New York: Cambridge University Press, 2008), pp. 238–66.

20. Long after writing this chapter, I came upon the unpublished screenplay for *The Thin Red Line* and was amazed to discover that my intuitions about "exposure" were echoed in the film's original conception and planning. Early on in the lengthy script, Malick describes the mindset of one of the main characters in exactly these terms: "Fife looks this way and that, to see if there is something or someone about to shoot at him. He has a singular feeling of exposure, like a man standing on the edge of a mountaintop." In the finished film, the character of Fife (played by Adrien Brody) is drastically reduced to a speechless face perpetu-ally overexposed by a deep gnawing fear he cannot overcome. Terrence Malick, *The Thin Red Line* (unpublished screenplay), p. 34.

21. Robert Sinnerbrink, *Terrence Malick: Filmmaker and Philosopher* (London and New York: Bloomsbury, 2019), p. 46.

22. I found some inspiration here from the words of philosopher-poet Jan Zwicky, who specializes in doing philosophy through poetry and making poetry out of philosophy. Her metaphor for the power of *insight* to perceive the whole through one of its parts runs as follows: "As though the weight of the universe were bal-anced on a single point, and that point entered us." Zwicky, *Wisdom and Metaphor* (Kentville, NS, Canada: Gaspereau Press, 2003), p. 54, left side.

23. My understanding of the concept of exposure has developed from both film and philosophy: specifically, the art of cinematography and Cora Diamond's spellbinding essay "The Difficulty of Reality and the Difficulty of Philosophy," in *Philosophy and Animal Life* (New York: Columbia University Press, 2008), pp. 43–89.

24. This unrecognizability and perhaps unknowability of characters who stand on the brink of death is related to George Toles's reading of the noir film *Red Light* (Roy Del Ruth, USA, 1949), a film in which a minor character meets his untimely end mechanically and meaninglessly, at a trivial juncture of the narrative and without any narrative justification or recuperation to speak of. According to Toles, the

viewer is deprived of the standard movie conventions to make sense of death, conventions whose comforts almost always thread death through the aesthetic and moral logic of the film. Seeing death in all its routine mechanicity, unsentimental and absurd, makes plain the fact that most movies strive to put a face on death, to *humanize* death, rendering it more bearable when it is the anonymity of death, hence our own anonymity, that may very well be the bliss we have been waiting for. Toles, "Film Death and the Failure to Signify: The Curious Case of Warni Hazard," *New Review of Film and Television Studies* (2017), 15 (2): p. 219.

25. See Susan Sontag, *Regarding the Pain of Others* (New York: Picador, 2004).

26. The questions keep coming because the film is a feat of thinking through questioning. And unlike philosophy, it need not answer its own questions—in fact, they ought to be left *unanswered* if the viewer is to participate in its thought process. Some philosophers may find this situation enviable, others may find it deplorable; either way, the artwork which refuses to answer its own questions (or which wouldn't know where to start) can account for why such questions never disappear completely, even if philosophy claims to have thoroughly answered them and put them to rest. They wake up. The answers of philosophy in its waking life are as if reprocessed as lingering or nagging questions in the great dream that is art.

27. Such a perspective is, of course, superficial and stereotypical, as if framing *out* parts of a picture like a postcard in denial of dilapidation and decay. As I had cause to mention before, this Eden adjacent to the war is partially filtered through Witt's romanticism and impassioned search for a spiritual unity, what he calls "the spark" that is diverted, diffused, or altogether eclipsed by ego-driven and materialistic ways of life. Robert Pippin goes so far as to argue that we see only what Witt sees, and what Witt sees is ultimately what he *thinks* he sees and *wants* to see—a reflection of his belief system which, as in any system, conveniently edits out contrary evidence. The less insight one has into the logic of one's own beliefs, the easier it is to reinforce them through experience; and the edits required to actually see what one believes are virtually seamless when performed by the unconscious. It is my belief, however, that Witt's beliefs also help him to see clearly and deeply. Witt's desire to see beauty and unity *opens his eyes* to their possibility. Robert Pippin, "Vernacular Metaphysics: On Terrence Malick's *The Thin Red Line*," in *The Philosophy of War Films*, ed. David LaRocca (Lexington: The University Press of Kentucky, 2014), pp. 392–4.

28. A similar subject position of power is assumed when nature is constructed in the image of a landscape. The relation between landscape and war was identified by Denis E. Cosgrove, *Social Formation and Symbolic Landscape* (London and Sydney: Croom Helm, 1984).

29. Lefebvre, "Between Setting and Landscape in the Cinema," p. 53.

30. Kaja Silverman, "All Things Shining," in *Loss: The Politics of Mourning*, ed. David L. Eng and David Kazanjian (Berkeley and Los Angeles: University of California Press, 2003), p. 327.

31. Paul Virilio, *War and Cinema: The Logistics of Perception*, trans. Patrick Camiller (London and New York: Verso, 1989), p. 7 (italics in original).

32. The paradisiacal vision of nature at the beginning of the film, with the two AWOL American soldiers living "in harmony" with the native Melanesians, contains, by contrast, not a single discrete *shot* of nature, for the idea is that they are living amongst those who are at one with nature, who still live there, and for a brief time (the length of an experiment, let's say) shed the Western consciousness skin whose instinct is to control rather than to connect.

33. Robert Silberman, "Terrence Malick, Landscape and 'This War at the Heart of Nature'," in *The Cinema of Terrence Malick: Poetic Visions of America*, ed. Hannah Patterson (London and New York: Wallflower Press, 2003), p. 167.

34. One of the many myths surrounding what are called baobab trees.

CHAPTER FIVE

1. The truth of their anonymous and repetitive life is perfectly captured by Samuel Beckett, whose work, I believe, is an inspiration for the film. The relevant passage is from his novel *Molloy*: "All the things you would do gladly, oh without enthusiasm, but gladly, all the things there seems no reason for your not doing, and that you do not do! Can it be we are not free? It might be worth looking into." Beckett, *Molloy: A Novel*, trans. Patrick Bowles, in collaboration with Samuel Beckett (New York: Grove Press, 1955), p. 48. I thank my friend Daniel Gerson for alerting me to what I take to be Beckett at his philosophical best here.

2. See Friedrich Nietzsche, *The Gay Science*, trans. Walter Kaufmann (New York: Vintage Books, 1974), pp. 181–2.

3. See especially the Fourth Part of Friedrich Nietzsche, *Thus Spoke Zarathustra*, in *The Portable Nietzsche*, trans. and ed. Walter Kaufmann (New York: Penguin Books, 1982), pp. 343–439.

4. See Siegfried Kracauer, *Theory of Film: The Redemption of Physical Reality* (Princeton, NJ: Princeton University Press, 1997), pp. 287–8.

5. In reality, Nietzsche's breakdown probably had nothing to do with his philosophy, but in the fictional world of *The Turin Horse* I believe it has *everything* to do with it. Fiction permits us to make the connection that stares us in the face and which we want so much to make yet so rarely do out of fear of being proven wrong. In this peculiar case the connection at stake is the *contradiction* between thought and feeling, possibility and actuality, philosophy and humanity, laughter and tears . . .

6. In his lecture course on Nietzsche, Martin Heidegger correctly points out that Nietzsche's "hammer" is used not only to destroy the false but to tap the surface of things which appear true, to see (or hear) whether or not there is still any substance left within them. Heidegger is a good reader of Nietzsche on many points, carefully listening to the secret sense of key terms. Heidegger, *Nietzsche, Volume 1: The Will to Power as Art*, trans. David Ferrell Krell (San Francisco: Harper & Row, 1979), p. 66.

7. Tony Pipolo, in his fine review of the film, does well to remind us that the barren and utterly dismal terrain of the film's setting can in no way be confused with the Italian countryside surrounding the small city of Turin. While this fact problematizes a strictly biographical reading of the film, it need not deny the relevant philosophical interpretation which the film clearly invites without, however, insisting upon it. See Pipolo, "The Turin Horse," *Cineaste* (Spring 2012), pp. 48–50.

8. It came as no surprise, at least to me and other fans, that Tarr announced his retirement after the release of this film, though I do find it surprising, or vexing rather, that the metanarrative about the death of film for Tarr is traced back and hitched to the moment preceding the birth of film. For this his final film, Tarr depicts the threshold of the *birth* of film, marked by the *death* of Nietzsche, the great philosopher of *Life*. Is all this fitting somehow?

9. I would point out here that the father's right hand and arm are disabled or, in automatist terms, have malfunctioned. This makes the clawing character of his one good hand that much more apparent, as when he ferociously whips the stubborn horse or tears off piping hot potato skins. On the other hand, so to speak, his disability prevents him from being able to dress himself or perform certain chores. He has to rely on his daughter to collect water from the well and change into his day and evening attire. In this sense he is half-will and half-animal, half-power and half-powerlessness. Overall, he compensates well and you might not notice for very long that he is restricted to the use of only one hand. Let your attention drift to his dormant hand (ironically the might-makes-right hand) and behold that side of him that is spared the regime of human striving, that sleeps through the agonizing consciousness of constant clutching and debasement.

Bibliography

Andersen, Nathan. *Film, Philosophy, and Reality: Ancient Greece to Godard* (London and New York: Routledge, 2019).

Arnheim, Rudolph. *Film as Art* (Berkeley: University of California Press, 2007).

Ayer, A. J. *Language, Truth, and Logic* (London: Penguin, 2001).

Bachelard, Gaston. *The Poetics of Space*, trans. Maria Jolas (New York: The Orion Press, 1964).

Badiou, Alain. "Cinema as Philosophical Experimentation," in *Cinema*, trans. Susan Spitzer, ed. Antoine de Baecque (Cambridge: Polity, 2013), pp. 202–32.

Balázs, Béla. *Béla Balázs: Early Film Theory: Visible Man and The Spirit of Film* (New York: Berghahn Books, 2010).

Barthes, Roland. *Camera Lucida: Reflections on Photography*, trans. Richard Howard (New York: The Noonday Press and Farrar, Straus and Giroux, 1981).

Bazin, André. *What is Cinema?* Volume 1, trans. and ed. Hugh Gray (Berkeley, Los Angeles, and London: University of California Press, 1967).

Beckett, Samuel. *Endgame and Act Without Words* (New York: Grove Press, 1957).

——. *Molloy: A Novel*, trans. Patrick Bowles, in collaboration with Samuel Beckett (New York: Grove Press, 1955).

Benjamin, Walter. "The Work of Art in the Age of Its Technological Reproducibility: Second Version," in *The Work of Art in the Age of Its Technological Reproducibility, and Other Writings on Media*, trans. Edmund Jephcott and Rodney Livingstone, ed. Michael W. Jennings, Brigid Doherty, and Thomas Levin (Cambridge, MA: Belknap Press of Harvard University Press, 2008), pp. 19–55.

——. *The Writer of Modern Life: Essays on Charles Baudelaire* (Cambridge, MA, and London: Belknap Press of Harvard University Press, 2006).

Bersani, Leo and Ulysse Dutoit. *Forms of Being: Cinema, Aesthetics, Subjectivity* (London: British Film Institute, 2004).

Blanchot, Maurice. *The Space of Literature*, trans. Ann Smock (Lincoln, London: University of Nebraska Press, 1989).

Bresson, Robert. *Notes on the Cinematograph*, trans. Jonathan Griffin (New York: New York Review of Books, 2016).

Bryson, Norman. "The Natural Attitude," in *Visual Culture: The Reader*, ed. Jessica Evans and Stuart Hall (London, Thousand Oaks, CA, and New Delhi: Sage, 1999), pp. 23–32.

Bull, Malcolm. *Anti-Nietzsche* (London and New York: Verso, 2011).

Carroll, Noël. "Forget the Medium!," in *Engaging the Moving Image* (New Haven, CT, and London: Yale University Press, 2003), pp. 1–9.

Cavell, Stanley. *Cavell on Film*, ed. William Rothman (Albany: State University of New York Press, 2005).

——. *The Claim of Reason: Wittgenstein, Skepticism, Morality and Tragedy* (Oxford and New York: Oxford University Press, 1999).

——. "Knowing and Acknowledging," in *Must We Mean What We Say?*, Updated Edition (New York: Cambridge University Press, 2008), pp. 238–66.

——. *A Pitch of Philosophy: Autobiographical Exercises* (Cambridge, MA, and London: Harvard University Press, 1994).

——. *Pursuits of Happiness: The Hollywood Comedy of Remarriage* (Cambridge, MA, and London: Harvard University Press, 1981).

——. *The World Viewed: Reflections on the Ontology of Film*, Enlarged Edition (London and Cambridge, MA: Harvard University Press, 1979).

Chion, Michel. *The Thin Red Line*, trans. Trista Selous (London: British Film Institute, 2004).

Clark, T. J. *Picasso and Truth: From Cubism to Guernica* (Princeton, NJ: Princeton University Press, 2013).

——. *The Sight of Death: An Experiment in Art Writing* (New Haven and London: Yale University Press, 2006).

Comolli, Jean-Luc and Jean Narboni. "Cinema/Criticism/Ideology," in *Film Theory and Criticism*, ed. Leo Braudy and Marshall Cohen, 5th Edition (New York and Oxford: Oxford University Press, 1999), pp. 752–9.

Cosgrove, Denis E. *Social Formation and Symbolic Landscape* (London and Sydney: Croom Helm, 1984).

Critchley, Simon. "Calm—On Terrence Malick's *The Thin Red Line*," in *The Thin Red Line*, ed. David Davies (London and New York: Routledge, 2009), pp. 11–27.

——. *Very Little … Almost Nothing*, Revised Edition (London and New York: Routledge, 2004).

Davies, David. "Vision, Touch, and Embodiment in *The Thin Red Line*," in *The Thin Red Line*, ed. David Davies (London and New York: Routledge, 2009), pp. 45–64.

Deleuze, Gilles. *Cinema 2: The Time-Image*, trans. Hugh Tomlinson and Robert Galeta (London and New York: Bloomsbury Academic, 2013).

Diamond, Cora. "The Difficulty of Reality and the Difficulty of Philosophy," in *Philosophy and Animal Life* (New York: Columbia University Press, 2008), pp. 43–90.

Doane, Mary Ann. *The Emergence of Cinematic Time: Modernity, Contingency, the Archive* (Cambridge, MA, and London: Harvard University Press, 2002).

——. "Indexicality: Trace and Sign: Introduction," *Differences* (May 1, 2007), 18 (1): 1–6.

Emerson, Ralph Waldo. "Nature," in *The Portable Emerson*, ed. Carl Bode and Malcolm Cowley (New York: Penguin Books, 1981), pp. 7–50.

——. "The Poet," in *The Portable Emerson*, ed. Carl Bode and Malcolm Cowley (New York: Penguin Books, 1981), pp. 241–65.

Epstein, Jean. "On Certain Characteristics of Photogénie," in *French Film Theory and Criticism: A History/Anthology 1907–1939*, Volume 1: 1907–1929, trans. Tom Milne, ed. Richard Abel (Princeton, NJ: Princeton University Press, 1988), pp. 314–18.

——. "The Senses I (b)," in *French Film Theory and Criticism: A History/Anthology 1907–1939*, Volume 1: 1907–1929, trans. Tom Milne, ed. Richard Abel (Princeton, NJ: Princeton University Press, 1988), pp. 241–6.

Frampton, Daniel. *Filmosophy* (London and New York: Wallflower Press, 2006).

Fried, Michael. *Why Photography Matters as Art as Never Before* (New Haven, CT: Yale University Press, 2008).

Gorky, Maxim. "Maxim Gorky on the Lumiére Program, 1896," trans. Leda Swan, in *Kino: A History of the Russian and Soviet Film*, ed. Jay Leyda (New York, Macmillan, 1960), pp. 407–9.

Hazlett, Allan. "Introduction," in *New Waves in Metaphysics* (Basingstoke and New York: Palgrave Macmillan, 2010), pp. 1–7.

Heidegger, Martin. *Being and Time*, trans. John Macquarrie and Edward Robinson (San Francisco: Harper & Row, 1962).

——. *The Fundamental Concepts of Metaphysics: World, Finitude, Solitude*, trans. William McNeill and Nicholas Walker (Bloomington: Indiana University Press, 1995).

——. "Memorial Address," in *Discourse on Thinking*, trans. John M. Anderson and E. Hans Freund (New York: Harper & Row, 1966), pp. 43–57.

——. *Nietzsche, Volume 1: The Will to Power as Art*, trans. David Ferrell Krell (San Francisco: Harper & Row, 1979).

——. *Poetry, Language, Thought*, trans. Albert Hofstadter (New York: Harper & Row, 1971).

——. *The Question Concerning Technology and Other Essays*, trans. William Lovitt (New York: Harper & Row, 1977).

Janouch, Gustav. *Conversations with Kafka*, 2nd Edition, trans. Goronwy Rees (New York: New Directions, 2012).

Kaes, Anton, Nicholas Baer and Michael Cowan (eds.). *The Promise of Cinema: German Film Theory, 1907–1933* (Oakland, CA: University of California Press, 2016).

Kafka, Franz. "The Metamorphosis," in *The Complete Stories*, trans. Willa and Edwin Muir, ed. Nahum N. Glatzer (New York: Schocken Books, 1971), pp. 89–139.

——. *The Zürau Aphorisms*, trans. Michael Hofmann (New York: Schocken Books, 2006).

Keats, John. *The Complete Poetical Works and Letters of John Keats* (Cambridge, UK: Houghton, Mifflin and Company, 1899).

Kleist, Heinrich von. "On the Marionette Theater," in *German Romantic Criticism*, trans. Christian-Albrecht Gollub, ed. A. Leslie Willson (New York: Continuum, 1982), pp. 238–44.

Kracauer, Siegfried. *Theory of Film: The Redemption of Physical Reality* (Princeton, NJ: Princeton University Press, 1997).

Kuhn, Thomas. *The Structure of Scientific Revolutions* (Chicago and London: University of Chicago Press, 2012).

Lefebvre, Martin. "The Art of Pointing: On Peirce, Indexicality, and Photographic Images," in *Photography Theory*, ed. James Elkins (New York and London: Routledge, 2007), pp. 220–44.

——. "Between Setting and Landscape in the Cinema," in *Landscape and Film*, ed. Martin Lefebvre (New York: Routledge, 2006), pp. 19–60.

——. "On Landscape in Narrative Cinema," *Canadian Journal of Film Studies* (Spring 2011), 20 (1): pp. 61–78.

Levinas, Emmanuel. *Time and the Other*, trans. Richard A. Cohen (Pittsburgh: Duquesne University Press, 1987).

Lyotard, Jean-François. "The Sublime and the Avant-Garde," trans. Lisa Liebmann, with Geoff Bennington and Marian Hobson, in *The Continental Aesthetics Reader*, ed. Clive Cazeaux (London and New York: Routledge, 2008), pp. 453–64.

McCann, Ben. "'Enjoying the Scenery': Landscape and the Fetishization of Nature in *Badlands* and *Days of Heaven*," in *The Cinema of Terrence Malick: Poetic Visions of America*, ed. Hannah Patterson (London and New York: Wallflower Press, 2003), pp. 75–85.

Malick, Terrence. *Days of Heaven: An Original Screenplay* (Hollywood: Script City, 1976).

——. *The Thin Red Line* (unpublished screenplay).

Merleau-Ponty, Maurice. "The Film and the New Psychology," in *Sense and Non-Sense*, trans. Hubert L. Dreyfus and Patricia Allen Dreyfus (Chicago: Northwestern University Press, 1964), pp. 48–59.

Mowchun, Trevor. "A Machine's First Glimpse in Time and Space," *Evental Aesthetics* (2015), 4 (2): pp. 77–102.

Mulhall, Stephen. *On Film*, 2nd Edition (London and New York: Routledge, 2008).

——. *Philosophical Myths of the Fall* (Princeton, NJ, and Oxford: Princeton University Press, 2007).

Mullarkey, John. *Refractions of Reality: Philosophy and the Moving Image* (New York: Palgrave Macmillan, 2009).

Münsterberg, Hugo. "The Photoplay: A Psychological Study," in *Hugo Münsterberg on Film: The Photoplay—A Psychological Study and Other Writings*, ed. Allan Langdale (New York: Routledge, 2002), pp. 45–164.

Nietzsche, Friedrich. *The Gay Science*, trans. Walter Kaufmann (New York: Vintage Books, 1974).

——. "On the Uses and Disadvantages of History for Life," in *Untimely Meditations*, ed. Daniel Breazeale, trans. R. J. Hollingdale (Cambridge, UK: Cambridge University Press, 2019), pp. 57-123.

——. *Thus Spoke Zarathustra*, in *The Portable Nietzsche*, trans. and ed. Walter Kaufmann (New York: Penguin Books, 1982), pp. 103–439.

——. *The Will to Power*, trans. Walter Kaufmann and R. J. Hollingdale, ed. Walter Kaufmann New York: Vintage Books, 1968).

Panofsky, Erwin. "Style and Medium in the Motion Pictures," in *Three Essays on Style*, ed. Irving Lavin (Cambridge, MA: MIT Press, 1995), pp. 91–128.

Pipolo, Tony. "*The Turin Horse*," *Cineaste* (Spring 2012), pp. 48–50.

Pippin, Robert. "Vernacular Metaphysics: On Terrence Malick's *The Thin Red Line*," in *The Philosophy of War Films*, ed. David LaRocca (Lexington: The University Press of Kentucky, 2014), pp. 385–411.

Price, Brian. "Heidegger and Cinema," in *European Film Theory*, ed. Temenuga Trifonova (New York: Routledge, 2009), pp. 190–210.

Rancière, Jacques. *Béla Tarr, the Time After*, trans. Erik Beranek (Minneapolis: Univocal, 2013).

Ray, Robert. *The Structure of Complex Images* (Cham, Switzerland: Palgrave Macmillan, 2020).

Rodowick, D. N. *Philosophy's Artful Conversation* (Cambridge, MA, and London: Harvard University Press, 2015).

——. *The Virtual Life of Film* (Cambridge, MA: Harvard University Press, 2007).

Rorty, Richard. *Philosophy and the Mirror of Nature* (Princeton, NJ: Princeton University Press, 1979).

Rosen, Philip. *Change Mummified: Cinema, Historicity, Theory* (Minneapolis: University of Minnesota Press, 2001).

Schrader, Paul. *Transcendental Style in Film: Ozu, Bresson, Dreyer* (Berkeley: Da Capo Press, 1972).

Silberman, Robert. "Terrence Malick, Landscape and 'This War at the Heart of Nature'," in *The Cinema of Terrence Malick: Poetic Visions of America*, ed. Hannah Patterson (London and New York: Wallflower Press, 2003), pp. 160–72.

Silverman, Kaja. "All Things Shining," in *Loss: The Politics of Mourning*, ed. David L. Eng and David Kazanjian (Berkeley and Los Angeles: University of California Press, 2003), pp. 323–42.

Sinnerbrink, Robert. *Terrence Malick: Filmmaker and Philosopher* (London and New York: Bloomsbury, 2019).

Smith, Justin E. H. *The Philosopher: A History in Six Types* (Princeton: Princeton University Press, 2016).

Sontag, Susan. *Against Interpretation, and Other Essays* (New York: Farrar, Straus and Giroux, 1986).

——. *Regarding the Pain of Others* (New York: Picador, 2004).

Tarkovsky, Andrei. *Sculpting in Time*, trans. Kitty Hunter-Blair (Austin: University of Texas Press, 2000).

Tiercelin, Claudine. "Metaphysical Knowledge" (Inaugural lecture delivered on Thursday, May 5, 2011), New Edition [online] (Paris: Collège de France, 2013).

Toles, George. "Film Death and the Failure to Signify: The Curious Case of Warni Hazard," *New Review of Film and Television Studies* (2017), 15 (2): pp. 211–30.

Turvey, Malcolm. *Doubting Vision: Film and the Revelationist Tradition* (Oxford and New York: Oxford University Press, 2008).

Vattimo, Gianni. *Art's Claim to Truth*, trans. Luca D'Isanto, ed. Santiago Zabala (New York: Columbia University Press, 2008).

Virilio, Paul. *War and Cinema: The Logistics of Perception*, trans. Patrick Camiller (London and New York: Verso, 1989).

Wittgenstein, Ludwig. *Culture and Value*, trans. Peter Winch, ed. G. H. Von Wright, in collaboration with Heikki Nyman (Oxford: Basil Blackwell, 1980).

——. *On Certainty*, trans. Denis Paul and G. E. M. Anscombe, ed. G. E. M. Anscombe and G. H. von Wright (Oxford: Blackwell, 1977).

——. *Philosophical Investigations*, trans. G. E. M. Anscombe (Oxford and Malden, MA: Blackwell, 2001).

——. *Tractatus Logico-Philosophicus*, trans. D. F. Pears and B. F. McGuinness (London and New York: Routledge, 2003).

Yacavone, Daniel. *Film Worlds: A Philosophical Aesthetics of Cinema* (New York: Columbia University Press, 2015).

Zwicky, Jan. *Wisdom and Metaphor* (Kentville, NS, Canada: Gaspereau Press, 2003).

Index